Placement and Diagnostic Assessment

Credits:

Oral Reading and Fluency: From Oral Reading and Fluency: 90 Years of Measurement.

Phoneme Deletion Test: CORE Phoneme Deletion Test by Orna Lenchner, Ph.D., Assessing Reading: Multiple Measures, 1999, Arena Press. Used by permission of Arena Press and Consortium on Reading Excellence, Inc. Permission granted to reproduce for classroom use. Other reproduction of this material is prohibited without permission from the publisher.

Metacomprehension Strategy: Adapted from Schmitt, Maribeth C. (1999). A Questionnaire to Measure Children's Awareness of Strategic Processes. In S.J. Barrentine (Ed.). Reading Assessment: Principles and Practices for Elementary Teachers (pp. 189-195). Newark, DE, International Reading Association.

Permission granted by ATP Assessments and Arena Press, publishers of Assessing Reading: Multiple Measures (www.academictherapy.com)

Acknowledgments:

The publisher gratefully acknowledges permission to reprint the following copyrighted material:

Excerpts "Critchlow Verbal Language Scales" by Donald E. Critchlow are from Consortium On Reading Excellence (CORE): Assessing Reading Multiple Measures for Kindergarten Through Eighth Grade. Copyright © 1999 by Consortium On Reading Excellence (CORE). Reprinted by permission of Arena Press.

Excerpt "Metacomprehension Strategy Index" by Maribeth C. Schmitt includes information from 2007 Applestar Productions Web site: http://www.applestar.org/Recent/Metacognition_presentation.pdf by Jean Marrapodi, Ph.D.

Excerpts "McLeod Assessment of Reading Comprehension" by John McLeod, Ph.D. and Rita McLeod, Ph.D. are from Consortium On Reading Excellence (CORE): Assessing Reading Multiple Measures for Kindergarten Through Eighth Grade. Copyright © 1999 by Consortium On Reading Excellence (CORE). Reprinted by permission of Arena Press.

Excerpt: "CORE Phoneme Deletion Test" by Orna Lenchner, Ph.D. from Consortium On Reading Excellence (CORE): Assessing Reading Multiple Measures for Kindergarten Through Eighth Grade. Copyright © 1999 by Consortium On Reading Excellence (CORE). Reprinted by permission of Arena Press.

www.mheonline.com/readingwonders

Send all inquiries to:
McGraw-Hill Education
Two Penn Plaza
New York, New York 10121

ISBN: 978-0-07-677954-3
MHID: 0-07-677954-8

Printed in the United States of America.

3 4 5 6 7 8 9 RHR 20 19 18 17 16
C

Table of Contents

Introduction

Phonological and Phonemic Awareness

Letter Naming and Sight Words for Grades K-2

Phonics and Decoding for Grades K-6

Oral Reading Fluency for Grades 1-6

Table of Contents

Introduction

Overview

The purpose of this *Placement and Diagnostic Assessment* book is to provide you with assessment options to measure critical components of the Common Core State Standards (CCSS) for English Language Arts across grades K–6. This book includes a large portion of the assessments recommended for use with *McGraw-Hill Wonders*. Its primary focus is on assessments that can be used for **screening** and **placement** into an instructional level of *Wonders*: on grade level, beyond level, or approaching level. This book is designed to help you manage the use of multiple assessments, compare and interpret the results, and then use that information for instructional planning. It provides basic definitions and clear guidance on how test scores can be a useful resource for addressing your students' needs.

Separate, self-contained assessment components, including assessments at weekly/unit/mid-year/end-of-year intervals, anthology selection tests, and fluency assessments, also are provided as a part of the *Wonders* materials.

What is assessment?

- Assessment is the process of systematically gathering evidence about what students know and can do.

- Assessments can be formal or informal as long as the information is systematically collected, scored, and recorded.

Types of assessment

Screening and **Diagnostic Assessments** often are used together and serve to complement each other.

A **screening** test is a short, skill-specific instrument that can be administered quickly to give a general idea of what a student knows. Screening tests are good for telling teachers one of two alternatives: "The student knows it" *or* "The student does not know it." Cut scores that identify these alternatives usually are conservative, or high, which will result in more of the "doesn't know it" students than may actually be the case. The consequence of not meeting the cut score of a screening test is taking the diagnostic test. The underlying premise of the conservative decision is that we do not want to set the expectations for a student higher than his or her skill level can handle in the classroom. Taking the time, early, to do a more thorough skill analysis using a diagnostic assessment is much better than trying to go back and pick up the missing pieces behind a failing child.

Introduction

A **diagnostic** assessment is an expanded screening test that provides more items and additional ways to determine a student's knowledge of a skill and to monitor the student's progress with that skill throughout the school year. The greater number of items creates a more reliable test, which can make you more confident about decision-making for instructional purposes. A diagnostic test can be administered individually or in a group, depending on the original design of the test. The results of the test can be used to determine a starting point for instruction and for assigning small skill-based groups for extra attention. Diagnostic tests are best administered after the cut score *is not made* on a related screening test, at the beginning of the school year, or when a new student enters the class. Diagnostic assessments can identify specific instructional targets in small groups as well as providing a picture of skill mastery for an entire class.

A **placement** test is a type of diagnostic test. Placement tests are group administered and help you decide on an appropriate instructional level for the student. However, a placement test alone may not provide specific, detailed information about the strengths and weaknesses of a student's skills. Instead, you should use the skill-specific tests included in this book, such as the Phonics Survey or Informal Reading Inventory, to help you make decisions about placing students in the *Wonders* program.

Progress monitoring assessments are used to keep tabs on the growth or maintenance of a student's skills. These tests can be categorized as **formative** assessments because they are given more than once, over time, and rarely have high stakes attached. The primary purpose of a progress monitoring or any other formative assessment is to allow you to make immediate, corrective instructional decisions. Formative test results allow you to try alternative teaching methods during the school year, before the administration of a high-stakes test, such as a state test, used for accountability purposes.

State tests with high-stakes decisions attached are called **summative,** or **outcome,** assessments. A summative assessment gives a judgment about whether the tested material has been learned. The consequences of summative assessments can be harsh. For example, a student with low test scores may have to repeat a grade or attend summer school. Therefore, the assessments usually are made with great care and are tested and reviewed by hundreds or thousands of people before they are administered.

The scores on these tests generally provide an accurate understanding of a student's general skill level. They cover the broad domain of a particular concept to give an overall perception of learning. Most often, they are not designed for diagnosing a student's specific skill weaknesses, but they can paint a picture of general strong and weak spots when a class, a school, or a district's scores are examined.

Introduction

Placement Assessments

Using Assessment to Place Students

Placement and Diagnostic Assessment offers assessments to help you make decisions about where to place students. Based on the assessment results, guidelines are offered to place students in

- *Wonders* On Level Materials
- *Wonders* Approaching Level Materials
- *Wonders* Beyond Level Materials
- *McGraw-Hill WonderWorks*

The ultimate goal for classroom assessments in making placement decisions is to minimize the amount of testing needed to get the most valid and reliable information so that you can provide the most suitable level of instruction for each student. Using an appropriate type of test, with the best order of delivery, will help you reach this goal. Careful planning of your testing needs can help eliminate the confusion and lost time caused by jumping from test to test to individually match ever-changing student needs. The charts that follow are designed as a guide to support your placement testing plan. The guidelines are designed to help support the placement decisions of teachers and specialists using *Wonders* and *McGraw-Hill WonderWorks*. They should be used as ONE PIECE of information and should not be considered as definitive placement recommendations.

Introduction

Kindergarten Placement Decisions

Directions: Administer the following assessments to students:

☑ **Phonological Awareness Subtests** and **Letter Naming Fluency Assessment**   OR

☑ **Listening Comprehension Tests**

IF STUDENTS SCORE

> 80% correct or higher on the **Phonological Awareness Subtests**
>
> AND
>
> At or above the appropriate benchmark for the **Letter Naming Fluency Assessment**

OR

> 80% correct or higher on the **Listening Comprehension Tests**

THEN

IF STUDENTS SCORE

> 60–79% correct on the **Phonological Awareness Subtests**
>
> AND
>
> At or above the appropriate benchmark for the **Letter Naming Fluency Assessment**

OR

> Less than 80% correct on the **Listening Comprehension Tests**

THEN

IF STUDENTS SCORE

> Below 60% correct on the **Phonological Awareness Subtests**

OR

> Below the appropriate benchmark for the **Letter Naming Fluency Assessment**

THEN

Introduction

Begin instruction with *Wonders* On Level materials. Use **Beyond Level** materials for students who score high on placement assessments and easily complete On Level assignments.

Beyond Level

On Level

Begin instruction with *Wonders* Approaching Level materials.

Approaching Level

Students require focused, intensive instruction. Place students in *Wonders* **Approaching Level** materials and in *WonderWorks* materials based on placement tests results.

WonderWorks **Intervention**

Introduction

Grade 1 Placement Decisions

Directions: Administer the following assessments to students:

☑ **Reading Comprehension Tests** *   OR

☑ **Phonemic Awareness Subtests** and **Letter Naming Fluency Assessment****

IF STUDENTS SCORE

80% correct or higher on the **Reading Comprehension Tests**

OR

80% correct or higher on the **Phonemic Awareness Subtests** AND At or above the appropriate benchmark for the **Letter Naming Fluency Assessment**

THEN

IF STUDENTS SCORE

Below 80% correct on the **Reading Comprehension Tests**

OR

60–79% correct on the **Phonemic Awareness Subtests** AND At or above the appropriate benchmark for the **Letter Naming Fluency Assessment**

THEN

IF STUDENTS SCORE

Below 60% correct on the **Phonemic Awareness Subtests**

OR

Below the appropriate benchmark for the **Letter Naming Fluency Assessment**

THEN

Introduction

* For mid-year placement, begin by administering an **Oral Reading Fluency Assessment (ORF)** and note student performance above and below the 50ᵗʰ percentile. Use additional assessments to verify placement.

** The **Sight Word Fluency Assessment (SWF)** can be given mid-year in lieu of the **Letter Naming Fluency Assessment (LNF)**.

		Beyond Level
Begin instruction with *Wonders* **On Level** materials. Use **Beyond Level** materials for students who score high on placement assessments and easily complete On Level assignments.		**On Level**
Begin instruction with *Wonders* **Approaching Level** materials.		**Approaching Level**
Students require focused, intensive instruction. Place students in *Wonders* **Approaching Level** materials and in *WonderWorks* materials based on placement tests results.		*WonderWorks* **Intervention**

Introduction

Grades 2-3 Placement Decisions

Directions: Administer the following assessments to students:

☑ **Oral Reading Fluency Assessment**
☐ **Sight Word Fluency Assessment** *(if applicable)*
☑ **Reading Comprehension Tests**
☐ **Phonics Survey Subtests** *(if applicable)*

IF STUDENTS SCORE

> In the 50th percentile or higher on the **Oral Reading Fluency Assessment**
>
> AND
>
> 80% correct or higher on the **Reading Comprehension Tests**

THEN . . . .

IF STUDENTS SCORE

> Below the 50th percentile on the **Oral Reading Fluency Assessment**
>
> OR
>
> 60% to 79% correct on the **Reading Comprehension Tests**

THEN . . . .

IF STUDENTS SCORE

> Below the 50th percentile on the **Oral Reading Fluency Assessment**
>
> AND
>
> 60% to 79% correct on the **Reading Comprehension Tests**

THEN . . . .

IF STUDENTS SCORE

> 80% correct or higher on the majority of the **Phonics Survey Subtests**
>
> OR
>
> Less than 40 correct words on the **Sight Word Fluency Assessment**

THEN . . . .

IF STUDENTS SCORE

> Below 60% correct on the majority of the **Phonics Survey Subtests**
>
> OR
>
> Less than 40 correct words on the **Sight Word Fluency Assessment**

THEN . . . .

> Below 60% correct on the **Reading Comprehension Tests**

THEN . . . .

Introduction

Begin instruction with *Wonders* **On Level** materials. Use **Beyond Level** materials for students who score high on placement assessments and easily complete On Level assignments.

Beyond Level

On Level

Begin instruction with *Wonders* **Approaching Level** materials.

Begin instruction with *Wonders* **Approaching Level** materials. For further leveling clarification/confirmation, administer the **Phonics Survey Subtests** to students who are struggling with decoding. Otherwise, administer the **Sight Word Fluency Assessment**.

Approaching Level

Continue using the *Wonders* **Approaching Level** materials.

Students require focused, intensive instruction. Place students in *Wonders* **Approaching Level** materials and engage students using appropriate lessons from the *WonderWorks* materials.

WonderWorks **Intervention**

Students require focused, intensive instruction. Place students in *Wonders* **Approaching Level** materials and in the *WonderWorks* materials.

Introduction

Grades 4-6 Placement Decisions

Directions: Administer the following assessments to students:

- ☑ **Oral Reading Fluency Assessment***
- ☑ **Reading Comprehension Tests**
- ☐ **Phonics Survey Subtests** *(if applicable)*

IF STUDENTS SCORE

In the 50th percentile or higher on the **Oral Reading Fluency Assessment**

AND

80% correct or higher on the **Reading Comprehension Tests**

THEN

IF STUDENTS SCORE

Below the 50th percentile on the **Oral Reading Fluency Assessment**

OR

60% to 79% correct on the **Reading Comprehension Tests**

THEN

IF STUDENTS SCORE

Below the 50th percentile on the **Oral Reading Fluency Assessment**

AND

60% to 79% correct on the **Reading Comprehension Tests**

THEN

IF STUDENTS SCORE

Below 60% correct on the majority of the **Phonics Survey Subtests**

THEN

IF STUDENTS SCORE

Below 60% correct on the **Reading Comprehension Tests**

THEN

Introduction

* Consult page 89 for Words Correct per Minute (WCPM) ranges.

Begin instruction with *Wonders* **On Level** materials. Use **Beyond Level** materials for students who score high on placement assessments and easily complete On Level assignments.

Beyond Level

On Level

Begin instruction with *Wonders* **Approaching Level** materials.

Approaching Level

Begin instruction with *Wonders* **Approaching Level** materials. Administer the **Phonics Survey Subtests** for further leveling clarification/confirmation.

Students require focused, intensive instruction. Place students in *Wonders* **Approaching Level** materials and engage students using appropriate decoding lessons from the *WonderWorks* materials.

WonderWorks **Intervention**

Students require focused, intensive instruction. Place students in *Wonders* **Approaching Level** materials and in *WonderWorks* materials based on placement tests results.

Introduction

Using Multiple Measures

The Assessment Process

The assessment process is about making instructional decisions based on assessment information. To the greatest extent possible, all instructional decisions should be based on **multiple sources** of valid and reliable information.

- The process starts with measurement and scoring (test results, observations).
- The next step is to compare and interpret the information you have gathered.
- The third step is to make instructional decisions based on your conclusions.
- This process is ongoing: measure, interpret, make decisions. . . .

The Assessment Process

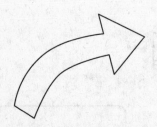

Measure and Score
Use multiple sources of evidence (test scores, observations).

Interpret
Compare and contrast scores and observations with other assessment results.

Make Instructional Decisions
Base these on your findings.

Introduction

Assessment Planning and Pacing Guide

Beyond the initial placement of students into the appropriate *Wonders* level of materials, students need to be tested periodically to determine whether they are progressing on a grade-level or faster pace. Many teachers administer these progress monitoring or benchmark tests on a regular schedule throughout the year: fall, winter, and spring, or over a regular period of time, such as every four to six weeks. The chart that follows provides a general testing scheduling guide.

ELA Component	Assessment	Grade Level						
		K	1	2	3	4	5	6
Phonological and Phonemic Awareness	**Phonological Awareness Subtests**	Beginning, Middle, and End of Year		Only if needed				
	Phonemic Awareness Subtests	Beginning, Middle, and End of Year			Only if needed			
Letter Naming and Sight Words	**Letter Naming Fluency**	Beginning, Middle, and End of Year	Beginning and Middle of Year		Not Applicable			
	Sight Word Fluency	End of Year	Beginning, Middle, and End of Year					
Phonics and Decoding	**Phonics Survey**	Beginning, Middle, and End of Year			Only if needed			
Fluency	**Oral Reading Fluency**	Not Applicable	Middle and End of Year		Beginning, Middle, and End of Year			
	Running Records*	Middle and End of Year			Every Three to Four Weeks			
	Informal Reading Inventory	Not Applicable	Beginning, Middle, and End of Year					
Spelling	**Inventories of Developmental Spelling**	End of Year	Beginning, Middle, and End of Year					
Vocabulary	**Critchlow Verbal Language Scales**	Middle and End of Year	Beginning, Middle, and End of Year					
Comprehension	**Comprehension Tests**	Beginning of Year						
	McLeod Assessment of Reading Comprehension	Not Applicable		Beginning of Year				
	Metacomprehension Strategy Index	Not Applicable			Beginning of Year			
Writing	**Writing Assessment**	Not Applicable	Middle and End of Year	Beginning, Middle, and End of Year				

* See Running Records/Benchmark Books

Introduction

Assessment Record Sheet

Student Name _____ Date/Time of Year _____

ELA Component	Assessment	Scores	Observations	Next Steps
Phonemic Awareness	Phonological Awareness Subtests			
	Phonemic Awareness Subtests			
Letter Naming and Sight Words	Letter Naming Fluency			
	Sight Word Fluency			
Phonics and Decoding	Phonics Survey			
Fluency	Oral Reading Fluency			
	Running Records*			
	Informal Reading Inventory			
Spelling	Inventories of Developmental Spelling			
Vocabulary	Critchlow Verbal Language Scales			
Comprehension	Comprehension Tests			
	McLeod Assessment of Reading Comprehension			
	Metacomprehension Strategy Index			
Writing	Writing Assessment			

* See *Running Records/Benchmark Books*

Introduction

Assessments in this Book

This book includes assessments in the following areas:

- **Phonological and Phonemic Awareness** Students who struggle with decoding often lack the ability to perceive and manipulate sounds (phonemes) in spoken words. Phonological and phonemic awareness strongly correlates to early reading growth and is a key assessment with beginning readers.

- **Letter Naming and Sight Word Fluency** Students use their knowledge of the alphabet and high-frequency words to recognize and name letters as well as common sight words.

- **Phonics and Decoding** Basic decoding proficiency and mastery of sound-spelling relationships is necessary for reading success. Decoding proficiency can be assessed using lists of real and pseudowords.

- **Oral Reading Fluency** The hallmark of a skilled reader is the ability to decode and comprehend simultaneously. Oral reading fluency assessments determine which students are above, on, or below level for reading grade-level text. Oral reading fluency assessments correlate strongly to standardized comprehension assessments and are a quick measure to determine students' overall reading proficiency. These assessments can also be used to monitor the effect of instructional modifications or interventions as they are very sensitive to reading growth.

- **Informal Reading Inventory** A skilled reader also reads silently and orally with comprehension and accuracy. This assessment measures independent, instructional, and frustrational reading levels and provides you with greater understanding of a student's strengths and weaknesses in word recognition, word meaning, reading strategies, and comprehension.

- **Spelling** Spelling ability supports fluent reading and writing. Students use their knowledge of spelling patterns when reading and writing.

- **Vocabulary** Vocabulary knowledge is also highly correlated to comprehension. The more words a student knows and the deeper that knowledge, the more likely he or she will be able to comprehend the text.

- **Reading Comprehension** The goal of reading is comprehension, or overall understanding of the text. Reading comprehension assessments determine at which grade level students successfully comprehend text. These assessments are useful for providing leveled practice materials and serve as a starting point for instruction as you move struggling students to grade-level proficiency.

- **Writing** Writing is a reflection of students' ability to comprehend ideas, express throughts, and master English language conventions. Assessing writing can help individualize instruction and monitor student progress.

Introduction

Screening Options

Screening Students K–3

Most states or school districts identify the screening assessment you should use with your students, such as DIBELS or TPRI. It is recommended that you use the approved screening assessment in your state to identify at-risk students. We provide the information needed to align both **DIBELS Next (pages 17–21)** and **TPRI (pages 22–24)** to *Wonders* on the indicated pages.

Program screening options are available.

At the start of Kindergarten, consider using the following screening assessments to identify students who may be at risk and in need of more instruction. As students progress through Grade K, subtests from phonological awareness (pages 37–45) can be used as additional screening instruments.

- Letter Naming Fluency (pages 72 and 73): Note whether students reach the recommended FALL benchmark score as a consideration of student readiness.

- Sight Word Fluency (pages 74 and 75): Students will not be asked to complete this full assessment until closer to the end of the year. However, you may ask students to read the following list of ten words from the assessment—*and, go, has, he, like, see, the, we, you, one*. Students who read **less than 6** correctly could be candidates for further instruction.

At the start of Grade 1, Letter Naming Fluency and Sight Word Fluency assessment benchmarks and performance in subtests of phonological awareness can be used to help identify students at risk. Students at the mid-point of Grade 1 can be administered subtests from phonemic awareness (pages 46–69) and oral reading fluency assessments (pages 92–99).

Students in Grades 2 and 3 can be administered Sight Word Fluency, subtests from phonemic awareness, and oral fluency assessments (pages 100–123) to identify students below benchmarks and goals as at-risk candidates.

<u>DIBELS</u> (Dynamic Indicators of Basic Early Literacy Skills), K–3

DIBELS are short, one-minute fluency measures. The probes are individually administered and measure all of the following:

Reading First Component	DIBELS Next Measure	Grade Level
Phonemic Awareness	First Sound Fluency (FSF)	K
Phonemic Awareness	Phoneme Segmentation Fluency (PSF)	K–1
Phonics	Nonsense Word Fluency (NWF)	K–1
Fluency (Connected Text)	Oral Reading Fluency (DORF)	1–3
Comprehension	Oral Reading and Retell Fluency	1–3

Screening Students 4–6

For screening students in the upper grades, we have provided an **Oral Reading Fluency Assessment** on **pages 86–162**. Fiction and nonfiction passages are provided along with comprehension questions. The screening assessment should be administered three times a year to measure students' fluency in the fall, winter, and spring.

Introduction

Using DIBELS Next for Screening

What is the DIBELS Next screening assessment?

- Dynamic Indicators of Basic Early Literacy Skills measures reading acquisition skills.
- DIBELS Next provides an indicator of how well children are likely to do in their overall reading performance by the end of the third grade.
- DIBELS Next identifies children who are at risk for reading difficulties before failure sets in and determines appropriate instructional support.

What does it do?

- The DIBELS Next measures identify emerging literacy skills and the risk of developing reading difficulties.

How does it work?

- Screening is administered to all students in the fall, mid-winter, and spring of each year, K–3.
- All measures are individually administered and include scripted administration instructions.
- Each measure is timed for one minute, except for Initial Sound Fluency.
- There are three or four short tasks at each grade level. Results help teachers identify skills, monitor progress, and intervene with students at risk.

What does it measure?

- **First Sound Fluency:** a student's ability to recognize and produce the initial sound in an orally presented word.
- **Phoneme Segmentation Fluency:** a student's ability to segment three- and four-phoneme words into their individual phonemes fluently.
- **Nonsense Word Fluency:** a student's knowledge of letter-sound correspondence and the student's ability to blend sounds into words.
- **Oral Reading and Retell Fluency:** a student's overall reading performance and potential need for additional instructional support in fluency and comprehension.

Introduction

Aligning the DIBELS Next Screening Schedule with *Wonders*

Kindergarten

Wonders	DIBELS Next Measure	Start Smart/ Beginning	Unit 4/ Middle	Unit 9/ End
Phonemic Awareness	FSF	Goal: 10 At Benchmark: 10+ Below Benchmark: 5–9 Well Below: 0–4	Goal: 30 At Benchmark: 30+ Below Benchmark: 20–29 Well Below: 0–19	Move to PSF
	PSF		Goal: 20 correct phonemes At Benchmark: 20+ Below Benchmark: 10–19 Well Below: 0–9	Goal: 40 correct phonemes At Benchmark: 40+ Below Benchmark: 25–39 Well Below: 0–24
Letter Recognition	*LNF	Goal: 8 correct letters Low Risk > 8 Some Risk 2–7 At Risk < 2	Goal: 27 correct letters Low Risk > 27 Some Risk 15–26 At Risk < 15	Goal: 40 correct letters Low Risk > 40 Some Risk 29–39 At Risk < 29
Alphabetic Principle/ Phonics	NWF–CLS		Goal: 17 correct letter sounds At Benchmark: 17+ Below Benchmark: 8–16 Well Below: 0–7	Goal: 28 correct letter sounds At Benchmark: 28+ Below Benchmark: 15–27 Well Below: 0–14

* No benchmarks set for DIBELS Next; earlier benchmarks noted

Introduction

Aligning the DIBELS Next Screening Schedule with *Wonders*

First Grade

Wonders	DIBELS Next Measure	Unit 1/ Beginning	Unit 3/ Middle	Unit 5/ End
Phonemic Awareness	PSF	Goal: 40 correct phonemes At Benchmark: 40+ Below Benchmark: 25–39 Well Below: 0–24		
Alphabetic Principle/ Phonics	NWF–CLS	Goal: 27 correct letter sounds At Benchmark: 27+ Below Benchmark: 18–26 Well Below: 0–17	Goal: 43 correct letter sounds At Benchmark: 43+ Below Benchmark: 33–42 Well Below: 0–32	Goal: 58 correct letter sounds At Benchmark: 58+ Below Benchmark: 47–57 Well Below: 0–46
	NWF–WWR	Goal: 1 whole word read At Benchmark: 1+ Below Benchmark: 0	Goal: 8 whole words read At Benchmark: 8+ Below Benchmark: 3–7 Well Below: 0–2	Goal: 13 whole words read At Benchmark: 13+ Below Benchmark: 6–12 Well Below: 0–5
Fluency	DORF Words Correct		Goal: 23 At Benchmark: 23+ Below Benchmark: 16–22 Well Below: 0–15	Goal: 47 At Benchmark: 47+ Below Benchmark: 32–46 Well Below: 0–31
	DORF Accuracy		Goal: 78% At Benchmark: 78% + Below Benchmark: 68%–77% Well Below: 0–67%	Goal: 90% At Benchmark: 90% + Below Benchmark: 82%–89% Well Below: 0–81%
	Retell			Goal: 15 At Benchmark: 15+ Below Benchmark: 0–14

Introduction

Aligning the DIBELS Next Screening Schedule with *Wonders*

Second Grade

Wonders	DIBELS Next Measure	Unit 1/ Beginning	Unit 3/ Middle	Unit 5/ End
Alphabetic Principle/ Phonics	NWF–CLS	Goal: 54 correct letter sounds At Benchmark: 54+ Below Benchmark: 35–53 Well Below: 0–34		
	NWF–WWR	Goal: 13 whole words read At Benchmark: 13+ Below Benchmark: 6–12 Well Below: 0–5		
Fluency	DORF Words Correct	Goal: 52 At Benchmark: 52+ Below Benchmark: 37–51 Well Below: 0–36	Goal: 72 At Benchmark: 72+ Below Benchmark: 55–71 Well Below: 0–54	Goal: 87 At Benchmark: 87+ Below Benchmark: 65–86 Well Below: 0–64
	DORF Accuracy	Goal: 90% At Benchmark: 90% + Below Benchmark: 81%–89% Well Below: 0–80%	Goal: 96% At Benchmark: 96% + Below Benchmark: 91%–95% Well Below: 0–90%	Goal: 97% At Benchmark: 97% + Below Benchmark: 93%–96% Well Below: 0–92%
	Retell	Goal: 16 At Benchmark: 16+ Below Benchmark: 8–15 Well Below: 0–7	Goal: 21 At Benchmark: 21+ Below Benchmark: 13–20 Well Below: 0–12	Goal: 27 At Benchmark: 27+ Below Benchmark: 18–26 Well Below: 0–17
	Retell Quality of Response		Goal: 2 At Benchmark: 2+ Below Benchmark: 1	Goal: 2 At Benchmark: 2+ Below Benchmark: 1

Introduction

Aligning the DIBELS Next Screening Schedule with *Wonders*

Third Grade

Wonders	DIBELS Next Measure	Unit 1/ Beginning	Unit 3/ Middle	Unit 5/ End
Fluency	DORF Words Correct	Goal: 70 At Benchmark: 70+ Below Benchmark: 55–69 Well Below: 0–54	Goal: 86 At Benchmark: 86+ Below Benchmark: 68–85 Well Below: 0–67	Goal: 100 At Benchmark: 100+ Below Benchmark: 80–99 Well Below: 0–79
	DORF Accuracy	Goal: 95% At Benchmark: 95% + Below Benchmark: 89%–94% Well Below: 0–88%	Goal: 96% At Benchmark: 96% + Below Benchmark: 92%–95% Well Below: 0–91%	Goal: 97% At Benchmark: 97% + Below Benchmark: 94%–96% Well Below: 0–93%
	Retell	Goal: 20 At Benchmark: 20+ Below Benchmark: 10–19 Well Below: 0–9	Goal: 26 At Benchmark: 26+ Below Benchmark: 18–25 Well Below: 0–17	Goal: 30 At Benchmark: 30+ Below Benchmark: 20–29 Well Below: 0–19
	Retell Quality of Response	Goal: 2 At Benchmark: 2+ Below Benchmark: 1	Goal: 2 At Benchmark: 2+ Below Benchmark: 1	Goal: 3 At Benchmark: 3+ Below Benchmark: 2 Well Below: 1
Comprehension	Daze Adjusted Score	Goal: 8 At Benchmark: 8+ Below Benchmark: 5–7 Well Below: 0–4	Goal: 11 At Benchmark: 11+ Below Benchmark: 7–10 Well Below: 0–6	Goal: 19 At Benchmark: 19+ Below Benchmark: 14–18 Well Below: 0–13

Introduction

Using TPRI for Screening

TPRI (Texas Primary Reading Inventory), K–3

The TPRI probes are individually administered, quick, and given at the beginning, middle, and end of the year. They measure all of the following:

Reading First Component	TPRI Measure	Grade Level
Phonemic Awareness	Blending: Onset-Rimes, Phonemes	K–1
Phonics	Graphophonemic Knowledge	K–1
Phonics	Word Reading	1–3
Fluency (Connected Text)	Reading Accuracy and Fluency	1–3
Comprehension	Listening/Reading Comprehension	K–1/1–3

What is the TPRI screening assessment?

- The Texas Primary Reading Inventory is a teacher-administered assessment that quickly identifies students who are NOT at risk of reading failure.

- It allows teachers to target their instruction and resources on those students who need further evaluation.

- It is a predictive assessment.

What does it do?

- The TPRI is designed to supplement and facilitate teacher judgment.

- It identifies students as developed or still developing literacy concepts.

How does it work?

- The screening test is a series of short (i.e. in three–five minutes), student-friendly tasks.

- The Kindergarten screening is administered in mid-January and mid-April.

- The Grade 1 screening is administered in mid-September and mid-April.

- The Grade 2 screening is administered in mid-September.

- The Grade 3 screening is administered in mid-September.

What do they measure?

- **Graphophonemic Knowledge:** the recognition of alphabet letters and the understanding of sound-symbol relationships.

- **Phonemic Awareness:** the ability to identify, think about, or manipulate the individual sounds in words.

- **Word Reading:** the correct identification of words. Students are identified as *Developed* or *Still Developing*.

Introduction

How to Sequence the TPRI Kit

Step 1: Screening Section

- All students take the screening assessment.

- Allows you to identify students who are not likely to experience difficultly learning to read.

- Provides a way to focus additional resources on students who need more evaluation.

Step 2: Inventory Section

- Students who are *Still Developing* move on to the Inventory Section.

- Optional: Administer to all students for additional diagnostic information.

Step 3: Reading Accuracy, Fluency, and Comprehension (Listening Comprehension in Grade K)

- Administer to all students.

Aligning the TPRI Screening Schedule with *Wonders*

Kindergarten

Unit 4/Mid-Year: Blending Onset-Rimes and Phonemes,
Graphophonemic Knowledge

Unit 9/End of Year: Blending Onset-Rimes and Phonemes,
Graphophonemic Knowledge

First Grade

Unit 1/Beginning of Year: Blending Onset-Rimes and Phonemes, Graphophonemic
Knowledge and Word Reading

Unit 5/End of Year: Blending Onset-Rimes and Phonemes and Word Reading

Second Grade

Unit 1/Beginning of Year: Word Reading

Third Grade

Unit 1/Beginning of Year: Word Reading

Introduction

Administering the TPRI Screening Assessment

1. Read the directions before beginning.

2. Begin with the practice items.

3. Administer the task to the student.

4. Be sure to pronounce the phonemes correctly.

5. Follow the Branching Rules.

6. Scoring criteria:
   Developed or *Still Developing*

7. Grade 2: Students who are identified as still developing on the TPRI screening at the beginning of grade 2 may be in need of intensive reading intervention.

8. Grade 3: The screening tasks should be simplified into one task. Administer all twenty items at one time. This makes it easier to administer and evaluate.

9. Third-grade students who do not read at least nineteen out of twenty words correctly on the combined tasks are at risk of falling below the 20th percentile on a standardized, end-of-the-year reading test.

Introduction

Diagnostic Options

Diagnostic Assessments

There are several diagnostic assessments you can use for identifying the strengths and weaknesses of your students. These can be used according to a schedule or at any time during the year when in-depth information about a student is needed.

TPRI (Texas Primary Reading Inventory), K–3

For developing students, the Inventory portion of the **TPRI** allows teachers to gather specific diagnostic information. The Inventory section measures:

- Book and Print Awareness (K)
- Phonemic Awareness (K–1)
- Listening Comprehension (K–1)
- Graphophonemic Knowledge (K–3)
- Reading Accuracy (1–3)
- Reading Fluency (1–3)
- Reading Comprehension (1–3)

Informal Reading Inventory, 1–6

IRIs are silent and oral reading passages that are used to determine students' Independent, Instructional, and Frustrational reading levels. Students read successively more difficult, grade-level text, and answer vocabulary and comprehension questions.

Placement, K–6

Use a combination of the skill-specific tests included in this book to help make decisions about placing students in the *Wonders* program. The Placement Decision charts on pages 6–11 provide cut scores and guidelines for decision making.

Introduction

Using TPRI as a Diagnostic

What is the TPRI Inventory assessment?

- The Inventory is a diagnostic tool intended to guide instruction.
- The Inventory reveals students' strengths and weaknesses to help teachers plan differentiated classroom instruction.

What does it do?

- It gives teachers an opportunity to acquire more data to help match reading instruction with specific student needs.

How does it work?

- The Inventory is administered to all students who fail the screening section.
- It takes about twenty minutes to administer, and materials are color coded.
- Concepts are considered *Developed* when students provide correct responses to the indicated number of items within a task. Teachers then proceed to the next task.
- If a student does not respond to the indicated number of items, the concept is considered *Still Developing.*
- At the beginning of the year, students are expected to score *Still Developing* on many of the Inventory tasks; they are expected to learn and develop the skills measured on the Inventory throughout the school year.

What does it measure?

- **Book and Print Awareness/Concepts of Print:** The ability to concentrate on the conventions and formats of print.
- **Phonemic Awareness:** The ability to attend to the sound structure of spoken language.
- **Graphophonemic Knowledge:** The ability to recognize letters and understand sound-spelling relationships.
- **Listening and Reading Comprehension:** Word lists help place students into the appropriate instructional reading level.
- **Reading Accuracy and Reading Fluency**

Introduction

Inventory Branching Rules

- All tasks are arranged from easiest to most difficult.

- A basic task is the first or easiest one, and an advanced task is the last or hardest one.

- Begin with the easiest task and stay within the same portion of the Inventory as long as the student continues to score as *Developed*.

- If a student scores *Still Developing* on a task, stop and move the student to the next portion of the Inventory.

How to Prevent Student Frustration

- If the student is reading the entire passage at a Frustrational Level, stop and ask the student to read the previous passage instead.

- At Grades 1 and 2, the Frustrational Level is defined as the point when the student cannot read three or more words in the *first* sentence.

- In Grade 1, the teacher can read the story aloud and treat this as Listening Comprehension.

- In Grade 2, the teacher should administer the First Grade Word List before going back to a first-grade story.

Aligning the TPRI Inventory Schedule with *Wonders*

Kindergarten

Unit 4/Middle of the Year and **Unit 9**/End of the Year:
Book and Print Awareness, Phonemic Awareness, Graphophonemic Knowledge, Reading/Listening Comprehension

First Grade

Unit 1/Beginning of Year, **Unit 3**/Middle of Year, and **Unit 5**/End of Year:
Phonemic Awareness, Graphophonemic Knowledge, Reading Accuracy, Fluency, and Reading/Listening Comprehension

Second and Third Grades

Unit 1/Beginning of Year, **Unit 3**/Middle of Year, and **Unit 5**/End of Year:
Graphophonemic Knowledge, Reading Accuracy, Fluency, and Reading/Listening Comprehension

Introduction

Other Assessment Opportunities

Assessment is an ongoing and continuous process. It does not end after you administer diagnostic and screening tests and assessments for placement. In fact, good teaching requires that you teach and assess simultaneously, thereby providing immediate corrective feedback and lesson modifications. The following pages detail how informal assessments can be used to confirm (or not) diagnostic assessment results and can lead you to administer additional diagnostic assessments based on observed student needs.

Informal Assessments

The reading classroom is full of assessment opportunities. Chances are you use some of them without realizing you are doing "assessment." Remember the definition of assessment is systematically gathering information about what students know and can do. In reading, you can do this in an informal way throughout instruction.

- **Teach students to monitor their own comprehension.** Monitoring comprehension is an important comprehension strategy explicitly taught in *Wonders* from Grades one through six. Students can ask themselves questions about what they have just read. Good readers learn to use these metacognitive skills unconsciously. Have you ever said to yourself, "I am not sure what I just read"? Your automatic monitoring system helps you improve your comprehension of the text.

- **Ask students to retell** or explain in their own words what they have just read. A good explanation shows you what a student understands, and a poor explanation makes the student's misconceptions and misunderstandings apparent so you can address them.

- **Teach students how to monitor their own progress.** If children realize they do not understand something they have read, they can try various reading strategies and/or ask for help from peers or from their teacher. Listen for the substance of the answer, and not merely if it is "correct" or not. Learn from the student's answer what he or she is thinking.

Introduction

Types of Informal Assessments

Quick Checks: *Wonders* provides many opportunities for you to observe students independently practice a strategy or skill taught in whole group instruction.

- The Quick Check reminds you to observe your students and see if any of them are having difficulty with a skill they have just learned.

- You can use this information to decide if this is a skill you need to address in small group instruction.

Assignments: Every assignment or activity allows you to assess reading behaviors. Assignments do not need to be formally graded, but they should be treated as a potential source of information about what students know, what they still need to learn, and what their misconceptions or difficulties are.

- Review assignments, noting both strengths and weaknesses, and present the student with oral or written feedback.

- Ask students to go over their own assignments in groups, where peers can point out their strengths and weaknesses to each other. Note that this is an opportunity to show students that looking at what is right and wrong is important.

- Ask students to go over their own work and reflect upon it. This, too, is a skill that needs to be modeled and taught.

Classroom Observations: You have opportunities to observe your students at work and at play, working alone, and interacting with other students. Be systematic with the way you do and record the observations.

- Does this student like to read or look at books? What topics is he or she interested in?

- How does this student work with others?

- You can ask students what kinds of stories or books they like. You should strive to create a print-rich environment, with materials at a wide range of reading levels on as many topics as possible. Expand on students' interests and introduce new ones.

Introduction

QUICK CHECKS OBSERVATIONS FORM (PRIMARY)					
Student's Name	Phonological Awareness	Phonics	Fluency	Comprehension	Vocabulary

Placement and Diagnostic Assessment • Introduction

Introduction

QUICK CHECKS OBSERVATIONS FORM (INTERMEDIATE)				
Student's Name	Phonics/Word Study	Fluency	Comprehension	Vocabulary

**Placement and
Diagnostic Assessment**

Phonological
and Phonemic
Awareness

Phonological and Phonemic Awareness Grades K–3

Overview

The ability to hear individual sounds (phonemes) in words is an important precursor to learning to read. Research has shown that deficits in phonological and phonemic awareness may be at the root of many difficulties in reading and spelling. For this reason, early assessment is important. By administering this assessment, you can objectively estimate a student's level of phonological and phonemic awareness. The results will give you a good idea of where to focus your instruction. The assessment can also help to identify students whose lack of phonological and phonemic awareness may be causing difficulty in their acquisition of reading and spelling skills.

Phonological and Phonemic Awareness Subtests

The Phonological and Phonemic Awareness Assessment consists of these subtests:

Phonological Awareness Subtests (Grade K–early Grade 1)

1. Recognize Rhyming Words
2. Produce Rhyming Words
3. Segment and Count Syllables
4. Blend Syllables
5. Blend and Segment Onsets and Rimes

Phonemic Awareness Subtests (Grades K–3)

1. Count Phonemes
2. Isolate and Pronounce Phonemes
3. Match Phonemes
4. Blend Phonemes to Produce Words
5. Segment Words into Phonemes
6. CORE Phoneme Deletion Test
7. Add Phonemes to Make New Words
8. Substitute Phonemes to Make New Words
9. Distinguish Long from Short Vowels

A set of phonics-based assessments, Represent Phonemes with Letters, is included after the subtests to help gauge student readiness in the transition to phonics.

How to Use the Assessment

The phonological subtests should be given to all kindergarten students mid-year and to all first-graders in the fall. The phonemic awareness subtests should be given to kindergarten students mid- to late-year and to first-graders early in the year. Continue to administer the phonemic awareness subtests every two months, throughout the year, to monitor progress in these key skills. Give these tests only to second-graders or third-graders who are not yet reading.

It is recommended that you administer the subtests on an individual basis. Students are led through the tasks by the teacher. Most of the subtests are conducted orally, with the teacher recording the student's responses on a record sheet. A few have a student page on which students indicate their answers by circling pictures or writing letters. Students unfamiliar with these types of tasks should receive practice in completing such tasks prior to administration of this assessment.

The subtests progress in difficulty according to the developmental sequence in which these skills are generally learned. Some of the subtests have multiple sections, and these sections are also sequenced by difficulty. If a student is unable to complete the first section of a subtest, do not go on to the second section. If a student is unable to complete two subtests, it is best to stop the assessment at that point.

How to Interpret the Results

Generally, students who do well on the phonological and phonemic awareness assessment are progressing well and have a good foundation for learning to read and spell. If a student does not do well on any part of the test, reassess the student to determine where the difficulty lies.

Normally progressing kindergarten students should be able to recognize and produce rhymes, segment and blend syllables, and isolate and match initial sounds by the middle of kindergarten. Segmenting a word into phonemes and manipulating words by adding, deleting, or substituting phonemes are skills that are typically mastered in Grade 1 and early Grade 2.

Phonemic awareness and phonics instruction go hand-in-hand. Phonemic awareness is a precursor to reading but also develops as students learn to read. Students who are able to hear the individual phonemes in words are ready for phonics instruction. By the time students are decoding words easily, they no longer need to be assessed in phonemic awareness skills.

Students who do not do well on the phonemic awareness subtests appropriate for their grade level may need more intensive phonemic awareness training. An intervention of about 14 hours of phonemic awareness instruction (3–4 days a week for 15–20 minutes for about ten weeks) is all that is needed by many students in Grades K–2.

Recognize Rhyming Words

This phonological awareness test assesses a student's ability to recognize words that rhyme. Say a word. Have the student circle the picture that names a word that rhymes

Instructions for Administering the Assessment

Make a copy of page 37 for each child.

Say these directions to the child.

1. *Look at Number 1* (point to the number). *Listen carefully as I say a word:* pet. *Now listen to these answer choices:* cap, net, bed. *Which word rhymes with* pet? *Circle the picture of the word that rhymes with* pet.

2. *Look at Number 2* (point to the number). *Listen carefully as I say a word:* van. *Now listen to these answer choices:* vase, fork, fan. *Which word rhymes with* van? *Circle the picture of the word that rhymes with* van.

3. *Look at Number 3* (point to the number). *Listen carefully as I say a word:* coat. *Now listen to these answer choices:* boat, hat, sock. *Which word rhymes with* coat? *Circle the picture of the word that rhymes with* coat.

4. *Look at Number 4* (point to the number). *Listen carefully as I say a word:* trunk. *Now listen to these answer choices:* drum, train, skunk. *Which word rhymes with* trunk? *Circle the picture of the word that rhymes with* trunk.

5. *Look at Number 5* (point to the number). *Listen carefully as I say a word:* gate. *Now listen to these answer choices:* goat, skate, fruit. *Which word rhymes with* gate? *Circle the picture of the word that rhymes with* gate.

Directions for Scoring

Give 1 point for each correct response. The highest score is 5.

Answers: **1.** net; **2.** fan; **3.** boat; **4.** skunk; **5.** skate

Name: _____ **Date:** _____

Recognize Rhyming Words

1

2

3

4

5

Score: _____ / 5

Produce Rhyming Words

This phonological awareness test assesses a student's ability to produce his or her own rhymes. Say a word. Ask the student to say a rhyming word. Accept nonsense words that rhyme with the target word.

Instructions for Administering the Assessment

Make a copy of the record sheet on page 39 for each child. Use the sheet to record the child's oral responses.

Say these directions to the child:

I am going to say a word. I want you to tell me a word that rhymes with it. If you want, you can make up a word. Let's try one. Listen: big. *Tell me a word that rhymes with* big. (Examples: dig, fig, gig, hig, jig, kig, pig, wig, and so on.)

Go to page 39.

Directions for Scoring

Give 1 point for each correct response. The highest score is 5.

Sample answers: **1.** not; **2.** club; **3.** bake; **4.** ride; **5.** pick

Record Sheet

Produce Rhyming Words

Tell me a word that rhymes with . . .

	Word	Response
1.	hot	_____
2.	rub	_____
3.	rake	_____
4.	slide	_____
5.	kick	_____

Score _____ / 5

Segment and Count Syllables

This phonological awareness test assesses a student's ability to count syllables in a word. Say a word. Have the student repeat the word and clap for each syllable, or word part, he or she hears. Then have the student tell the number of syllables in the word.

Instructions for Administering the Assessment

Make a copy of the record sheet on page 41 for each child. Use the sheet to record the child's oral responses.

Say these directions to the child:

I am going to say a word. I want you to repeat the word slowly and clap for each syllable, or word part, you hear. Let's do one together. Ready? The word is picnic. *Say and clap it with me:* pic-nic. *How many claps?* (2) *How many syllables?* (2)

Go to page 41.

Directions for Scoring

Give 1 point for each correct response. The highest score is 5.

Answers: **1.** three syllables; **2.** four syllables; **3.** two syllables; **4.** one syllable; **5.** two syllables

Name: _____ Date: _____

Record Sheet

Segment and Count Syllables

The word is . . . . Say and clap the word. . . . How many syllables?

Word	Number of Syllables
1. umbrella	_____
2. caterpillar	_____
3. pumpkin	_____
4. kite	_____
5. turtle	_____

Score _____ / 5

Blend Syllables

This phonological awareness test assesses a student's ability to combine syllables to form compound and multi-syllabic words. Say the parts of a word. Have the student say the complete word.

There are three sets of words. The sets progress in difficulty. If a student is unable to correctly say the first set of words, do not go on to the next set.

Instructions for Administering the Assessment

Make a copy of the record sheet on page 43 for each child. Use the sheet to record the child's oral responses.

Say these directions to the child:

I am going to say the parts of a word. I want you to put the word parts together and say the whole word. Let's try one. Listen: can-dle. *Again:* can-dle. *What is the whole word?* (candle)

Go to page 43.

Directions for Scoring

Give 1 point for each correct response. The highest score for each set of items is 5.

Answers for each set

Compound Words: **1.** pancake; **2.** baseball; **3.** popcorn; **4.** rainbow; **5.** airplane

Words with 2 Syllables: **1.** trumpet; **2.** costume; **3.** reptile; **4.** table; **5.** tiger

Words with 3 or More Syllables: **1.** cucumber; **2.** computer; **3.** alphabet; **4.** apartment; **5.** kindergarten

Phonological Awareness Grades K–1

Name: _____ Date: _____

Record Sheet

Blend Syllables

What is the whole word?

Compound Words

	Word Parts	Response
1.	pan-cake	_____
2.	base-ball	_____
3.	pop-corn	_____
4.	rain-bow	_____
5.	air-plane	_____

Score ___ / 5

Words with 3 or More Syllables

	Word Parts	Response
1.	cu-cum-ber	_____
2.	com-pu-ter	_____
3.	al-pha-bet	_____
4.	a-part-ment	_____
5.	kin-der-gar-ten	_____

Score ___ / 5

Words with 2 Syllables

	Word Parts	Response
1.	trum-pet	_____
2.	cos-tume	_____
3.	rep-tile	_____
4.	ta-ble	_____
5.	ti-ger	_____

Score ___ / 5

Blend and Segment Onsets and Rimes

This phonological awareness test assesses a student's ability to combine onsets and rimes to form a word. Say the initial sound in a word (the onset) and then say the rest of the word (the rime). Have the student put the word together and repeat the whole word back to you.

Instructions for Administering the Assessment

Make a copy of the record sheet on page 45 for each child. Use the sheet to record the child's oral responses.

Say these directions to the child:

I am going to say a word in two parts. I want you to put the parts together and say the whole word. Let's try one. Listen: /g/-ame. Again: /g/-ame. What is the whole word? (game) *That's right, the word is* game.

Go to page 45.

Directions for Scoring

Give 1 point for each correct response. The highest score is 5.

Answers: **1.** sit; **2.** bear; **3.** call; **4.** toe; **5.** pants

Name: _____ Date: _____

Blend and Segment Onsets and Rimes

What is the whole word?

Onset and Rime	Response
1. /s/-it	_____
2. /b/-ear	_____
3. /k/-all	_____
4. /t/-oe	_____
5. /p/-ants	_____

Score ___ / 5

Count Phonemes

This phonemic awareness test assesses a student's ability to break a word into its separate sounds (phonemes) and count the sounds. Name each picture. Have the student repeat the word, segment it into sounds, and tell the number of sounds in the word.

Instructions for Administering the Assessment

Make a copy of page 47 for each child. Record the child's oral responses.

Say these directions to the child.

I am going to say a word. I want you to say the word very slowly and tell me how many sounds you hear. Let's try one. Listen: fan. *Say it very slowly. (/f/ /a/ /n/) How many sounds do you hear? (three)*

1. *Look at Number 1* (point to the number). *This is a picture of a rock. Say the word* rock *very slowly. How many sounds do you hear?*

2. *Look at Number 2* (point to the number). *This is a picture of a bee. Say the word* bee *very slowly. How many sounds do you hear?*

3. *Look at Number 3* (point to the number). *This is a picture of a snake. Say the word* snake *very slowly. How many sounds do you hear?*

4. *Look at Number 4* (point to the number). *This is a picture of a plant. Say the word* plant *very slowly. How many sounds do you hear?*

5. *Look at Number 5* (point to the number). *This is a picture of feet. Say the word* feet *very slowly. How many sounds do you hear?*

Directions for Scoring

Give 1 point for each correct response. The highest score is 5.

Answers: **1.** three sounds; **2.** two sounds; **3.** four sounds; **4.** five sounds; **5.** three sounds

Name: _____ **Date:** _____

Count Phonemes

1

_____

2

_____

3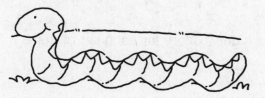

_____

4

_____

5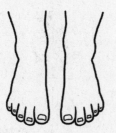

_____

Score: _____ / 5

Isolate and Pronounce Phonemes

This phonemic awareness test assesses a student's ability to recognize individual sounds (phonemes) in a word. Say a word. Have the student say the first, last, or medial sound in the word.

Instructions for Administering the Assessment

Make a copy of the record sheet on page 49 for each child. Use the sheet to record the child's oral responses.

Use the following directions depending on what is being assessed:

I am going to say a word. I want you to tell me the initial, or beginning, sound. Let's do an example. Listen: tag. *Say the initial, or beginning, sound in* tag. (/t/)

I am going to say a word. I want you to tell me the final, or ending, sound. Let's do an example. Listen: tag. *Say the final, or ending, sound in* tag. (/g/)

I am going to say a word. I want you to tell me the medial, or middle, sound. Let's do an example. Listen: tag. *Say the medial, or middle, sound in* tag. (/a/)

Go to page 49.

Directions for Scoring

Give 1 point for each correct response. The highest score for each set of items is 5.

Answers for each grouping

Initial Sounds: **1.** /b/; **2.** /f/; **3.** /l/; **4.** /d/; **5.** /n/

Final Sounds: **1.** /d/; **2.** /g/; **3.** /m/; **4.** /n/; **5.** /p/

Medial Sounds: **1.** /a/; **2.** /ē/; **3.** /e/; **4.** /ā/; **5.** /i/

Phonemic Awareness Grades K–3

Name: _____ Date: _____

Record Sheet

Isolate and Pronounce Phonemes

Initial Sounds

Say the initial, or beginning, sound in . . .

Word	Response
1. bag	_____
2. fun	_____
3. log	_____
4. dip	_____
5. net	_____

Score ____ / 5

Medial Sounds

Say the medial, or middle, sound in . . .

Word	Response
1. ran	_____
2. team	_____
3. set	_____
4. wait	_____
5. tip	_____

Score ____ / 5

Final Sounds

Say the final, or ending, sound in . . .

Word	Response
1. hid	_____
2. wag	_____
3. hum	_____
4. pen	_____
5. top	_____

Score ____ / 5

Match Phonemes

This phonemic awareness test assesses a student's ability to recognize the same sounds in different words. Say three words. Have the student say the words that have the same initial, final, or medial sound.

Instructions for Administering the Assessment

Make a copy of the record sheet on page 51 for each child. Use the sheet to record the child's oral responses.

Use the following directions depending on what is being assessed:

I am going to say three words. I want you to tell me which two words begin with the same sound. Let's do an example. Listen: lap, pat, let. (Repeat.) *Which two words begin with the same sound?* (lap, let)

I am going to say three words. I want you to tell me which two words end with the same sound. Let's do an example. Listen: lap, pat, let. (Repeat.) *Which two words end with the same sound?* (pat, let)

I am going to say three words. I want you to tell me which two words have the same sound in the middle. Let's do an example. Listen: lap, pat, let. (Repeat.) *Which two words have the same sound in the middle?* (lap, pat)

Go to page 51.

Directions for Scoring

Give 1 point for each correct response. The highest score for each set of words is 5.

Answers for each grouping

Initial Sounds: **1.** mob, mess; **2.** tack, toad; **3.** neck, nose; **4.** cut, cape; **5.** get, game

Final Sounds: **1.** seed, wood; **2.** hog, rag; **3.** take, pick; **4.** team, gum; **5.** foot, heat

Medial Sounds: **1.** red, net; **2.** mine, side; **3.** sail, fade; **4.** robe, loaf; **5.** cub, jug

Name: _____ **Date:** _____

Record Sheet

Match Phonemes

Initial Sounds

Which two words begin with the same sound?

Words	Response
1. mob, mess, pod	_____
2. lick, tack, toad	_____
3. neck, keep, nose	_____
4. cut, hut, cape	_____
5. get, game, sum	_____

Score ___ / 5

Medial Sounds

Which two words have the same sound in the middle?

Words	Response
1. red, net, nut	_____
2. mane, mine, side	_____
3. sail, tall, fade	_____
4. lot, robe, loaf	_____
5. cub, jug, web	_____

Score ___ / 5

Final Sounds

Which two words end with the same sound?

Words	Response
1. seed, wood, sat	_____
2. hip, hog, rag	_____
3. take, tab, pick	_____
4. men, team, gum	_____
5. foot, heat, has	_____

Score ___ / 5

Blend Phonemes to Produce Words

This phonemic awareness test assesses a student's ability to combine phonemes to form words. Slowly say each sound in a word. Have the student say the word.

Instructions for Administering the Assessment

Make a copy of the record sheet on page 53 for each child. Use the sheet to record the child's oral responses.

Say these directions to the child:

I am going to say a word, sound by sound. I want you to blend the sounds together and say the word. Let's try one. Listen: /s/ /a/ /d/. What word do you make when you blend the sounds /s/ /a/ /d/? (sad)

Go to page 53.

Directions for Scoring

Give 1 point for each correct response. The highest score for each set of items is 5.

Answers for each grouping

Words with 3 Phonemes: **1.** fed; **2.** him; **3.** jug; **4.** fly; **5.** chin

Words with 4 Phonemes: **1.** brake (or break); **2.** sleep; **3.** nest; **4.** lamp; **5.** pinch

Phonemic Awareness Grades K–3

Name: _____ Date: _____

Record Sheet

Blend Phonemes to Produce Words

What word do you make when you blend the sounds . . .?

Words with 3 Phonemes

Phonemes	Response
1. /f/ /e/ /d/	_____
2. /h/ /i/ /m/	_____
3. /j/ /u/ /g/	_____
4. /f/ /l/ /ī/	_____
5. /ch/ /i/ /n/	_____

Score ___ / 5

Words with 4 Phonemes

Phonemes	Response
1. /b/ /r/ /ā/ /k/	_____
2. /s/ /l/ /ē/ /p/	_____
3. /n/ /e/ /s/ /t/	_____
4. /l/ /a/ /m/ /p/	_____
5. /p/ /i/ /n/ /ch/	_____

Score ___ / 5

Segment Words into Phonemes

This phonemic awareness test assesses a student's ability to break a word into its separate sounds. Say a word. Have the student segment the word into its sounds.

Instructions for Administering the Assessment

Make a copy of the record sheet on page 55 for each child. Use the sheet to record the child's oral responses.

Say these directions to the child:

I am going to say a word. I want you to tell me all the sounds in the word. Let's try one. Tell me all the sounds you hear in the word pig. (/p/ /i/ /g/)

Go to page 55.

Directions for Scoring

Give 1 point for each correct response. The highest score for each set of items is 5.

Answers for each grouping

Words with 3 Phonemes:
1. /r/ /u/ /b/; **2.** /g/ /o/ /t/; **3.** /f/ /ī/ /v/; **4.** /m/ /u/ /d/; **5.** /sh/ /ā/ /k/

Words with 4 Phonemes:
1. /t/ /r/ /ā/ /d/; **2.** /p/ /l/ /a/ /n/; **3.** /b/ /l/ /ē/ /d/; **4.** /d/ /e/ /s/ /k/;
5. /k/ /a/ /m/ /p/

Name: _____ Date: _____

Record Sheet

Segment Words into Phonemes

Tell me all the sounds you hear in the word . . . .

Words with 3 Phonemes

Word	Response
1. rub	_____
2. got	_____
3. five	_____
4. mud	_____
5. shake	_____

Score ____ / 5

Words with 4 Phonemes

Word	Response
1. trade	_____
2. plan	_____
3. bleed	_____
4. desk	_____
5. camp	_____

Score ____ / 5

CORE Phoneme Deletion Test

This assessment includes four phoneme deletion tasks arranged in order of difficulty. The first task assesses the student's ability to delete initial phonemes. For example, the examiner may say the word *cat* and ask the student to say *cat* without the initial /k/ sound. The remaining tasks assess the student's ability to delete final phonemes, such as /t/ in the word *seat*; initial phonemes in blends, such as /s/ in the word *slip*; and phonemes embedded in blends, such as /l/ in the word *play*. The assessment contains minimal grade-level expectations for Grades 1 to 3, but can also be used with older students.

These tasks may help to determine whether deficits in phonemic, or sound, awareness account for the student's reading or spelling delays. According to research, the lack of phonemic awareness is the most powerful determinant of the likelihood of a student's failure to learn to read.

How to Use the Assessment

Before administering each task, administer the Practice Items. For all students, begin with the tasks in Part A of the test. Assess as far as the student can go, regardless of his or her grade placement. Do not correct errors; instead encourage students by praising their willingness to participate. Remember that this is an auditory assessment—students do not see the items on the test. The Correct Response column tells how the student's answer should sound, not how it should be spelled.

Phonemic Awareness Grades K–3

Part A

Begin by saying to the student, "We are going to play a word game. This game will give me information to help teach you better." Then administer the following two Practice Items.

Initial Sound
(Late K and Grade 1)

Practice Item 1

TEACHER: Say *cat*.

STUDENT: *cat*

TEACHER: Now say it without the /k/.

STUDENT: *at*

If the student responds incorrectly say, "Let's try that again." For example, if the student says *kit*, model the correct response by emphasizing the /k/ and artificially separating it from the *at*. Help the student to give the correct response by saying each sound slowly. Repeat the Practice Item until the student gives the correct response—even if the student does not seem to understand the task. After the student repeats the correct response, proceed to Practice Item 2.

Practice Item 2

TEACHER: Say *table*.

STUDENT: *table*

TEACHER: Now say it without the /t/.

STUDENT: *able*

If the student responds incorrectly say, "Let's try that again." For example, if the student says *bull*, model the correct response by emphasizing the /t/ and artificially separating it from *able*. Encourage the student to repeat the correct response.

If the student can correctly respond to these two Practice Items, proceed to the Test Items. If the student cannot correctly respond to these Practice Items, skip Part A and proceed to the Practice Items for Part B. Some students may be able to delete a final sound, but not an initial sound.

Part B

Final Sound
(Grade 1)

Say to the student, "We are going to play another word game. The rules of this game are a little different. Pay close attention." Then administer the following Practice Item.

Practice Item

TEACHER: Say *seat*.

STUDENT: *seat*

TEACHER: Now say it without the /t/.

STUDENT: *sea*

If the student responds incorrectly say, "Let's try that again." For example, if the student says *keat*, model the correct response by elongating *sea* and artificially separating it from the /t/. Then say, "*Seat* without the /t/ is *sea*." Encourage the student to repeat the correct response.

If the student can correctly respond to the Practice Item, proceed to the Test Items. If the student cannot correctly respond to any of the Part A or B Practice Items, discontinue the assessment.

Part C

First Sound of a
Consonant Blend
(Grade 2)

Say to the student, "We are going to do something different now. Pay close attention." Then administer the following Practice Item.

Practice Item

TEACHER: Say *slip*.

STUDENT: *slip*

TEACHER: Now say it without the /s/.

STUDENT: *lip*

If the student responds incorrectly say, "Let's try that again." For example, if the student deletes the entire /sl/ blend and says *ip*, model a correct response by emphasizing the /s/ and separating it from *lip*. Say, "Be careful, you're taking off too much. Try to say it without the /s/." If necessary, help the student to repeat the correct response.

If the student can correctly respond to, or repeat, the Practice Item, proceed to the Test Items. If the student can respond correctly to at least two of the Test Items, proceed to Part D; otherwise, discontinue the assessment.

Part D

Embedded Sound of a Consonant Blend (Grade 3)

Say to the student, "We are going to play another word game. The rules of this game are a little different." Then administer the following Practice Item.

Practice Item

TEACHER: Say *play*.

STUDENT: *play*

TEACHER: Now say it without the /l/.

STUDENT: *pay*

If the student responds incorrectly say, "Let's try that again." For example, if the student deletes the entire blend and says *ay*, say: "You are taking off too much. I just wanted you to say it without /l/." Model a correct response by separating all three sounds of the word: /p/ /l/ /ay/, and say: "Without the /l/ it is just /p/ /ay/—*pay*. So, what is *play* without the /l/? Yes, it is *pay*." If necessary, help the student to repeat the correct response.

If the student can correctly respond to, or repeat, the Practice Item, proceed to the Test Items.

▶ **WHAT IT MEANS** Use the guidelines below to determine the student's performance level.

Minimal Grade-Level Expectations

1–6 correct	late K / early Grade 1
7–10 correct	end of Grade 1
11–13 correct	early Grade 2
14–15 correct	end of Grade 2
16–18 correct	early Grade 3
19–20 correct	end of Grade 3

▶ **WHAT'S NEXT** Students who are able to do Part A: Initial Sound are especially ready for formal reading instruction. Students who do not meet grade expectations will benefit from more intense phonemic awareness instruction.

CORE Phoneme Deletion Test

Name: _____ **Grade:** _____ **Date:** _____

Directions: Follow the format used in the Practice Items to administer the items for each level. Mark "+" to indicate a correct response or "–" to indicate an incorrect response. Write down incorrect responses, but do not correct the student. If the student cannot complete any of the items in Parts A or B, discontinue testing. If the student cannot do at least two items in Part C, discontinue testing. Remember that this is an auditory assessment. Students do not see the items.

Part A: Initial Sound

Practice Items

Say *cat* ... now say it without the /k/ ___(at)

Say *table* ... now say it without the /t/ ___(able)

TEST ITEM		CORRECT RESPONSE		
1. (t)ower	our	(+) (–)	_____
2. (c)old	old	(+) (–)	_____
3. (b)ake	ache	(+) (–)	_____
4. (s)ize	eyes	(+) (–)	_____
5. (l)ow	owe	(+) (–)	_____

Part B: Final Sound

Practice Items

Say *seat* ... now say it without the /t/ ___(sea)

Say *rake* ... now say it without the /k/ ___(ray)

TEST ITEM		CORRECT RESPONSE		
6. to(n)e	toe	(+)(–)	_____
7. droo(p)	drew	(+)(–)	_____
8. ti(m)e	tie	(+)(–)	_____
9. ro(d)e	row	(+)(–)	_____
10. pla(c)e	play	(+)(–)	_____

Items Correct _____ **Grade Level** _____

Part C: First Sound of a Consonant Blend

Practice Items

Say *slip* ... now say it without the /s/ ___(lip)

Say *cloud* ... now say it without the /k/ ___(loud)

TEST ITEM		CORRECT RESPONSE		
11. (f)reight	rate	(+) (–)	_____
12. (p)layed	laid	(+) (–)	_____
13. (s)weet	wheat	(+) (–)	_____
14. (b)reak	rake	(+) (–)	_____
15. (s)pill	pill	(+) (–)	_____

Part D: Embedded Sound of a Consonant Blend

Practice Items

Say *slip* ... now say it without the /l/ ___(sip)

Say *play* ... now say it without the /l/ ___(pay)

TEST ITEM		CORRECT RESPONSE		
16. b(l)end	bend	(+)(–)	_____
17. t(w)in	tin	(+)(–)	_____
18. g(r)ow	go	(+)(–)	_____
19. be(s)t	bet	(+)(–)	_____
20. li(f)t	lit	(+)(–)	_____

Name: _____ Date: _____

Add Phonemes to Make New Words

This phonemic awareness test assesses a student's ability to manipulate sounds in words by adding a phoneme to a word to make a new word. Say a word. Have the student add a phoneme and say the new word. Make a copy of this page for each child, and record the child's oral responses. Give 1 point for each correct response.

The highest score for each set of items is 5.

Add Initial Sound

Listen to the word I say. Then add the sound I say to the beginning of the word.

	Word		Response
1.	an	Add /k/ to the beginning of an.	_____ (can)
2.	ice	Add /m/ to the beginning of ice.	_____ (mice)
3.	eel	Add /s/ to the beginning of eel.	_____ (seal)
4.	out	Add /p/ to the beginning of out.	_____ (pout)
5.	ox	Add /f/ to the beginning of ox.	_____ (fox)

Score ___ / 5

Add Final Sound

Listen to the word I say. Then add the sound I say to the end of the word.

	Word		Response
1.	bee	Add /d/ to the end of bee.	_____ (bead)
2.	way	Add /v/ to the end of way.	_____ (wave)
3.	he	Add /t/ to the end of he.	_____ (heat)
4.	no	Add /z/ to the end of no.	_____ (nose)
5.	boo	Add /m/ to the end of boo.	_____ (boom)

Score ___ / 5

Add First Sound of Consonant Blend

Listen to the word I say. Then add the sound I say to the beginning of the word.

	Word		Response
1.	ranch	Add /b/ to the beginning of ranch.	_____ (branch)
2.	loud	Add /k/ to the beginning of loud.	_____ (cloud)
3.	win	Add /t/ to the beginning of win.	_____ (twin)
4.	tar	Add /s/ to the beginning of tar.	_____ (star)
5.	ray	Add /g/ to the beginning of ray.	_____ (gray)

Score ___ / 5

Name: _____ **Date:** _____

Substitute Phonemes to Make New Words

This phonemic awareness test assesses a student's ability to manipulate sounds in words by substituting one phoneme for another to make a new word. Say a word. Have the student replace one phoneme and say the new word. Make a copy of this page for each child, and record the child's oral responses. Give 1 point for each correct response.

The highest score for each set of items is 5.

Initial Sound Substitution

Listen to the word I say. Then change the sound I say at the beginning of the word.

	Word		Response
1.	ham	Change the /h/ to /r/.	_____ (ram)
2.	face	Change the /f/ to /p/.	_____ (pace)
3.	jet	Change the /j/ to /s/.	_____ (set)
4.	line	Change the /l/ to /n/.	_____ (nine)
5.	house	Change the /h/ to /m/.	_____ (mouse)

Score ___ / 5

Final Sound Substitution

Listen to the word I say. Then change the sound I say at the end of the word.

	Word		Response
1.	has	Change the /z/ to /t/.	_____ (hat)
2.	fig	Change the /g/ to /n/.	_____ (fin)
3.	safe	Change the /f/ to /m/.	_____ (same)
4.	hot	Change the /t/ to /p/.	_____ (hop)
5.	rode	Change the /d/ to /z/.	_____ (rose)

Score ___ / 5

Medial Sound Substitution

Listen to the word I say. Then change the sound I say in the middle of the word.

	Word		Response
1.	lip	Change the /i/ to /a/.	_____ (lap)
2.	sad	Change the /a/ to /ī/.	_____ (side)
3.	rake	Change the /ā/ to /o/.	_____ (rock)
4.	rode	Change the /ō/ to /e/.	_____ (red)
5.	pile	Change the /ī/ to /i/.	_____ (pill)

Score ___ / 5

Distinguish Long from Short Vowels

This phonemic awareness test assesses a student's ability to distinguish between long and short vowels. Say a pair of words. Ask the student to identify the word with a long or short vowel sound.

Instructions for Administering the Assessment

Make a copy of the record sheet on page 64 for each child. Record the child's oral responses.

Say these directions to the child based on the assessment focus:

I am going to say two words. I want you to tell me which word has a short vowel sound. Let's try an example. Listen: cot, coat. *Which word has a short vowel sound:* cot *or* coat? (cot)

I am going to say two words. I want you to tell me which word has a long vowel sound. Let's try an example. Listen: cot, coat. *Which word has a long vowel sound:* cot *or* coat? (coat)

Go to page 64.

Directions for Scoring

Give 1 point for each correct response. The highest score for each set of items is 5.

Answers for each grouping

Short Vowels: **1.** man; **2.** rip; **3.** met; **4.** hop; **5.** slid

Long Vowels: **1.** pine; **2.** robe; **3.** tape; **4.** cube; **5.** bead

Name: _____ Date: _____

Record Sheet

Distinguish Long from Short Vowels

Short Vowels

Which word has a short vowel sound?

Words	Response
1. man *or* mane?	_____
2. ripe *or* rip?	_____
3. meet *or* met?	_____
4. hop *or* hope?	_____
5. slide *or* slid?	_____

Score ____ / 5

Long Vowels

Which word has a long vowel sound?

Words	Response
1. pine *or* pin?	_____
2. rob *or* robe?	_____
3. tap *or* tape?	_____
4. cub *or* cube?	_____
5. bead *or* bed?	_____

Score ____ / 5

Phonics

Represent Phonemes with Letters

This test assesses a student's ability to connect sound to letter. Name a picture. Have the student circle the letter for the first, last, or middle sound in the picture name.

Instructions for Administering the Assessment

Make a copy of pages 67, 68, and 69 for each child.

Say these directions to the child.

Page 67: Initial Consonants

1. *Look at Number 1* (point to the number). *This is a picture of a cup. Circle the letter that stands for the sound at the beginning of* cup.

2. *Look at Number 2* (point to the number). *This is a picture of a note. Circle the letter that stands for the sound at the beginning of* note.

3. *Look at Number 3* (point to the number). *This is a picture of a dog. Circle the letter that stands for the sound at the beginning of* dog.

4. *Look at Number 4* (point to the number). *This is a picture of a goat. Circle the letter that stands for the sound at the beginning of* goat.

5. *Look at Number 5* (point to the number). *This is a picture of a van. Circle the letter that stands for the sound at the beginning of* van.

Page 68: Final Consonants

1. *Look at Number 1* (point to the number). *This is a picture of a cat. Circle the letter that stands for the sound at the end of* cat.

2. *Look at Number 2* (point to the number). *This is a picture of a tub. Circle the letter that stands for the sound at the end of* tub.

3. *Look at Number 3* (point to the number). *This is a picture of a hen. Circle the letter that stands for the sound at the end of* hen.

4. *Look at Number 4* (point to the number). *This is a picture of a toad. Circle the letter that stands for the sound at the end of* toad.

5. *Look at Number 5* (point to the number). *This is a picture of a drum. Circle the letter that stands for the sound at the end of* drum.

Phonics

Page 69: Vowels

1. *Look at Number 1* (point to the number). *This is a picture of a bib. Circle the letter that stands for the sound you hear in the middle of* bib.

2. *Look at Number 2* (point to the number). *This is a picture of a bag. Circle the letter that stands for the sound you hear in the middle of* bag.

3. *Look at Number 3* (point to the number). *This is a picture of a pot. Circle the letter that stands for the sound you hear in the middle of* pot.

4. *Look at Number 4* (point to the number). *This is a picture of a sun. Circle the letter that stands for the sound you hear in the middle of* sun.

5. *Look at Number 5* (point to the number). *This is a picture of a bed. Circle the letter that stands for the sound you hear in the middle of* bed.

Directions for Scoring

Give 1 point for each correct response. The highest score for each set of items is 5.

Answers for each page

Page 67: **1.** c; **2.** n; **3.** d; **4.** g; **5.** v

Page 68: **1.** t; **2.** b; **3.** n; **4.** d; **5.** m

Page 69: **1.** i; **2.** a; **3.** o; **4.** u; **5.** e

Placement and Diagnostic Assessment

Name: _____ Date: _____

Represent Phonemes with Letters:
Initial Consonants

1  **b** **f** **c**

2  **m** **n** **w**

3  **d** **t** **l**

4  **k** **g** **p**

5  **b** **s** **v**

Score ___ / 5

Name: _____ Date: _____

Represent Phonemes with Letters:
Final Consonants

1  **d**   **t**   **g**

2  **b**   **p**   **v**

3  **m**   **d**   **n**

4  **g**   **d**   **p**

5  **n**   **m**   **k**

Score ____ / 5

Placement and Diagnostic Assessment

Name: _____ Date: _____

Represent Phonemes with Letters: Vowels

1  **a**   **i**   **o**

2 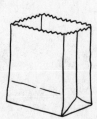 **e**   **u**   **a**

3  **a**   **o**   **u**

4  **u**   **i**   **e**

5  **i**   **o**   **e**

Score ____ / 5

Letter Naming
and Sight Words

Letter Naming Fluency Assessment

Instructions for Administering Letter Naming Fluency

1. Make a copy of the Letter Naming Fluency sheet for the student to use. Then make a copy of the sheet for yourself to record the student's oral responses.

2. Say these directions to the student:

   Here are some letters. Tell me the names of as many letters as you can. When I say, "Begin" start here (point to the first letter) *and go across the page. Point to each letter and tell me the name of that letter. If you come to a letter that you don't know, I'll tell it to you. Put your finger on the first letter. Ready, begin.*

3. Start your stopwatch. Follow along with your copy of the Letter Naming Fluency record sheet. Put a slash (/) through letters named incorrectly. Place a check above letters named correctly.

4. **At the end of 1 minute, place a bracket (]) after the last letter named and say,** *Stop.*

Directions for Scoring

1. Each row has 10 letters and there are 120 letters in the entire sheet. If the student does not get any correct letter names within the first 10 letters (1 row), discontinue the task and record a score of zero.

2. If the student hesitates for 3 seconds on a letter, score the letter incorrect, and provide the correct letter to the student.

3. If the student provides the letter sound rather than the letter name, say: *Remember to tell me the letter name, not the sound it makes.* If the student continues providing letter sounds, mark each letter as incorrect, and make a note of this behavior at the bottom of the page.

4. Score a point for each correct letter the student names and make a record of the total number of correct letters.

5. Use the following benchmarks to gauge student achievement in this assessment.

   Grade K

   • Fall: 10 or more correct letters

   • Winter: 30 or more correct letters

   • Spring: 40 or more correct letters

   Grade 1

   • Fall: 40 or more correct letters

   • Winter: 50 or more correct letters

   • Spring: 60 or more correct letters

Name: _____ **Date:** _____

Fluency Sheet

Letter Naming Fluency

g	H	t	X	r	F	C	j	T	z
K	I	q	z	b	n	y	s	l	O
A	e	V	u	Q	Y	z	M	j	a
f	i	W	R	g	U	d	z	S	c
k	M	g	D	o	J	n	p	m	h
C	N	E	b	u	a	g	w	V	f
G	Y	i	d	e	n	S	T	t	c
R	F	a	m	Z	l	w	v	C	n
f	s	P	o	Y	W	E	j	k	Q
D	U	g	e	A	b	i	y	B	d
N	f	p	R	F	q	l	K	p	M
L	a	W	f	U	c	O	b	x	Z

Sight Word Fluency Assessment

Instructions for Administering the Assessment

Make a copy of the sheet for the student to use. Then make a copy of the sheet for yourself to record the student's oral responses. Give the student the assessment sheet, and have the student put his or her finger on the first word in the first row. Explain that you would like the student to read as many words as he or she can in one minute. Tell the student to point to each word and say the word. Then say: *When you are ready, you may begin.* Start your stopwatch, timing the student for one minute as he or she reads the words.

1. Follow along as the student reads. Place a check above each word that is said correctly.

2. Place a line through each word that is read incorrectly or omitted.

3. If the student substitutes or mispronounces a word, put a line through the word and write the word the student said above it.

4. If the student does not correctly say a word within 3 seconds, say the word for the student and mark the word as incorrect.

5. Say *Stop* at the end of one minute and place a bracket (]) after the last word read by the student.

Directions for Scoring

1. There are five words per line and sixty words in total. Count the total number of words read. This includes the words that are read correctly and incorrectly. Record that number.

2. Count the number of errors and record them. Subtract this number from the total number of words read to get the number of words read correctly.

3. Use this formula to score Oral Reading Accuracy:

$$\frac{\text{Total No. of Words Read} - \text{No. of Errors}}{\text{Total Number of Words Read}} \times 100$$

For students at the end of Kindergarten or the start of Grade 1, **10–16** words read correctly is an appropriate benchmark.

For students at the end of Grade 1 or in Grades 2 or 3, **40+** words read correctly is an appropriate benchmark.

Name: _____ **Date:** _____

Fluency Sheet

Sight Word Fluency				
and	are	do	for	go
has	have	he	here	is
like	little	look	me	my
play	said	see	she	to
the	this	was	we	what
where	with	you	jump	not
up	too	yes	over	run
come	good	on	that	very
help	use	now	could	one
two	they	her	does	who
some	of	at	live	into
many	out	want	under	show

Copyright © McGraw-Hill Education

**Placement and
Diagnostic Assessment**

Phonics and Decoding

- Hasbrouck's Phonics Survey

Phonics Survey, Standard Version

based on **The Quick Phonics Screener**
Jan Hasbrouck, Ph.D.
© 2006-2010 JH Consulting

*The purpose of the Phonics Survey (PS)
is to provide informal diagnostic information that can be used
to help (a) PLAN a student's instructional program in basic word
reading skills, and (b) MONITOR THE PROGRESS or
IMPROVEMENT in phonics skill development. The PS has
not been normed or standardized. It is meant to be used as
an informal classroom assessment tool.*

Directions for Administration and Scoring

1. Say to the student:

   "I'm going to ask you to read some letters, words, and sentences to me so I can find out what kinds of words are easy for you to read and what kinds of words you still need to learn. I want you to try to do your best. We probably won't do this whole page; we'll stop if it gets too hard. Do you have any questions?"

   Start the PS assessment where you believe the student's skills are fairly strong. For beginning readers (K–1 level), start with sounds or letter names.

   For Task 1, first (a) have the student tell the name of each letter. Then (b) have the student tell the sound each letter makes.

   For the *NAMES* task, have the student name the letter Q, not the *qu* digraph. For the *SOUNDS* task, have the student give you the short sound for each of the vowels. If the student says the long sound (letter name), say: *"That is one sound that letter makes. Do you know the <u>short</u> sound for that letter?"* For the letter *c,* ask for the "hard sound" /k/, as in *cat.* For the letter *g* ask for the "hard sound" /g/, as in *gas.* For the letter *y* ask for the /y/ sound, as in *yes.* If the student offers a correct alternative sound for these letters, you should say, *"Yes, that is one sound for that letter. Do you know another sound that letter makes?"*

   Most students in 4th grade and above would not be given the letter names/sounds task. Letter names would usually only be given to K–1st students. (If a student reads 6/10 or more in Task 2a, you may skip Task 1 Letter Sounds.)

2. If the student has difficulty (half or fewer correct on any task) move up the page to an easier task. If the student does well (more than half correct on a task), move down to a harder task.

3. On Tasks 2–6: If the student reads all or almost all words correctly on part (a) of the task (reading words), you may want to skip part (b) of the task (reading sentences). If the next task is difficult for the student, you can go back and complete the part of a previous task that was skipped.

4. When the student is reading the words in text, only count errors on the target words (those underlined and in italics).

5. Stop the assessment when the student appears frustrated or tired. It is OK to stop in the middle of a task. Not all tasks must be administered, but try to assess as many as possible so you will have sufficient information to plan instruction or monitor progress.

Phonics and Decoding Grades K–6

6. Mark errors and make notes or comments to help you remember how the student responded. Note that in Task 9, students read the entire word, not syllable-by-syllable. The teacher's copy is written in syllables to facilitate marking/recording of errors within a word.

7. The PS is scored by each individual task *only*. Record the ratio of correct responses over the total number possible, (e.g., 13/21 or 8/10 for each task). A chart format can be helpful for reporting PS results.

1. Letters		Score
(a) Names	N/A not administered	_____ /26
(b) Sounds		18 _____ /21 cons. 4 _____ /5 vowels
2. VC and CVC		**Score**
(a) List		8 /10
(b) Text		17 /20
3. Digraphs		**Score**
(a) List		6 /10
(b) Text		4 /10

8. The grade level listed above each task is an approximate level at which those phonics skills are often taught. **NOTE:** *Results from the PS **CAN ONLY** be used to determine a student's strengths/needs in key phonics and decoding skills, **NOT** his or her grade-level performance in reading.*

Phonics and Decoding Grades K–6

	Phonics Survey — Standard Version
Task 1(a)	m t a s i r d f o g l h u c n b j k
Task 1(b)	y e w p v qu x z
Task 2(a)	wat fod leb tum pon sib cug raf mip hev
Task 2(b)	Sam and Ben hid the gum. Pat had a nap in bed. Mom had a top on a big pot. Tim can sit in a tub.
Task 3(a)	shap ming gack whum pith chan thog kosh mich whaf
Task 3(b)	That duck had a wet wing. Dad hit a log with a whip. When can Chip pack? A fish is in that tub.
Task 4(a)	clab trin snaf greb slad fosp lonk mant jast sund
Task 4(b)	Glen will swim past the raft in the pond. The frog must flip and spin and jump.
Task 5(a)	sice nole fune moze vate rine lade sile gane fote
Task 5(b)	Mike and Jane use a rope to ride the mule. Pete had five tapes at home.

Copyright © McGraw-Hill Education

Phonics and Decoding Grades K–6

	Phonics Survey — Standard Version						
Task 6(a)	cort	pirk	varb	serl	surd		
	tarn	forp	murk	tirn	kerm		
Task 6(b)	The tar on his torn shirt burned and hurt him.						
	The bird hid under the short ferns in the park.						
Task 7(a)	litch	mudge	glux	quam	celp		
	gerb	knaz	gnap	wrill	ralk		
Task 7(b)	The milk is in the wrong cup.						
	She ran to the center of the bridge.						
	I will stitch a knot on the quilt.						
	The giant dog will gnaw on the box.						
Task 8	foat	roast	frea	creak	moom	scoop	raim	waist
	folt	scold	dray	gray	chout	mount	poid	join
	moy	royal	vaul	fault	praw	straw	koe	toe
	frew	jewel	palk	scald	pigh	fight		
Task 9(a)	mascot	basket	moment	bacon	handle		
	puzzle	cartoon	order	escape	chowder		
Task 9(b)	amputate	liberty	dominate	elastic	entertain		
	practical	innocent	electric	volcano	segregate		
Task 9(c)	particular	contaminate	community	superior	vitality		
	evaporate	inventory	prehistoric	solitary	emergency		
Task 10	discount	dismiss	nonsense	nonstop	index	intent	
	prefix	prepare	return	replay	unable	uncertain	
	confident	concert	station	motion	famous	joyous	
	coolness	wildness	portable	drinkable	fastest	dampest	
	mouthful	fearful	honorary	literary	instrument	fragment	

Phonics and Decoding Grades K–6

Grades K-1

1. Letters

(a) Names							Score		(b) Sounds							Score
	m	t	a	s	i	r				/m/ /t/ /a/ /s/ /i/ /r/						Consonants:
	d	f	o	g	l	h				/d/ /f/ /o/ /g/ /l/ /h/						/21
	u	c	n	b	j	k				/u/ /k/ /n/ /b/ /j/ /k/						
	y	e	w	p	v	qu				/y/ /e/ /w/ /p/ /v/ /kw/						Vowels:
	x	z					/26			/ks/ /z/						/5

Grade 1

2. VC and CVC

					Comments	Score
(a) In List	wat	fod	leb	tum		
	pon	sib	cug	raf		
	mip	hev				/10
(b) In Text	Sam and Ben hid the gum. Pat had a nap in bed.					
	Mom had a top on a big pot. Tim can sit in a tub.					/20

Grade 1

3. Consonant Digraphs

					Comments	Score
(a) In List	shap	ming	gack	whum		
	pith	chan	thog	kosh		
	mich	whaf				/10
(b) In Text	That duck had a wet wing. Dad hit a log with a whip.					
	When can Chip pack? A fish is in that tub.					/10

Grade 1

4. CVCC and CCVC

					Comments	Score
(a) In List	clab	trin	snaf	greb		
	slad	fosp	lonk	mant		
	jast	sund				/10
(b) In Text	Glen will swim past the raft in the pond.					
	The frog must flip and spin and jump.					/10

Grades 1-2

5. Silent e

					Comments	Score
(a) In List	sice	nole	fune	moze		
	vate	rine	lade	sile		
	gane	fote				/10
(b) In Text	Mike and Jane use a rope to ride the mule.					
	Pete had five tapes at home.					/10

Phonics and Decoding Grades K–6

Grades 1 - 2

6. r-Controlled Vowels		Comments	Score
(a) In List	cort pirk varb serl surd tarn forp murk tirn kerm		/10
(b) In Text	The _tar_ on his _torn shirt burned_ and _hurt_ him. The _bird_ hid _under_ the _short ferns_ in the _park_.		/10

Grades 1 - 3

7. Advanced Consonants (-tch, -dge, -x, qu, soft c & g, kn, gn, wr, -lk)		Comments	Score
(a) In List	litch mudge glux quam celp gerb knaz gnap wrill ralk		/10
(b) In Text	The _milk_ is in the _wrong_ cup. She ran to the _center_ of the _bridge_. I will _stitch_ a _knot_ on the _quilt_. The _giant_ dog will _gnaw_ on the _box_.		/10

Grades 1 - 3

8. Vowel Teams								Comments	Score
oa, ea, oo, **ai, ol, ay,** **ou, oi, oy,** **au, aw, oe,** **ew, al, igh**	foat roast frea creak moom scoop raim waist folt scold dray gray chout mount poid join moy royal vaul fault praw straw koe toe frew jewel palk scald pigh fight								/30

Grades 2, 3, 4 - 6+

9. Multi-Syllable		Comments	Score
(a) 2-Syllable	mas-cot bas-ket mo-ment ba-con han-dle puz-zle car-toon or-der es-cape chow-der		/10
(b) 3-Syllable	am-pu-tate lib-er-ty dom-in-ate e-las-tic en-ter-tain prac-ti-cal in-no-cent e-lec-tric vol-ca-no seg-re-gate		/10
(c) 4-Syllable	par-tic-u-lar con-tam-i-nate com-mu-ni-ty su-per-i-or vi-tal-i-ty e-vap-or-ate in-ven-tor-y pre-his-tor-ic sol-i-tar-y e-mer-gen-cy		/10

Grades 2, 3, 4 - 6+

10. Prefixes and Suffixes					Comments	Score
dis-, non-, **in-, pre-, re-,** **un-, con-,** **-tion, -ous,** **-ness, -able,** **-est, -ful,** **-ary, -ment**	discount intent unable motion portable fearful	dismiss prefix uncertain famous drinkable honorary	nonsense prepare confident joyous fastest literary	nonstop return concert coolness dampest instrument	index replay station wildness mouthful fragment	/30

Oral Reading
Fluency

- Fluency Passages for Grades 1–6
- National Fluency Norms

Introduction

What Is Fluency?

Fluency is the critical bridge between two key elements of reading—decoding and comprehension. In its 2000 report, the National Reading Panel defined it as "the ability to read text quickly, accurately, and with proper expression." Fluency has several dimensions. Successful readers must decode words accurately. But they must move beyond decoding and recognize words in connected text quickly and automatically. They must also read with expression in order to bring meaningful interpretation to the text. All three dimensions—accurate decoding, automaticity, and ability to read expressively—work together to create effective comprehension and overall success in reading.

In its 1994 study of reading, the National Assessment of Educational Progress (NAEP) established a clear connection between fluency and comprehension. NAEP defined fluency as the ease or "naturalness" of reading. It recognized certain key elements as contributing to fluency. These included the reader's grouping or phrasing of words as shown through intonation, stress, and pauses and the reader's adherence to the author's syntax. They also included expressiveness as reflected by the reader's interjection of a sense of feeling, anticipation, or characterization in oral reading. These elements are called *prosody*. When readers use appropriate volume, tone, emphasis, and phrasing, they give evidence of comprehension. They demonstrate that they are actively constructing meaning from the text.

Why Is Fluency Important?

Fluency is critical because it directly impacts the comprehension process. For years, teachers thought that if students could decode words accurately, they would become strong readers. Fluency, which has been referred to as a "neglected" aspect of reading, received little attention. Now it is recognized as one of the five critical components of reading.

Researchers have pointed out that people can successfully focus on only one thing at a time. They can, however, do more than one thing at a time if one of those things is so well learned that it can be done automatically. In its simplest form, reading can be seen as (1) word identification or decoding and (2) comprehension, or the active construction of meaning. Effective readers cannot focus on both of these processes at the same time. If a reader is focused almost entirely on decoding, that reader will have few resources left over for constructing meaning. Only when readers can read the words in connected text automatically are they free to focus their attention on making inferences, drawing conclusions, and applying other critical thinking skills associated with constructing meaning.

Oral Reading Fluency Grades 1–6

A fluent reader generally reads with speed and accuracy, but in addition usually displays these kinds of behaviors:

- Recognizes words automatically
- Applies graphophonic, semantic, and syntactic cues to recognize unfamiliar words
- Segments texts into meaningful chunks
- Emulates the sounds and rhythms of spoken language while reading aloud

A nonfluent reader, in contrast, may display these kinds of behaviors:

- Reads slowly and laboriously
- Processes text word-by-word in a choppy manner
- Frequently ignores punctuation
- Fails to use meaningful phrasing
- Shows little certainty when reading high-frequency words

Fluency does not mean only rapid reading. Occasionally, you will come across a nonfluent reader who is able to read text rapidly but fails to use appropriate phrasing. This reader often ignores meaning and punctuation. As a result, this reader struggles to answer questions about what has been read and fails to grasp the intent of the text.

Why Assess Fluency?

Students need to be fluent in order to be proficient readers. Their oral reading fluency can be improved through explicit training, but you need to assess their fluency level before you can determine what specific fluency-building activities and materials will be appropriate. In addition, students excel in reading when they are given opportunities to read as much connected text as possible at their independent level. Fluency assessment helps you determine what this level is.

The oral reading fluency assessments in this book answer this question: *How many words can a student read aloud per minute and how many of these words are read correctly?* This book also helps you observe reading performance beyond speed and accuracy by providing a rubric similar to the one developed by NAEP. This 4-level rubric on page 88 takes into account additional aspects of fluency, such as prosody.

How and When to Assess
Kindergarten Through Early First Grade

Until children can decode and automatically recognize many words by sight, they cannot be expected to read aloud effortlessly and expressively. That is why formally assessing their oral reading fluency at this early stage is not recommended. However, it is highly recommended that kindergarten children be involved in fluency-building activities, such as listening to books being read aloud and imitating auditory models of natural speech. Toward the end of kindergarten, children can be given opportunities to reread familiar, predictable, and decodable text to build fluency.

Oral Reading Fluency Grades 1–6

Some assessments for children at these grade levels are considered valuable. By assessing letter naming, phoneme segmentation, and sight word fluency during kindergarten and the early part of Grade 1, teachers can determine what type of fluency-building activities and materials to provide. Assessments for these skill areas appear in other sections of this book.

Midyear of Grade 1 Through Grade 6

Curriculum-based assessment of oral reading fluency is administered by asking a student to do a timed reading of a carefully selected on-level passage. As the student reads, you follow along in a copy of the same text and record errors such as omissions, substitutions, misreadings, insertions of words or parts of words, and hesitations of more than three seconds. Self-corrections and repetitions are not considered errors. To calculate the number of words read correctly in one minute, subtract the number of errors from the total number of words read. This process should be repeated periodically throughout the school year to monitor growth.

The Fluency Passages

The fluency passages serve two purposes. They can be administered as benchmark tests to determine if students are on track. They can also be used every unit so that you can monitor progress and determine if students are meeting instructional goals.

For Grade 1, the first passage is below the LEXILE band; the remaining passages are within the band.

For Grades 2–6, the first two passages approach or are at the low end of the LEXILE grade band; the next two passages are within the band; and the final two are at the high end or exceed the high end of the band.

Oral Fluency Scale

Prosody Rubric

Level 4
- **The student:** reads in large, meaningful phrases; may occasionally repeat words or short phrases, but the overall structure and syntax of the passage is not affected; reads at an appropriate rate of speed with expressive interpretation.

Level 3
- **The student:** reads in three- and four-word phrases; reads primarily in phrases that preserve the passage's syntax and structure; attempts to read expressively; generally reads at an appropriate rate of speed.

Level 2
- **The student:** reads mainly in two-word phrases, with some longer phrases and at times word-by-word; may group words awkwardly and not connect phrases to the larger context of the passage; reads sections of the passage excessively slowly or quickly.

Level 1
- **The student:** reads word-by-word, with some longer phrases; does not phrase meaningfully or with an appropriate rate of speed; reads the passage excessively slowly.

Oral Reading Fluency Grades 1–6

Curriculum-Based Oral Reading Fluency Norms

Use these norms to interpret your students' oral reading fluency abilities and to tailor instruction to their individual needs. Results are based on a one-minute timed sampling of students reading aloud. A more detailed chart appears on pages 160–161.

Grade	Percentile	Fall WCPM	Winter WCPM	Spring WCPM
1	90	NA	81	111
	75	NA	47	82
	50	NA	23	53
	25	NA	12	28
	10	NA	6	15
	SD	NA	32	39
2	90	106	125	142
	75	79	100	117
	50	51	72	89
	25	25	42	61
	10	11	18	31
	SD	37	41	42
3	90	128	146	162
	75	99	120	137
	50	71	92	107
	25	44	62	78
	10	21	36	48
	SD	40	43	44
4	90	145	166	180
	75	119	139	152
	50	94	112	123
	25	68	87	98
	10	45	61	72
	SD	40	41	43
5	90	166	182	194
	75	139	156	168
	50	110	127	139
	25	85	99	109
	10	61	74	83
	SD	45	44	45
6	90	177	195	204
	75	153	167	177
	50	127	140	150
	25	98	111	122
	10	68	82	93
	SD	42	45	44
7	90	180	192	202
	75	156	165	177
	50	128	136	150
	25	102	109	123
	10	79	88	98
	SD	40	43	41
8	90	185	193	199
	75	161	173	177
	50	133	146	151
	25	106	115	124
	10	77	84	97
	SD	43	45	41

A student's scores should fall within a range of ten WCPM above or below the score shown.

KEY
WCPM: Words correct per minute
SD: Average standard deviation of scores

SOURCE Hasbrouck, J. & Tindal, G. (2005) Norms for oral reading fluency. Eugene, OR: Behavioral Research & Teaching, University of Oregon.

Administering Fluency Assessments and Using the Fluency Record

Directions

Give a student a reading passage he or she has not seen before. Fluency assessments are always done as "cold reads"; that is, they are done with material that is new to the person being tested. Explain that you would like the student to read the passage out loud and then answer two questions about it. Then say: *When you are ready, you may begin.* Start your stopwatch when the student reads the first word.

1. Follow along on your copy of the passage as the student reads. Place a line through each word that is read incorrectly or omitted.

2. Place a check above each word that is read correctly.

3. If the student substitutes or mispronounces a word, put a line through the word and write the word the student said above it.

4. If the student does not correctly say the word within 3 seconds, say the word for the student and circle the word to mark it as incorrect. Self-corrections and repetitions are not marked as errors.

5. At the end of one minute, stop your stopwatch and place a bracket (]) after the last word read by the student.

6. Have the student finish reading the passage.

7. Read the comprehension questions to the student. Have the student answer the comprehension questions orally.

Oral Reading Fluency Grades 1–6

How to Score

1. Look at the number to the left of the same line in which you placed the bracket. (Note: In hyphenated words, count each individual word.) Subtract from this number all the words that follow the bracket to arrive at the number of words a student was able to read in one minute. Place this number in the "Words Read" section of the scoring table right below the questions on the recording sheet.

2. Count each word you circled or put a line through. This the number of errors made. Place this number in the "Errors" section of the scoring table right below the questions on the recording sheet.

3. Subtract "Errors" from "Words Read" to arrive at your Oral Reading Fluency Rate or Words Correct Per Minute (WCPM) score.

4. Check off the box that best matches the administration date and compare this WCPM with the 50th percentile score listed on the recording sheet.

5. To arrive at the Oral Reading Accuracy Rate, divide the WCPM by the total number of words read. Use the scoring table on the recording sheet to capture the information.

6. Use the Prosody scoring table on the recording sheet to measure a student's ability in the following key areas—Reading in Phrases, Pace, Syntax, Self-correction, and Intonation. Score students from Level 1 (L1) to Level 4 (L4) based on the descriptions in the Oral Fluency Scale found on page 88.

7. Write comments about oral reading performance on the recording sheet, including a student's ability to answer the comprehension questions.

The Bug

I see a bug. It has six legs.
It is red. It is very small.
It is fun to look at it.
The bug is very busy.
I see it go up a hill.
I see it come down.
I see it dig. I see it stop.
The sun is out now. It is a hot sun.
It is time for a nap.
The bug naps in the sun.
I will nap in the sun, too.

✔ What is this story mostly about?

✔ Why does the bug take a nap?

Name: _____ **Date:** _____

The Bug

8	I see a bug. It has six legs.
15	It is red. It is very small.
22	It is fun to look at it.
27	The bug is very busy.
34	I see it go up a hill.
39	I see it come down.
47	I see it dig. I see it stop.
57	The sun is out now. It is a hot sun.
63	It is time for a nap.
69	The bug naps in the sun.
76	I will nap in the sun, too.

✔ What is this story mostly about?
✔ Why does the bug take a nap?

Words Read	–	Errors	=	WCPM

☐ **Winter (23 WCPM)**
☐ **Spring (53 WCPM)**

WCPM	/	Words Read	=	Accuracy %

PROSODY				
	L1	L2	L3	L4
Reading in Phrases	○	○	○	○
Pace	○	○	○	○
Syntax	○	○	○	○
Self-correction	○	○	○	○
Intonation	○	○	○	○

Ben's Birthday

Today is Ben's birthday.

I am helping Mom make a cake.

We mix eggs and milk.

Then Mom adds more good things.

The batter is thick and white.

Mom puts the batter into a pan.

She puts the pan into the oven.

"I think Ben will like his cake," I say.

Time passes. Then I think I smell smoke.

Is it the cake? Mom runs in. But the cake is fine.

Now we are ready for Ben's birthday.

Dad picks Ben up to see his cake.

Ben smiles and claps his hands.

"You are one year old today!" we all say.

- ✔ What is the story about?
- ✔ Explain why Ben could not bake the cake.

Oral Reading Fluency Grades 1–6

Name: _____ **Date:** _____

Ben's Birthday

4	Today is Ben's birthday.
11	I am helping Mom make a cake.
16	We mix eggs and milk.
22	Then Mom adds more good things.
28	The batter is thick and white.
35	Mom puts the batter into a pan.
42	She puts the pan into the oven.
51	"I think Ben will like his cake," I say.
59	Time passes. Then I think I smell smoke.
71	Is it the cake? Mom runs in. But the cake is fine.
78	Now we are ready for Ben's birthday.
86	Dad picks Ben up to see his cake.
92	Ben smiles and claps his hands.
101	"You are one year old today!" we all say.

✓ What is the story about?

✓ Explain why Ben could not bake the cake.

Words Read	–	Errors	=	WCPM

☐ **Winter (23 WCPM)**

☐ **Spring (53 WCPM)**

WCPM	/	Words Read	=	Accuracy %

PROSODY				
	L1	L2	L3	L4
Reading in Phrases	○	○	○	○
Pace	○	○	○	○
Syntax	○	○	○	○
Self-correction	○	○	○	○
Intonation	○	○	○	○

You and Your Shadow

Do you like to play with your shadow?

You can use your hands to make pictures on a wall.

You can make animal heads and funny shapes.

Light makes the shadows.

Light might hit you on one side.

Your shadow would fall on the other side.

When you are outside, sunlight makes shadows.

The sun may make long shadows or short ones.

In the morning and evening, the sun is low.

Shadows are long.

At noon, the sun is high. Shadows are short.

Is your shadow in front of you?

Then the light is behind you.

Is your shadow behind you?

Then the light is in front of you.

You are never alone. You always have your shadow.

- ☑ What makes shadows?
- ☑ What would your shadow look like in the morning?

Name: _____ **Date:** _____

You and Your Shadow

8	Do you like to play with your shadow?
19	You can use your hands to make pictures on a wall.
27	You can make animal heads and funny shapes.
31	Light makes the shadows.
38	Light might hit you on one side.
46	Your shadow would fall on the other side.
53	When you are outside, sunlight makes shadows.
62	The sun may make long shadows or short ones.
71	In the morning and evening, the sun is low.
74	Shadows are long.
83	At noon, the sun is high. Shadows are short.
90	Is your shadow in front of you?
96	Then the light is behind you.
101	Is your shadow behind you?
109	Then the light is in front of you.
118	You are never alone. You always have your shadow.

✔ What makes shadows?
✔ What would your shadow look like in the morning?

Words Read	–	Errors	=	WCPM

☐ Winter (23 WCPM)
☐ Spring (53 WCPM)

WCPM	/	Words Read	=	Accuracy %

PROSODY				
	L1	L2	L3	L4
Reading in Phrases	○	○	○	○
Pace	○	○	○	○
Syntax	○	○	○	○
Self-correction	○	○	○	○
Intonation	○	○	○	○

Our American Flag

Our flag is special to us.

It stands for our country. It is red, white, and blue.

The flag has 13 stripes. It has 50 stars.

There were 13 states when our country was born.

There are 50 states in our country now.

We call our flag the Stars and Stripes.

That is what we see when we look at the flag.

Here are some rules about the flag.

Fly the flag outside in good weather.

Take the flag down at night.

Take the flag inside when it rains.

Never let the flag touch the ground.

Follow these rules.

They show that you are proud of your flag.

✔ What does each star stand for on the flag?

✔ How can you care for your flag?

Name: _____ **Date:** _____

Our American Flag

6	Our flag is special to us.
17	It stands for our country. It is red, white, and blue.
26	The flag has 13 stripes. It has 50 stars.
35	There were 13 states when our country was born.
43	There are 50 states in our country now.
51	We call our flag the Stars and Stripes.
62	That is what we see when we look at the flag.
69	Here are some rules about the flag.
76	Fly the flag outside in good weather.
82	Take the flag down at night.
89	Take the flag inside when it rains.
96	Never let the flag touch the ground.
99	Follow these rules.
108	They show that you are proud of your flag.

✓ What does each star stand for on the flag?

✓ How can you care for your flag?

Words Read	–	Errors	=	WCPM

☐ **Winter (23 WCPM)**

☐ **Spring (53 WCPM)**

WCPM	/	Words Read	=	Accuracy %

PROSODY				
	L1	L2	L3	L4
Reading in Phrases	○	○	○	○
Pace	○	○	○	○
Syntax	○	○	○	○
Self-correction	○	○	○	○
Intonation	○	○	○	○

The Picnic

Tamara and Marcus looked out at the rain.

"Why are you frowning?" asked Mrs. Green.

"We wanted to go to the park," Tamara said.

"We wanted to have a picnic," Marcus added.

Mrs. Green got paper and found crayons.

"What would you do at the park?" asked

Mrs. Green. "Draw a picture of it."

Tamara drew a swing, Marcus drew people

playing ball, and Mrs. Green drew a picnic table.

Then Mrs. Green taped the pictures on the wall.

"This can be the park," Mrs. Green said.

"Now we will make a picnic."

Tamara and Marcus smiled. Everyone got

busy. Mrs. Green made sandwiches, Tamara got

drinks, and Marcus got a blanket. He spread it out on

the floor. Then the family sat down to eat.

"What a pretty park!" Tamara said.

"What a good day for a picnic!" said Marcus.

✔ Why can't Tamara and Marcus go to the park?

✔ Where do Tamara and Marcus have a picnic?

Name: _____ **Date:** _____

The Picnic

8	Tamara and Marcus looked out at the rain.
15	"Why are you frowning?" asked Mrs. Green.
24	"We wanted to go to the park," Tamara said.
32	"We wanted to have a picnic," Marcus added.
39	Mrs. Green got paper and found crayons.
47	"What would you do at the park?" asked
54	Mrs. Green. "Draw a picture of it."
61	Tamara drew a swing, Marcus drew people
70	playing ball, and Mrs. Green drew a picnic table.
79	Then Mrs. Green taped the pictures on the wall.
87	"This can be the park," Mrs. Green said.
93	"Now we will make a picnic."
99	Tamara and Marcus smiled. Everyone got
106	busy. Mrs. Green made sandwiches, Tamara got
117	drinks, and Marcus got a blanket. He spread it out on
126	the floor. Then the family sat down to eat.
132	"What a pretty park!" Tamara said.
139	"What a good day for a picnic!" said Marcus.

✓ Why can't Tamara and Marcus go to the park?
✓ Where do Tamara and Marcus have a picnic?

Words Read	–	Errors	=	WCPM

☐ **Fall (51 WCPM)**
☐ **Winter (72 WCPM)**
☐ **Spring (89 WCPM)**

WCPM	/	Words Read	=	Accuracy %

PROSODY				
	L1	L2	L3	L4
Reading in Phrases	○	○	○	○
Pace	○	○	○	○
Syntax	○	○	○	○
Self-correction	○	○	○	○
Intonation	○	○	○	○

The Farmer's Market

It is early Saturday morning. The park is already a busy place. People are putting up small tents. They are setting up tables. Soon tables will be filled. There will be baskets full of fresh food. It is time to start!

A farmer's market is a place where you sell things you grow. Some farmers grow fruits. They will sell apples and oranges. Other farmers grow vegetables. They will sell beans and peas.

Farmers raise animals, too. They will sell foods that come from animals. Farmers who have cows will sell milk and cheese. Farmers who raise chickens will sell eggs.

Some farmer's markets have other kinds of fresh foods. Bakers sell bread and cookies. Other people sell jam they put in jars.

The neighbors who live close to the park visit the farmer's market. They can taste the fresh food. They like to buy it.

By the end of the day, the food is gone. The farmer's market closes. It will open again next Saturday with more fresh food.

✔ What is this passage about?

✔ What are three foods that people can buy at a farmer's market?

Name: _____ **Date:** _____

The Farmer's Market

8	It is early Saturday morning. The park is
17	already a busy place. People are putting up small
26	tents. They are setting up tables. Soon tables will
36	be filled. There will be baskets full of fresh food.
41	It is time to start!
49	A farmer's market is a place where you
57	sell things you grow. Some farmers grow fruits.
65	They will sell apples and oranges. Other farmers
73	grow vegetables. They will sell beans and peas.
80	Farmers raise animals, too. They will sell
88	foods that come from animals. Farmers who have
97	cows will sell milk and cheese. Farmers who raise
101	chickens will sell eggs.
108	Some farmer's markets have other kinds of
116	fresh foods. Bakers sell bread and cookies. Other
123	people sell jam they put in jars.
132	The neighbors who live close to the park visit
141	the farmer's market. They can taste the fresh food.
146	They like to buy it.
157	By the end of the day, the food is gone. The
165	farmer's market closes. It will open again next
170	Saturday with more fresh food.

✔ What is this passage about?

✔ What are three foods that people can buy at a farmer's market?

Words Read	–	Errors	=	WCPM

☐ Fall (51 WCPM)

☐ Winter (72 WCPM)

☐ Spring (89 WCPM)

WCPM	/	Words Read	=	Accuracy %

PROSODY				
	L1	L2	L3	L4
Reading in Phrases	○	○	○	○
Pace	○	○	○	○
Syntax	○	○	○	○
Self-correction	○	○	○	○
Intonation	○	○	○	○

Sharks

Sharks have lived on Earth for many years. Today there are more than 350 different kinds. Sharks come in many sizes. The whale shark can be thirty-six feet in length. The smallest shark grows only to about six inches. Some sharks have big, sharp teeth. Others have very small teeth. But all sharks have one thing in common. They all must open their mouths to breathe. Sharks must keep their mouths open when they swim, or they will die.

Every year sharks are killed for many reasons. They get caught in fishing nets. Some are caught to be sold for shark meat or shark fin soup. Shark skin is sometimes used for belts. Other people hunt them because they think sharks are dangerous. Will sharks be around much longer?

☑ How does a shark breathe?

☑ Why are sharks in danger?

Name: _____ **Date:** _____

Sharks

8	Sharks have lived on Earth for many years.
16	Today there are more than 350 different kinds.
26	Sharks come in many sizes. The whale shark can be
35	thirty-six feet in length. The smallest shark grows
44	only to about six inches. Some sharks have big,
53	sharp teeth. Others have very small teeth. But all
62	sharks have one thing in common. They all must
70	open their mouths to breathe. Sharks must keep
80	their mouths open when they swim, or they will die.
87	Every year sharks are killed for many
95	reasons. They get caught in fishing nets. Some
106	are caught to be sold for shark meat or shark fin
114	soup. Shark skin is sometimes used for belts.
121	Other people hunt them because they think
128	sharks are dangerous. Will sharks be around
130	much longer?

☑ How does a shark breathe?
☑ Why are sharks in danger?

Words Read	–	Errors	=	WCPM

☐ **Fall (51 WCPM)**
☐ **Winter (72 WCPM)**
☐ **Spring (89 WCPM)**

WCPM	/	Words Read	=	Accuracy %

PROSODY				
	L1	L2	L3	L4
Reading in Phrases	○	○	○	○
Pace	○	○	○	○
Syntax	○	○	○	○
Self-correction	○	○	○	○
Intonation	○	○	○	○

Fun for Marge

Marge the cat did not feel like chasing mice today. She wanted some fun for a change. Marge strolled across the street and into a schoolyard. She wanted to watch what the children were doing there.

Marge slid through the door and hid in a cardboard box. Not much later, someone picked up the box. Marge swayed as she was carried through a narrow hall. Then the swaying stopped.

In a flash, Marge was out of the box. She could not believe her eyes. All the children were running and chasing balls. Marge thought they were all pretending to be cats, and joined in the game.

Soon the children were chasing Marge, but she did not like this kind of fun. Marge ran down the hall and out the door. After that day, Marge thought chasing mice was just enough fun for a feline.

✔ Why did Marge go to the schoolyard?

✔ Why would Marge think the children were pretending to be cats?

Oral Reading Fluency Grades 1–6

Name: _____ **Date:** _____

Fun for Marge

9	Marge the cat did not feel like chasing mice
18	today. She wanted some fun for a change. Marge
26	strolled across the street and into a schoolyard.
34	She wanted to watch what the children were
36	doing there.
45	Marge slid through the door and hid in a
52	cardboard box. Not much later, someone picked
61	up the box. Marge swayed as she was carried
69	through a narrow hall. Then the swaying stopped.
79	In a flash, Marge was out of the box. She
88	could not believe her eyes. All the children were
96	running and chasing balls. Marge thought they were
106	all pretending to be cats, and joined in the game.
112	Soon the children were chasing Marge,
123	but she did not like this kind of fun. Marge ran
133	down the hall and out the door. After that day,
140	Marge thought chasing mice was just enough
144	fun for a feline.

☑ Why did Marge go to the schoolyard?

☑ Why would Marge think the children were pretending to be cats?

Words Read	–	Errors	=	WCPM

☐ Fall (51 WCPM)

☐ Winter (72 WCPM)

☐ Spring (89 WCPM)

WCPM	/	Words Read	=	Accuracy %

PROSODY				
	L1	L2	L3	L4
Reading in Phrases	○	○	○	○
Pace	○	○	○	○
Syntax	○	○	○	○
Self-correction	○	○	○	○
Intonation	○	○	○	○

Why Possum's Tail Is Bare

Long ago, Possum had a huge, bushy tail.

"My tail is the most beautiful in the world!" Possum always told everybody.

Rabbit, who had a short tail, hated listening to Possum and decided to play a trick on her.

"There is a dance Saturday," Rabbit said. "All the animals will see your tail if you come."

"What a great idea!" agreed Possum.

"I will send Cricket to help you get ready, so your tail will look its best," Rabbit said.

On Saturday, Cricket visited Possum. "Shut your eyes so you will be surprised!" he said.

Cricket carefully cut off all the hair on Possum's tail, and then wrapped a cloth around it. Possum raced to the dance and proudly walked to the middle of the dance floor.

"See my beautiful tail," Possum sang, as she pulled off the cloth. The animals laughed loudly.

Seeing her bare tail, Possum dropped to the ground and pretended to be dead until everybody left. To this day, possums have bare tails and play dead when they are surprised.

☑   Why does Rabbit play a trick on Possum?

☑   What happens after Possum takes the cloth off her tail?

Oral Reading Fluency Grades 1–6

Name: _____ **Date:** _____

Why Possum's Tail Is Bare

8	Long ago, Possum had a huge, bushy tail.
17	"My tail is the most beautiful in the world!"
21	Possum always told everybody.
29	Rabbit, who had a short tail, hated listening
39	to Possum and decided to play a trick on her.
46	"There is a dance Saturday," Rabbit said.
56	"All the animals will see your tail if you come."
62	"What a great idea!" agreed Possum.
72	"I will send Cricket to help you get ready, so
80	your tail will look its best," Rabbit said.
86	On Saturday, Cricket visited Possum. "Shut
95	your eyes so you will be surprised!" he said.
103	Cricket carefully cut off all the hair on
111	Possum's tail, and then wrapped a cloth around
120	it. Possum raced to the dance and proudly walked
127	to the middle of the dance floor.
135	"See my beautiful tail," Possum sang, as she
143	pulled off the cloth. The animals laughed loudly.
151	Seeing her bare tail, Possum dropped to the
159	ground and pretended to be dead until everybody
169	left. To this day, possums have bare tails and play
174	dead when they are surprised.

 Why does Rabbit play a trick on Possum?

 What happens after Possum takes the cloth off her tail?

Words Read	–	Errors	=	WCPM

☐ Fall (51 WCPM)
☐ Winter (72 WCPM)
☐ Spring (89 WCPM)

WCPM	/	Words Read	=	Accuracy %

PROSODY				
	L1	L2	L3	L4
Reading in Phrases	○	○	○	○
Pace	○	○	○	○
Syntax	○	○	○	○
Self-correction	○	○	○	○
Intonation	○	○	○	○

A Cowboy's Job

In the past, movies and songs made a cowboy's job seem fun. After all, cowboys got to ride horses and sit by the campfire. In real life, though, cowboys worked hard.

Long ago, ranches didn't have fences, so the cows walked around freely. The cattle could easily travel many miles from the ranch house. When cowboys had to find the cattle, they often rode their horses all day without stopping. They could be gone for many days, too. On the longer trips, cowboys took dried meat and rolls to eat. They slept on the ground with only a blanket for cover.

The weather was another hard part of a cowboy's job. Even in the hot summer, cowboys still dressed in shirts, pants, and boots. When it was wet, they used long raincoats, which made it hard to work with the cattle. Winter weather was the most difficult of all because it was unsafe for the horses to walk in the snow and ice. If a horse was hurt, the cowboy could not do the job.

✔ What is this article about?

✔ How did weather make a cowboy's job hard?

Name: _____ Date: _____

A Cowboy's Job

8	In the past, movies and songs made a
16	cowboy's job seem fun. After all, cowboys got
27	to ride horses and sit by the campfire. In real life,
31	though, cowboys worked hard.
39	Long ago, ranches didn't have fences, so the
47	cows walked around freely. The cattle could easily
55	travel many miles from the ranch house. When
64	cowboys had to find the cattle, they often rode
72	their horses all day without stopping. They could
82	be gone for many days, too. On the longer trips,
91	cowboys took dried meat and rolls to eat. They
101	slept on the ground with only a blanket for cover.
109	The weather was another hard part of a
117	cowboy's job. Even in the hot summer, cowboys
126	still dressed in shirts, pants, and boots. When it
135	was wet, they used long raincoats, which made it
144	hard to work with the cattle. Winter weather was
154	the most difficult of all because it was unsafe for
166	the horses to walk in the snow and ice. If a horse
175	was hurt, the cowboy could not do the job.

☑ What is this article about?

☑ How did weather make a cowboy's job hard?

Words Read	–	Errors	=	WCPM

☐ Fall (51 WCPM)

☐ Winter (72 WCPM)

☐ Spring (89 WCPM)

WCPM	/	Words Read	=	Accuracy %

PROSODY				
	L1	L2	L3	L4
Reading in Phrases	○	○	○	○
Pace	○	○	○	○
Syntax	○	○	○	○
Self-correction	○	○	○	○
Intonation	○	○	○	○

Silk Threads

A spider can spin a silk thread. Some of the silk is sticky. Some of it is not sticky. The silk is important in a spider's life.

Spiders use silk to spin a web. A web is a spider's home. A spider uses both sticky and non-sticky silk. Bugs cannot see the thread. They fly or jump into the web and get trapped. The sticky silk holds the bugs still. The spider walks to the trapped bug on the silk that is not sticky.

Spiders spin silk cases, too. Some cases hold the eggs. A spider also spins a case around a trapped bug. The spider eats the bug when it is hungry.

Finally, spiders use silk to help them travel. They go "ballooning." Spiders climb as high as they can. They stand on their front legs. Then they spin long silk threads. The wind catches the silk. It carries the spiders away. Sometimes the spiders go a few feet. Other times the spiders travel over a hundred miles away.

✔ What is this article mostly about?
✔ What are three ways that spiders use their silk?

Name: _____ **Date:** _____

Silk Threads

13	A spider can spin a silk thread. Some of the silk is sticky.
27	Some of it is not sticky. The silk is important in a spider's life.
40	Spiders use silk to spin a web. A web is a spider's home.
52	A spider uses both sticky and non-sticky silk. Bugs cannot see
65	the thread. They fly or jump into the web and get trapped. The
77	sticky silk holds the bugs still. The spider walks to the trapped
85	bug on the silk that is not sticky.
95	Spiders spin silk cases, too. Some cases hold the eggs.
108	A spider also spins a case around a trapped bug. The spider eats
114	the bug when it is hungry.
124	Finally, spiders use silk to help them travel. They go
135	"ballooning." Spiders climb as high as they can. They stand on
146	their front legs. Then they spin long silk threads. The wind
156	catches the silk. It carries the spiders away. Sometimes the
168	spiders go a few feet. Other times the spiders travel over a
171	hundred miles away.

✔ What is this article mostly about?

✔ What are three ways that spiders use their silk?

Words Read	–	Errors	=	WCPM

☐ Fall (71 WCPM)

☐ Winter (92 WCPM)

☐ Spring (107 WCPM)

WCPM	/	Words Read	=	Accuracy %

PROSODY				
	L1	L2	L3	L4
Reading in Phrases	○	○	○	○
Pace	○	○	○	○
Syntax	○	○	○	○
Self-correction	○	○	○	○
Intonation	○	○	○	○

Why Bears Sleep All Winter

Long ago in the winter, Bear laughed at Turtle for being slow.

"I am fast!" Turtle exclaimed. "We should race around the lake. You can run, and I will swim."

"Ice covers the water," Bear said. "How will I know if you are swimming around the lake?"

"I will look out of some holes as I swim," Turtle answered.

So Bear and Turtle met the next morning. Bear yelled, "Go!" and started jogging. Soon Turtle's head popped up through the first hole.

"I'm ahead of you!" Turtle called.

Bear ran faster. Turtle's head popped up again. "You are slow!"

Bear raced as fast as he could. Finally, Turtle's head popped up through the last hole, and he shouted, "I won!"

Bear was so tired that he ran home and slept the rest of the winter. Turtle tapped on the ice, and a green head popped up through each hole.

"Thank you, cousins," Turtle said. "We may move slowly, but we do not think slowly."

To this day, bears sleep all winter so they will not have to race turtles.

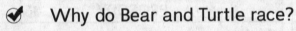 Why do Bear and Turtle race?

How does Turtle win the race?

Oral Reading Fluency Grades 1–6

Name: _____ **Date:** _____

Why Bears Sleep All Winter

12	Long ago in the winter, Bear laughed at Turtle for being slow.
22	"I am fast!" Turtle exclaimed. "We should race around the
30	lake. You can run, and I will swim."
42	"Ice covers the water," Bear said. "How will I know if you
47	are swimming around the lake?"
59	"I will look out of some holes as I swim," Turtle answered.
69	So Bear and Turtle met the next morning. Bear yelled,
78	"Go!" and started jogging. Soon Turtle's head popped up
82	through the first hole.
88	"I'm ahead of you!" Turtle called.
97	Bear ran faster. Turtle's head popped up again. "You
99	are slow!"
109	Bear raced as fast as he could. Finally, Turtle's head
120	popped up through the last hole, and he shouted, "I won!"
133	Bear was so tired that he ran home and slept the rest of
146	the winter. Turtle tapped on the ice, and a green head popped up
149	through each hole.
158	"Thank you, cousins," Turtle said. "We may move slowly,
164	but we do not think slowly."
177	To this day, bears sleep all winter so they will not have to
179	race turtles.

✔ Why do Bear and Turtle race?
✔ How does Turtle win the race?

Words Read	–	Errors	=	WCPM

☐ **Fall (71 WCPM)**
☐ **Winter (92 WCPM)**
☐ **Spring (107 WCPM)**

WCPM	/	Words Read	=	Accuracy %

PROSODY				
	L1	L2	L3	L4
Reading in Phrases	○	○	○	○
Pace	○	○	○	○
Syntax	○	○	○	○
Self-correction	○	○	○	○
Intonation	○	○	○	○

Knights

Some fairytales tell about the adventures of knights. These brave men might fight a fierce dragon or save a pretty princess. While fairytales are make-believe, the story characters are based on real people. Knights were a group of men who lived long ago. They probably did save princesses. They also did go to battle—just not with dragons.

Knights wore armor when they went to fight. The armor was a metal suit that covered their whole body, even their heads. The men used different tools to fight. A knight might swing a sword or an ax. Sometimes knights carried a long pole, called a lance. They used the lance to push another knight off a horse.

Knights made a promise to serve one ruler, such as a king or queen. It was a knight's job to keep that ruler safe. They guarded the palace. They watched over the people who lived in the kingdom. Knights worked long hours and were often in danger. It was a difficult job, but it was a job full of honor.

✔ How is a real knight not like a knight in a fairytale?
✔ Why does the author say a knight's job is full of honor?

Name: _____ **Date:** _____

Knights

8	Some fairytales tell about the adventures of knights.
20	These brave men might fight a fierce dragon or save a pretty
29	princess. While fairytales are make-believe, the story characters
41	are based on real people. Knights were a group of men who
52	lived long ago. They probably did save princesses. They also did
59	go to battle—just not with dragons.
69	Knights wore armor when they went to fight. The armor
81	was a metal suit that covered their whole body, even their heads.
93	The men used different tools to fight. A knight might swing a
105	sword or an ax. Sometimes knights carried a long pole, called a
117	lance. They used the lance to push another knight off a horse.
129	Knights made a promise to serve one ruler, such as a king
142	or queen. It was a knight's job to keep that ruler safe. They
153	guarded the palace. They watched over the people who lived in
163	the kingdom. Knights worked long hours and were often in
177	danger. It was a difficult job, but it was a job full of honor.

✔ How is a real knight not like a knight in a fairytale?
✔ Why does the author say a knight's job is full of honor?

Words Read	–	Errors	=	WCPM

☐ Fall (71 WCPM)
☐ Winter (92 WCPM)
☐ Spring (107 WCPM)

WCPM	/	Words Read	=	Accuracy %

PROSODY				
	L1	L2	L3	L4
Reading in Phrases	○	○	○	○
Pace	○	○	○	○
Syntax	○	○	○	○
Self-correction	○	○	○	○
Intonation	○	○	○	○

Skunked

Mario and Anna sat outside their home in the dark relaxing one quiet summer evening. The silence was suddenly interrupted by the howling of their dog, Blue.

"It sounds like Blue discovered something," Mario said.

Anna began sniffing and then wrinkled her nose. "Yuck! I think Blue found a skunk!" Holding her nose, Anna pointed to the backyard.

Mario looked up to see a skunk running toward the house with its tail raised up in the air. Blue trailed closely behind.

"Come here, Blue!" Mario called excitedly. "Stay away from that—." Before Mario could finish the sentence, he saw a small cloud float up into the air. Blue gave a sharp yip and swiftly backed up. The skunk disappeared into the bushes.

"Oh, no," Anna groaned. "After being sprayed five times before, you would think that Blue would have learned."

Mario sighed, "I will get Blue, if you will go get the tomato juice for his bath."

"I hope Mom has lots of cans of juice," laughed Anna. "Blue will need to be bathed at least three times to get that horrible smell off."

✔ What happened to Blue?

✔ What do you think Anna and Mario will do next?

Name: _____ **Date:** _____

Skunked

10	Mario and Anna sat outside their home in the dark
19	relaxing one quiet summer evening. The silence was suddenly
27	interrupted by the howling of their dog, Blue.
35	"It sounds like Blue discovered something," Mario said.
44	Anna began sniffing and then wrinkled her nose. "Yuck!
56	I think Blue found a skunk!" Holding her nose, Anna pointed to
58	the backyard.
69	Mario looked up to see a skunk running toward the house
81	with its tail raised up in the air. Blue trailed closely behind.
89	"Come here, Blue!" Mario called excitedly. "Stay away
100	from that—." Before Mario could finish the sentence, he saw a
113	small cloud float up into the air. Blue gave a sharp yip and
122	swiftly backed up. The skunk disappeared into the bushes.
131	"Oh, no," Anna groaned. "After being sprayed five times
140	before, you would think that Blue would have learned."
152	Mario sighed, "I will get Blue, if you will go get the
157	tomato juice for his bath."
168	"I hope Mom has lots of cans of juice," laughed Anna.
181	"Blue will need to be bathed at least three times to get that
184	horrible smell off."

✔ What happened to Blue?

✔ What do you think Anna and Mario will do next?

Words Read	–	Errors	=	WCPM

☐ **Fall (71 WCPM)**

☐ **Winter (92 WCPM)**

☐ **Spring (107 WCPM)**

WCPM	/	Words Read	=	Accuracy %

PROSODY				
	L1	L2	L3	L4
Reading in Phrases	○	○	○	○
Pace	○	○	○	○
Syntax	○	○	○	○
Self-correction	○	○	○	○
Intonation	○	○	○	○

Special Times

Martin's grandfather was moving, and Martin was sad about the change.

"Grandpa Howard is not moving too far away," Martin's mom said. "You will still see him every week."

Martin sat in the backyard of Grandpa Howard's old house and thought about all the hours they had spent reading books and playing. Martin wanted to do something to remind his grandpa of all those great times.

He went home and printed photographs off the computer that showed Grandpa Howard and him reading or playing. He wrote sentences under each photo and stapled the pages together like a book. Then Martin took the book to Grandpa Howard the following week.

"How do you like your new home?" asked Martin.

"I like it," said Grandpa Howard, "but I miss having a backyard. I so enjoyed the time I spent with you outside."

Martin handed the book to Grandpa Howard and said, "I miss the backyard, too, so I made a book about our special times together."

Grandpa Howard smiled at the photographs. "You know, there is a park nearby. Let's go see if it has a playground."

- ✔ Why was Martin sad?
- ✔ What do you think Grandpa Howard and Martin will do next?

Name: _____ **Date:** _____

Special Times

8	Martin's grandfather was moving, and Martin was sad
11	about the change.
20	"Grandpa Howard is not moving too far away," Martin's
29	mom said. "You will still see him every week."
38	Martin sat in the backyard of Grandpa Howard's old
49	house and thought about all the hours they had spent reading
59	books and playing. Martin wanted to do something to remind
66	his grandpa of all those great times.
75	He went home and printed photographs off the computer
85	that showed Grandpa Howard and him reading or playing. He
95	wrote sentences under each photo and stapled the pages together
107	like a book. Then Martin took the book to Grandpa Howard the
109	following week.
118	"How do you like your new home?" asked Martin.
129	"I like it," said Grandpa Howard, "but I miss having a
140	backyard. I so enjoyed the time I spent with you outside."
149	Martin handed the book to Grandpa Howard and said,
162	"I miss the backyard, too, so I made a book about our special
164	times together."
172	Grandpa Howard smiled at the photographs. "You know,
185	there is a park nearby. Let's go see if it has a playground."

 Why was Martin sad?

 What do you think Grandpa Howard and Martin will do next?

Words Read	–	Errors	=	WCPM

☐ Fall (71 WCPM)
☐ Winter (92 WCPM)
☐ Spring (107 WCPM)

WCPM	/	Words Read	=	Accuracy %

PROSODY				
	L1	L2	L3	L4
Reading in Phrases	○	○	○	○
Pace	○	○	○	○
Syntax	○	○	○	○
Self-correction	○	○	○	○
Intonation	○	○	○	○

A Good Mother

Crocodiles look fierce with their bumpy skin and sharp teeth. Yet these fierce-looking creatures take good care of their young. For example, after laying eggs, a mother crocodile waits near the nest. She makes sure other animals do not eat the babies.

A mother crocodile also helps her babies hatch. The babies grunt and bark while they are inside the egg. It lets the mother crocodile know they are ready to hatch. The babies use a special tooth, called an "egg tooth," on the end of their noses to cut the shell. If a baby has trouble, a mother crocodile will help it break its shell.

Since many mother crocodiles lay their eggs on riverbanks, they often carry their babies to the water. If another animal gets too close, the mother will scare it away. Sometimes a mother crocodile will open her mouth and let the babies climb inside. The other animal leaves, thinking the mother has swallowed the babies. Other times a mother crocodile will give the babies a ride on her back. She carries them to a safe place.

☑ What is this article about?

☑ How does a mother crocodile keep her babies safe from other animals?

Oral Reading Fluency Grades 1–6

Name: _____ **Date:** _____

A Good Mother

9	Crocodiles look fierce with their bumpy skin and sharp
20	teeth. Yet these fierce-looking creatures take good care of their
30	young. For example, after laying eggs, a mother crocodile waits
43	near the nest. She makes sure other animals do not eat the babies.
52	A mother crocodile also helps her babies hatch. The
65	babies grunt and bark while they are inside the egg. It lets the
77	mother crocodile know they are ready to hatch. The babies use a
90	special tooth, called an "egg tooth," on the end of their noses to
103	cut the shell. If a baby has trouble, a mother crocodile will help
107	it break its shell.
115	Since many mother crocodiles lay their eggs on
126	riverbanks, they often carry their babies to the water. If another
137	animal gets too close, the mother will scare it away. Sometimes
149	a mother crocodile will open her mouth and let the babies climb
158	inside. The other animal leaves, thinking the mother has
168	swallowed the babies. Other times a mother crocodile will give
182	the babies a ride on her back. She carries them to a safe place.

✔ What is this article about?

✔ How does a mother crocodile keep her babies safe from other animals?

Words Read	–	Errors	=	WCPM

☐ **Fall (71 WCPM)**
☐ **Winter (92 WCPM)**
☐ **Spring (107 WCPM)**

WCPM	/	Words Read	=	Accuracy %

PROSODY				
	L1	L2	L3	L4
Reading in Phrases	○	○	○	○
Pace	○	○	○	○
Syntax	○	○	○	○
Self-correction	○	○	○	○
Intonation	○	○	○	○

Play Ball

What do baseball players need? To start with, they need a bat and ball. A baseball bat is long and round. Most bats are made of ash wood. A bat cannot be longer than forty-six inches. It cannot be thicker than $2\frac{3}{4}$ inches at any point. Baseballs are hard and round. Each ball weighs about five ounces. It has a tiny cork ball at the center. Layers of rubber and yarn are tightly wrapped around this cork ball. The cover of the ball is made of two pieces of white cowhide. These are sewn together with thick red thread.

Next, players need a special padded leather glove. They also need shoes with spikes on the soles. The spikes help them stop and start quickly.

At bat, players wear a batting helmet. This is a special hard cap. The helmet protects batters in case they are hit in the head with the ball.

In baseball, a pitcher throws the ball to a catcher. Catchers have special equipment to protect them. They wear a metal mask over their faces. They also wear padded cloth covers over their chests. To protect their legs, they wear hard shin guards.

Baseball can be safe and fun. Are you ready to play ball?

- ✔ What is a baseball made of?
- ✔ Why do baseball players wear special clothing?

Name: _____ **Date:** _____

Play Ball

11	What do baseball players need? To start with, they need a
24	bat and ball. A baseball bat is long and round. Most bats are
36	made of ash wood. A bat cannot be longer than forty-six
48	inches. It cannot be thicker than $2\frac{3}{4}$ inches at any point. Baseballs
61	are hard and round. Each ball weighs about five ounces. It has a
74	tiny cork ball at the center. Layers of rubber and yarn are tightly
87	wrapped around this cork ball. The cover of the ball is made of
98	two pieces of white cowhide. These are sewn together with thick
100	red thread.
109	Next, players need a special padded leather glove. They
121	also need shoes with spikes on the soles. The spikes help them
125	stop and start quickly.
136	At bat, players wear a batting helmet. This is a special
149	hard cap. The helmet protects batters in case they are hit in the
153	head with the ball.
164	In baseball, a pitcher throws the ball to a catcher. Catchers
175	have special equipment to protect them. They wear a metal mask
186	over their faces. They also wear padded cloth covers over their
196	chests. To protect their legs, they wear hard shin guards.
208	Baseball can be safe and fun. Are you ready to play ball?

☑ What is a baseball made of?
☑ Why do baseball players wear special clothing?

Words Read	–	Errors	=	WCPM

☐ Fall (94 WCPM)
☐ Winter (112 WCPM)
☐ Spring (123 WCPM)

WCPM	/	Words Read	=	Accuracy %

PROSODY	L1	L2	L3	L4
Reading in Phrases	○	○	○	○
Pace	○	○	○	○
Syntax	○	○	○	○
Self-correction	○	○	○	○
Intonation	○	○	○	○

The Yard Sale

"Here is another box of old toys to add to your yard sale," Tran told his mother. "My bicycle is too small, so may I sell it, too?"

"You have so much stuff that you should have your own yard sale," laughed Mrs. Chung.

"Can I keep the money if I sell my things?" Tran asked.

"Yes, then you can buy that new bicycle you want," answered Mrs. Chung.

The yard sale was only two days away, so Tran needed a quick way to tell people about all the great stuff he was selling. He remembered seeing a poster advertising a recent yard sale. He decided to make a poster, too.

Tran took photos of the items he was selling. Then he loaded the photos onto the computer and printed them out. Next, he taped them on the poster. Using his best handwriting, Tran wrote the prices. He also included the yard sale date and address. When he was done, Mrs. Chung and Tran hung up the poster next to the neighborhood entrance.

An hour later, Tran heard the doorbell. Mrs. Chung came into the den excitedly.

"Your advertising is working," she said. "Your friend Mike and his dad are here. They want to buy your bicycle."

Tran hoped his other things would sell just as quickly.

✔ What did Tran do right after he loaded his photos?

✔ Who buys Tran's bicycle?

Name: _____ **Date:** _____

The Yard Sale

13	"Here is another box of old toys to add to your yard sale,"
28	Tran told his mother. "My bicycle is too small, so may I sell it, too?"
39	"You have so much stuff that you should have your own
44	yard sale," laughed Mrs. Chung.
56	"Can I keep the money if I sell my things?" Tran asked.
66	"Yes, then you can buy that new bicycle you want,"
69	answered Mrs. Chung.
81	The yard sale was only two days away, so Tran needed a
94	quick way to tell people about all the great stuff he was selling.
104	He remembered seeing a poster advertising a recent yard sale.
111	He decided to make a poster, too.
122	Tran took photos of the items he was selling. Then he
133	loaded the photos onto the computer and printed them out. Next,
144	he taped them on the poster. Using his best handwriting, Tran
155	wrote the prices. He also included the yard sale date and
167	address. When he was done, Mrs. Chung and Tran hung up the
173	poster next to the neighborhood entrance.
183	An hour later, Tran heard the doorbell. Mrs. Chung came
187	into the den excitedly.
195	"Your advertising is working," she said. "Your friend
207	Mike and his dad are here. They want to buy your bicycle."
217	Tran hoped his other things would sell just as quickly.

✔ What did Tran do right after he loaded his photos?

✔ Who buys Tran's bicycle?

Words Read	–	Errors	=	WCPM

☐ **Fall (94 WCPM)**

☐ **Winter (112 WCPM)**

☐ **Spring (123 WCPM)**

WCPM	/	Words Read	=	Accuracy %

PROSODY				
	L1	L2	L3	L4
Reading in Phrases	○	○	○	○
Pace	○	○	○	○
Syntax	○	○	○	○
Self-correction	○	○	○	○
Intonation	○	○	○	○

Before and Now

You don't have to be an explorer to be interested
in traveling to new places. Many people living today are just
as curious as explorers once were. These brave people leave
their beloved homelands behind and move to new countries
to live. These people are called *immigrants*, and they show
extraordinary courage! Try to imagine leaving everything
you know and love behind, and moving to a place you have
never even seen before. Perhaps your parents or grandparents
did just that. Maybe you are an immigrant yourself.

But what about the countries left behind? What did
they look like? If you know any immigrants, ask them if they
have any old photographs you can look at. What would you
see in those photos? What would the automobiles look like,
the buildings, even the clothes the people wore? What would
these things tell you about the other place the person had
lived? If you do not know anyone who has moved to this
country, or you do not have any photos to look at, you can
go to your local library. Look up travel books and videos.
If you are extremely lucky, you may know someone who
kept a diary or journal describing what life was like where
he or she came from. This type of keepsake will help bring
the old country and the new one together.

- ✔ What is the passage mostly about?
- ✔ What do you call people who move to new countries?

Oral Reading Fluency Grades 1–6

Name: _____ **Date:** _____

Before and Now

10	You don't have to be an explorer to be interested
21	in traveling to new places. Many people living today are just
31	as curious as explorers once were. These brave people leave
40	their beloved homelands behind and move to new countries
50	to live. These people are called *immigrants*, and they show
57	extraordinary courage! Try to imagine leaving everything
69	you know and love behind, and moving to a place you have
78	never even seen before. Perhaps your parents or grandparents
87	did just that. Maybe you are an immigrant yourself.
96	But what about the countries left behind? What did
108	they look like? If you know any immigrants, ask them if they
119	have any old photographs you can look at. What would you
129	see in those photos? What would the automobiles look like,
139	the buildings, even the clothes the people wore? What would
150	these things tell you about the other place the person had
162	lived? If you do not know anyone who has moved to this
175	country, or you do not have any photos to look at, you can
186	go to your local library. Look up travel books and videos.
196	If you are extremely lucky, you may know someone who
207	kept a diary or journal describing what life was like where
219	he or she came from. This type of keepsake will help bring
227	the old country and the new one together.

✔ What is the passage mostly about?

✔ What do you call people who move to new countries?

Words Read	–	Errors	=	WCPM

☐ **Fall (94 WCPM)**
☐ **Winter (112 WCPM)**
☐ **Spring (123 WCPM)**

WCPM	/	Words Read	=	Accuracy %

PROSODY				
	L1	L2	L3	L4
Reading in Phrases	○	○	○	○
Pace	○	○	○	○
Syntax	○	○	○	○
Self-correction	○	○	○	○
Intonation	○	○	○	○

Why Winter Comes

Centuries ago, people noticed that Earth was warm and green some of the time and bitter cold at other times. This was a cycle that repeated itself over and over. To explain these changes, ancient people told stories. There were myths to explain just about every cycle in nature. Some stories explained why the sun disappeared each night and reappeared each morning. Other myths told what caused the moon to wax and wane.

Why winter arrived each year is explained in one myth about a Greek goddess named Demeter. The myth said that Demeter had a beautiful daughter named Persephone. Hades, the god of the underworld, snatched Persephone and brought her to his kingdom. Demeter was so depressed by her daughter's sudden disappearance that she caused Earth to become cold and barren. Nothing grew during the time that Persephone was in the underworld.

Demeter begged Hades to return her daughter. Eventually, Hades gave in and allowed the girl to return to her mother. But Demeter had to promise that Persephone would spend part of every year with him. When she saw Persephone again, Demeter was overjoyed, and she allowed plants to grow again.

This early explanation told that when winter arrived Persephone had to go back to the underworld.

☑ What is the author's purpose for writing this passage?

☑ According to the myth, what causes winter?

Name: _____ Date: _____

Why Winter Comes

8	Centuries ago, people noticed that Earth was warm
20	and green some of the time and bitter cold at other times.
32	This was a cycle that repeated itself over and over. To explain
41	these changes, ancient people told stories. There were myths
52	to explain just about every cycle in nature. Some stories explained
62	why the sun disappeared each night and reappeared each morning.
73	Other myths told what caused the moon to wax and wane.
84	Why winter arrived each year is explained in one myth about
94	a Greek goddess named Demeter. The myth said that Demeter
104	had a beautiful daughter named Persephone. Hades, the god of
113	the underworld, snatched Persephone and brought her to his
122	kingdom. Demeter was so depressed by her daughter's sudden
131	disappearance that she caused Earth to become cold and
140	barren. Nothing grew during the time that Persephone was
143	in the underworld.
151	Demeter begged Hades to return her daughter. Eventually,
163	Hades gave in and allowed the girl to return to her mother.
172	But Demeter had to promise that Persephone would spend
183	part of every year with him. When she saw Persephone again,
193	Demeter was overjoyed, and she allowed plants to grow again.
201	This early explanation told that when winter arrived
209	Persephone had to go back to the underworld.

 What is the author's purpose for writing this passage?

 According to the myth, what causes winter?

Words Read	–	Errors	=	WCPM

☐ Fall (94 WCPM)

☐ Winter (112 WCPM)

☐ Spring (123 WCPM)

WCPM	/	Words Read	=	Accuracy %

PROSODY				
	L1	L2	L3	L4
Reading in Phrases	○	○	○	○
Pace	○	○	○	○
Syntax	○	○	○	○
Self-correction	○	○	○	○
Intonation	○	○	○	○

How Rhinoceros Got Its Wrinkly Skin

Long ago, Rhinoceros had a tight skin that he wore like a coat. One day a delicious smell drifted across the land. Rhinoceros followed it to where he saw a man holding a huge cake. The man dropped the cake fearfully and climbed to the top of a tree. Rhinoceros thrust his horn into the cake, tossed it into the air, and swallowed it whole.

Several weeks later, the sun baked the land. Rhinoceros, feeling hot, decided to go for a swim. So he undid the buttons and dropped his skin on the ground. Before long, Rhinoceros happily paddled in the cool sea.

The man, who had been watching Rhinoceros, gathered all the old cake bits he could find. He quietly filled Rhinoceros's coat with the dry pieces and then climbed up the tree again to watch Rhinoceros.

Soon the huge horned animal finished his swim and slipped on his coat. Rhinoceros felt a tickle, so he scratched, but the itch did not go away. Then Rhinoceros lay on the ground and rolled around, but the itch still did not go away. Rhinoceros, getting grumpy, ran to the tree and rubbed and rubbed until his skin was stretched and pulled and folded, but the itch remained. To this day, the rhinoceros has baggy skin and a bad temper.

✔ Why did the author write this story?

✔ What made Rhinoceros itch?

Name: _____ **Date:** _____

How Rhinoceros Got Its Wrinkly Skin

12	Long ago, Rhinoceros had a tight skin that he wore like a
22	coat. One day a delicious smell drifted across the land.
34	Rhinoceros followed it to where he saw a man holding a huge
46	cake. The man dropped the cake fearfully and climbed to the top
59	of a tree. Rhinoceros thrust his horn into the cake, tossed it into
65	the air, and swallowed it whole.
74	Several weeks later, the sun baked the land. Rhinoceros,
87	feeling hot, decided to go for a swim. So he undid the buttons
97	and dropped his skin on the ground. Before long, Rhinoceros
103	happily paddled in the cool sea.
111	The man, who had been watching Rhinoceros, gathered
123	all the old cake bits he could find. He quietly filled Rhinoceros's
136	coat with the dry pieces and then climbed up the tree again to
138	watch Rhinoceros.
147	Soon the huge horned animal finished his swim and
159	slipped on his coat. Rhinoceros felt a tickle, so he scratched, but
171	the itch did not go away. Then Rhinoceros lay on the ground
183	and rolled around, but the itch still did not go away. Rhinoceros,
195	getting grumpy, ran to the tree and rubbed and rubbed until his
206	skin was stretched and pulled and folded, but the itch remained.
218	To this day, the rhinoceros has baggy skin and a bad temper.

- ✓ Why did the author write this story?
- ✓ What made Rhinoceros itch?

Words Read	–	Errors	=	WCPM

☐ Fall (94 WCPM)

☐ Winter (112 WCPM)

☐ Spring (123 WCPM)

WCPM	/	Words Read	=	Accuracy %

PROSODY				
	L1	L2	L3	L4
Reading in Phrases	○	○	○	○
Pace	○	○	○	○
Syntax	○	○	○	○
Self-correction	○	○	○	○
Intonation	○	○	○	○

Moons

Many years ago, Native Americans did not have calendars to tell them what month or day it was. Instead, they had the moon. By keeping track of the time it took for the moon to go from one full moon phase to the next, they measured their days.

Each phase was called a moon, and each moon was about the length of a month. They noted how cold the winds were and what the Earth looked like around them. They observed what color the rabbits' fur was, and if choke cherries were on the bushes. Then they named that moon phase for what they saw and felt.

March might be the Moon of the Long Rains to a Native American living in the Northeast. To a Native American in a dry climate, March might be the Moon of the Desert Blooms. Moons could also be named after feasts and ceremonies, such as the Moon of Summer Encampment. Children learned about the moons from their elders, and looked forward to what each new moon would bring.

✔ How did Native Americans keep track of what month or day it was?

✔ How did Native Americans decide what to name a moon phase?

Name: _____ Date: _____

Moons

9	Many years ago, Native Americans did not have calendars
23	to tell them what month or day it was. Instead, they had the moon.
38	By keeping track of the time it took for the moon to go from one
48	full moon phase to the next, they measured their days.
60	Each phase was called a moon, and each moon was about the
73	length of a month. They noted how cold the winds were and what
83	the Earth looked like around them. They observed what color
95	the rabbits' fur was, and if choke cherries were on the bushes.
107	Then they named that moon phase for what they saw and felt.
119	March might be the Moon of the Long Rains to a Native
131	American living in the Northeast. To a Native American in a dry
142	climate, March might be the Moon of the Desert Blooms. Moons
153	could also be named after feasts and ceremonies, such as the
161	Moon of Summer Encampment. Children learned about the
172	moons from their elders, and looked forward to what each new
175	moon would bring.

✔ How did Native Americans keep track of what month or day it was?

✔ How did Native Americans decide what to name a moon phase?

Words Read	–	Errors	=	WCPM

☐ Fall (94 WCPM)
☐ Winter (112 WCPM)
☐ Spring (123 WCPM)

WCPM	/	Words Read	=	Accuracy %

PROSODY				
	L1	L2	L3	L4
Reading in Phrases	○	○	○	○
Pace	○	○	○	○
Syntax	○	○	○	○
Self-correction	○	○	○	○
Intonation	○	○	○	○

Seeing Pink

"Do you know where my soccer jersey and shorts are?" Marco asked his mother. "We are playing the championship game tomorrow, so I am getting my equipment ready."

Mrs. Cantu looked up from the book she was reading. "I washed a load of white clothes earlier today," she answered. "They are still in the washing machine. You will have to put them in the dryer."

Marco whistled happily as he walked down the hallway. He was thinking about how his team, the Sharks, would be the city soccer champions after the game tomorrow. The whistling stopped abruptly when Marco looked inside the washing machine.

"I thought you did a load of white clothes," Marco called out. "All the clothes here are pink!"

"Oh, no!" she groaned. "One of Amy's red socks must have gotten in with the whites. The color ran and dyed everything."

Marco watched in horror as his mother pulled out a pair of pink soccer shorts followed by a pink jersey.

"Mom, the big game is tomorrow!" gasped Marco. "I have to wear my *white* uniform."

"I will wash your clothes again with bleach," answered Mrs. Cantu calmly. "If that does not remove the pink color, we will have to go shopping later today."

Marco sighed in relief. The big game was not until tomorrow.

✔ Why did the white clothes change color?

✔ What is Mrs. Cantu's solution to the problem?

Name: _____ **Date:** _____

Seeing Pink

10	"Do you know where my soccer jersey and shorts are?"
20	Marco asked his mother. "We are playing the championship game
28	tomorrow, so I am getting my equipment ready."
40	Mrs. Cantu looked up from the book she was reading. "I washed
53	a load of white clothes earlier today," she answered. "They are still in
65	the washing machine. You will have to put them in the dryer."
75	Marco whistled happily as he walked down the hallway. He
87	was thinking about how his team, the Sharks, would be the city
96	soccer champions after the game tomorrow. The whistling stopped
104	abruptly when Marco looked inside the washing machine.
115	"I thought you did a load of white clothes," Marco called
122	out. "All the clothes here are pink!"
133	"Oh, no!" she groaned. "One of Amy's red socks must have
144	gotten in with the whites. The color ran and dyed everything."
156	Marco watched in horror as his mother pulled out a pair of
164	pink soccer shorts followed by a pink jersey.
174	"Mom, the big game is tomorrow!" gasped Marco. "I have
179	to wear my *white* uniform."
188	"I will wash your clothes again with bleach," answered
200	Mrs. Cantu calmly. "If that does not remove the pink color, we
207	will have to go shopping later today."
218	Marco sighed in relief. The big game was not until tomorrow.

✔ Why did the white clothes change color?

✔ What is Mrs. Cantu's solution to the problem?

Words Read	–	Errors	=	WCPM

☐ Fall (110 WCPM)

☐ Winter (127 WCPM)

☐ Spring (139 WCPM)

WCPM	/	Words Read	=	Accuracy %

PROSODY				
	L1	L2	L3	L4
Reading in Phrases	○	○	○	○
Pace	○	○	○	○
Syntax	○	○	○	○
Self-correction	○	○	○	○
Intonation	○	○	○	○

Egyptian Writing

Egyptian picture writing, or hieroglyphics, began almost 5,000 years ago. At first, the Egyptians just drew pictures to stand for objects. For example, the sun was a circle with a dot in it. A house was a small rectangle. Over time, it became too difficult to come up with a new picture for each word. So the Egyptians began to combine words to make sounds. For example, the Egyptian word for "go out" sounds like the words for "house" and "sun." Writers just combined these two pictures when they needed to write the word that means "go out."

Over the centuries, the ability to understand Egyptian writing was lost. Experts puzzled over Egyptian texts without any idea of what they meant. Then, in 1799, an officer in the French army found the Rosetta Stone in Egypt. The strange black stone had three sections of writing carved into it. The first section was a story in Greek. The other two sections were translations of the same story into Egyptian picture writing. Using these translations, experts quickly decoded the Rosetta Stone. Using what they deciphered, they soon solved the puzzle of Egyptian hieroglyphics.

Picture writing was used for thousands of years. But by 1000 B.C., the Phoenicians, a people who also lived in the Middle East, created a less clumsy writing system. Instead of combining pictures to make sounds, they developed an alphabet. Each letter in the alphabet stood for a sound.

☑ How is ancient Egyptian writing different from the way we write?

☑ What is the importance of the Rosetta Stone?

Name: _____ **Date:** _____

Egyptian Writing

7	Egyptian picture writing, or hieroglyphics, began almost
19	5,000 years ago. At first, the Egyptians just drew pictures to stand
34	for objects. For example, the sun was a circle with a dot in it. A
46	house was a small rectangle. Over time, it became too difficult to
59	come up with a new picture for each word. So the Egyptians began
69	to combine words to make sounds. For example, the Egyptian
81	word for "go out" sounds like the words for "house" and "sun."
92	Writers just combined these two pictures when they needed to write
98	the word that means "go out."
106	Over the centuries, the ability to understand Egyptian
116	writing was lost. Experts puzzled over Egyptian texts without any
129	idea of what they meant. Then, in 1799, an officer in the French
140	army found the Rosetta Stone in Egypt. The strange black stone
153	had three sections of writing carved into it. The first section was a
164	story in Greek. The other two sections were translations of the
173	same story into Egyptian picture writing. Using these translations,
182	experts quickly decoded the Rosetta Stone. Using what they
191	deciphered, they soon solved the puzzle of Egyptian hieroglyphics.
201	Picture writing was used for thousands of years. But by
213	1000 B.C., the Phoenicians, a people who also lived in the Middle
223	East, created a less clumsy writing system. Instead of combining
234	pictures to make sounds, they developed an alphabet. Each letter in
240	the alphabet stood for a sound.

☑ How is ancient Egyptian writing different from the way we write?

☑ What is the importance of the Rosetta Stone?

Words Read	–	Errors	=	WCPM

☐ Fall (110 WCPM)

☐ Winter (127 WCPM)

☐ Spring (139 WCPM)

WCPM	/	Words Read	=	Accuracy %

PROSODY				
	L1	L2	L3	L4
Reading in Phrases	○	○	○	○
Pace	○	○	○	○
Syntax	○	○	○	○
Self-correction	○	○	○	○
Intonation	○	○	○	○

Quick Thinking

Mr. Ryan closed the dishwasher door just as Daniel turned off the vacuum.

"The house is sparkling clean, and there are no dishes in the sink," remarked Daniel. "When Mom gets home from her business trip, she will be able to relax. It will be a nice surprise for her!"

"She will be home in an hour, so we need to start dinner," said Mr. Ryan. "Where did you put the chicken to defrost it?"

"I thought you were taking out the chicken," said Daniel.

"Oh, well," sighed Mr. Ryan, "we'll have to cook something else. Mom has been eating at restaurants and hotels all week, so I know she would appreciate a home-cooked meal. Take a look in the pantry to see if there is anything that we can quickly and easily prepare while I look in the refrigerator."

Searching on all the shelves, Daniel finally pulled out a jar of spaghetti sauce and a bag of noodles. Mr. Ryan held up a package of mushrooms.

"These are two of my favorites," said Daniel. "Can we cut up the mushrooms to make spaghetti with mushroom sauce?"

Mr. Ryan answered, "We don't have a choice if we are going to surprise Mom with dinner when she gets home."

"I think that Mom will love it," remarked Daniel.

✅ Why did Mr. Ryan and Daniel clean the house?

✅ What do you think Mr. Ryan and Daniel will do next?

Name: _____ **Date:** _____

Quick Thinking

10	Mr. Ryan closed the dishwasher door just as Daniel turned
13	off the vacuum.
25	"The house is sparkling clean, and there are no dishes in the
35	sink," remarked Daniel. "When Mom gets home from her business
50	trip, she will be able to relax. It will be a nice surprise for her!"
63	"She will be home in an hour, so we need to start dinner,"
75	said Mr. Ryan. "Where did you put the chicken to defrost it?"
85	"I thought you were taking out the chicken," said Daniel.
95	"Oh, well," sighed Mr. Ryan, "we'll have to cook something
108	else. Mom has been eating at restaurants and hotels all week, so I
120	know she would appreciate a home-cooked meal. Take a look in
134	the pantry to see if there is anything that we can quickly and easily
141	prepare while I look in the refrigerator."
152	Searching on all the shelves, Daniel finally pulled out a jar
165	of spaghetti sauce and a bag of noodles. Mr. Ryan held up a
168	package of mushrooms.
178	"These are two of my favorites," said Daniel. "Can we
188	cut up the mushrooms to make spaghetti with mushroom sauce?"
200	Mr. Ryan answered, "We don't have a choice if we are going
209	to surprise Mom with dinner when she gets home."
218	"I think that Mom will love it," remarked Daniel.

✓ Why did Mr. Ryan and Daniel clean the house?

✓ What do you think Mr. Ryan and Daniel will do next?

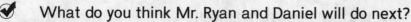

Words Read	–	Errors	=	WCPM

☐ **Fall (110 WCPM)**

☐ **Winter (127 WCPM)**

☐ **Spring (139 WCPM)**

WCPM	/	Words Read	=	Accuracy %

PROSODY				
	L1	L2	L3	L4
Reading in Phrases	○	○	○	○
Pace	○	○	○	○
Syntax	○	○	○	○
Self-correction	○	○	○	○
Intonation	○	○	○	○

Cell Phones Unplugged

A battery is a small, lightweight device that stores electric energy. It is used as a power source in handheld toys, tools, and machines. It is especially useful in small machines people carry, such as cell phones and laptop computers. A battery can be a problem, though. Heavy use drains the stored energy. The equipment turns off when there is no energy. A battery must be recharged through an electric power supply before the machine will operate. Scientists are now experimenting with a new power supply that will be able to create its own energy. It uses gas and is small like a battery, which makes it ideal for cell phones and laptop computers.

Some animals, like cows, eat grass. They belch a lot, which produces an invisible gas that has no odor. This same gas can also be produced from rotting vegetables. While large amounts of this gas can harm the environment, scientists have found a way to process it to make it safe. They are putting it into a device called a *fuel cell.* The fuel cell uses the gas to make electricity. So far, the experiments are successful. The gas-powered fuel cells are making their own energy. Scientists are excited that some day cell phones and laptops might be free of plugs.

✅ What is the main idea of this article?

✅ What is the power supply for a fuel cell?

Name: _____ **Date:** _____

Cell Phones Unplugged

10	A battery is a small, lightweight device that stores electric
23	energy. It is used as a power source in handheld toys, tools, and
33	machines. It is especially useful in small machines people carry,
45	such as cell phones and laptop computers. A battery can be a
54	problem, though. Heavy use drains the stored energy. The
66	equipment turns off when there is no energy. A battery must be
75	recharged through an electric power supply before the machine
85	will operate. Scientists are now experimenting with a new power
100	supply that will be able to create its own energy. It uses gas and is
112	small like a battery, which makes it ideal for cell phones and
114	laptop computers.
125	Some animals, like cows, eat grass. They belch a lot, which
138	produces an invisible gas that has no odor. This same gas can also
148	be produced from rotting vegetables. While large amounts of this
159	gas can harm the environment, scientists have found a way to
174	process it to make it safe. They are putting it into a device called a
188	*fuel cell.* The fuel cell uses the gas to make electricity. So far, the
198	experiments are successful. The gas-powered fuel cells are making
209	their own energy. Scientists are excited that some day cell phones
216	and laptops might be free of plugs.

☑ What is the main idea of this article?

☑ What is the power supply for a fuel cell?

Words Read	–	Errors	=	WCPM

☐ **Fall (110 WCPM)**

☐ **Winter (127 WCPM)**

☐ **Spring (139 WCPM)**

WCPM	/	Words Read	=	Accuracy %

PROSODY				
	L1	L2	L3	L4
Reading in Phrases	○	○	○	○
Pace	○	○	○	○
Syntax	○	○	○	○
Self-correction	○	○	○	○
Intonation	○	○	○	○

The Last Frontier

Many people claim that space is the last frontier. By this they mean that every country on Earth has already been discovered and explored. To be true explorers, they say, we must journey to distant planets.

While it may be true that space is an open frontier, plenty of frontier still exists here on our planet. This is because the deepest spots of our planet, deep areas beneath the oceans, are still unexplored. The average depth of the world's oceans is 12,200 feet, but parts of the ocean plunge much deeper. The deepest known spot is in the western Pacific and is 36,198 feet below sea level.

Divers can go only so far with the deep sea breathing equipment we have today. To really reach the ocean's depths, people need to travel in special vehicles especially built for underwater exploration. Only a handful of people have done that.

We know that plant life is rare deep below the ocean's surface. That's because sunlight is necessary for plant survival and solar rays can penetrate only about 660 feet below the surface of the water. Deeper than that, the waters are completely dark and plants are unable to survive. Many sea creatures depend on plants for food. What do we assume about animal activity in deep water?

We know that some animals have adapted to life in the dark by becoming luminous, giving off a glow. Other creatures have become scavengers, feeding on whatever drops to the ocean floor.

- ☑ In the author's opinion, what really is the last frontier?
- ☑ Why don't we know more about life in deep water?

Name: _____ **Date:** _____

The Last Frontier

11	Many people claim that space is the last frontier. By this
22	they mean that every country on Earth has already been discovered
34	and explored. To be true explorers, they say, we must journey to
36	distant planets.
48	While it may be true that space is an open frontier, plenty
60	of frontier still exists here on our planet. This is because the
72	deepest spots of our planet, deep areas beneath the oceans, are still
83	unexplored. The average depth of the world's oceans is 12,200 feet,
94	but parts of the ocean plunge much deeper. The deepest known
107	spot is in the western Pacific and is 36,198 feet below sea level.
118	Divers can go only so far with the deep sea breathing
128	equipment we have today. To really reach the ocean's depths,
138	people need to travel in special vehicles especially built for
148	underwater exploration. Only a handful of people have done that.
159	We know that plant life is rare deep below the ocean's
169	surface. That's because sunlight is necessary for plant survival and
181	solar rays can penetrate only about 660 feet below the surface of
192	the water. Deeper than that, the waters are completely dark and
203	plants are unable to survive. Many sea creatures depend on plants
215	for food. What do we assume about animal activity in deep water?
227	We know that some animals have adapted to life in the dark
237	by becoming luminous, giving off a glow. Other creatures have
247	become scavengers, feeding on whatever drops to the ocean floor.

 In the author's opinion, what really is the last frontier?

 Why don't we know more about life in deep water?

Words Read	−	Errors	=	WCPM

☐ **Fall (110 WCPM)**

☐ **Winter (127 WCPM)**

☐ **Spring (139 WCPM)**

WCPM	/	Words Read	=	Accuracy %

PROSODY				
	L1	L2	L3	L4
Reading in Phrases	○	○	○	○
Pace	○	○	○	○
Syntax	○	○	○	○
Self-correction	○	○	○	○
Intonation	○	○	○	○

Grocery Difficulty

Rachel always looked forward to Tuesday because she got to walk with Grandma Edwards to the grocery store. There was a skateboard park nearby, so Rachel met friends there to cruise the course and practice stunts while her grandma shopped.

This Tuesday was no different, and Rachel contentedly chatted with her friends as they took turns dropping into the pipe to practice different combinations. When Grandma Edwards finished shopping, she sat on the bench to watch. Rachel took one final run on the course and then joined her grandma.

"That was an excellent run," Grandma Edwards applauded.

Rachel removed her helmet and laughed, "I avoided falling, so it was a success!"

Grandma Edwards stood up and struggled to lift the grocery bag. "I purchased too many canned goods, so the bag is heavier than normal," she commented.

"Let me carry the groceries," Rachel offered.

"Then what do we do with the skateboard?" her grandma asked.

Rachel remembered a recent school lesson explaining that simple tools made work easier, and a wheel was surely a simple tool.

"I have a solution to our grocery difficulty," said Rachel. She plopped the bag of food on the skateboard, leaned over, and pushed.

"I guess it's time for us to roll, Rachel," said Grandma with a grin.

✔ What is the main problem in the story?

✔ What is Rachel's solution to the problem?

Name: _____ **Date:** _____

Grocery Difficulty

10	Rachel always looked forward to Tuesday because she got to
21	walk with Grandma Edwards to the grocery store. There was a
32	skateboard park nearby, so Rachel met friends there to cruise the
40	course and practice stunts while her grandma shopped.
48	This Tuesday was no different, and Rachel contentedly
61	chatted with her friends as they took turns dropping into the pipe to
68	practice different combinations. When Grandma Edwards finished
81	shopping, she sat on the bench to watch. Rachel took one final run
89	on the course and then joined her grandma.
97	"That was an excellent run," Grandma Edwards applauded.
106	Rachel removed her helmet and laughed, "I avoided falling,
111	so it was a success!"
121	Grandma Edwards stood up and struggled to lift the grocery
133	bag. "I purchased too many canned goods, so the bag is heavier
137	than normal," she commented.
144	"Let me carry the groceries," Rachel offered.
155	"Then what do we do with the skateboard?" her grandma asked.
163	Rachel remembered a recent school lesson explaining that
176	simple tools made work easier, and a wheel was surely a simple tool.
187	"I have a solution to our grocery difficulty," said Rachel. She
199	plopped the bag of food on the skateboard, leaned over, and pushed.
213	"I guess it's time for us to roll, Rachel," said Grandma with a grin.

✔ What is the main problem in the story?
✔ What is Rachel's solution to the problem?

Words Read	–	Errors	=	WCPM

☐ **Fall (110 WCPM)**
☐ **Winter (127 WCPM)**
☐ **Spring (139 WCPM)**

WCPM	/	Words Read	=	Accuracy %

PROSODY				
	L1	L2	L3	L4
Reading in Phrases	○	○	○	○
Pace	○	○	○	○
Syntax	○	○	○	○
Self-correction	○	○	○	○
Intonation	○	○	○	○

Odysseus and the Sirens

Odysseus was a distinguished Greek hero celebrated in many legends. One of these legends tells about an adventure Odysseus had while sailing home from Troy.

Odysseus knew that he and his crew would have to pass perilously close to the island of the Sirens. The Sirens were a dangerous group of singers whose voices were extremely beautiful. Every time a ship got close to the island, the Sirens would deliberately stand on a hilltop, waving and singing rhythmically. The ship's crew would forget about steering and head directly for the beautiful melody. Before long, their boat would crash and break against the rocky shore.

Odysseus was a man with common sense. He did not want his boat to be destroyed by the Sirens. He came up with a good plan. He instructed his crew to plug their ears with wax while the ship was steering past the island. Then the crew would not be able to hear the song, and the boat would be safe.

But Odysseus yearned to hear the Sirens' song. So he thought of another scheme. He had the crew strap him tightly to the mast. Then, as the crew rowed near the island, Odysseus listened to the most beautiful music imaginable. He struggled in vain to get free, to throw himself into the water and swim toward the Sirens. Finally, the boat passed the island. The sailors took the wax out of their ears and loosened the knots tying Odysseus.

✔ What danger did Odysseus face near the island of the Sirens?

✔ Why did the crew tie Odysseus to the mast?

Oral Reading Fluency Grades 1–6

Name: _____ Date: _____

Odysseus and the Sirens

8	Odysseus was a distinguished Greek hero celebrated in
18	many legends. One of these legends tells about an adventure
25	Odysseus had while sailing home from Troy.
36	Odysseus knew that he and his crew would have to pass
48	perilously close to the island of the Sirens. The Sirens were a
57	dangerous group of singers whose voices were extremely beautiful.
69	Every time a ship got close to the island, the Sirens would
78	deliberately stand on a hilltop, waving and singing rhythmically.
89	The ship's crew would forget about steering and head directly for
99	the beautiful melody. Before long, their boat would crash and
104	break against the rocky shore.
115	Odysseus was a man with common sense. He did not want
129	his boat to be destroyed by the Sirens. He came up with a good
142	plan. He instructed his crew to plug their ears with wax while the
155	ship was steering past the island. Then the crew would not be able
165	to hear the song, and the boat would be safe.
175	But Odysseus yearned to hear the Sirens' song. So he
187	thought of another scheme. He had the crew strap him tightly to
198	the mast. Then, as the crew rowed near the island, Odysseus
208	listened to the most beautiful music imaginable. He struggled in
221	vain to get free, to throw himself into the water and swim toward
233	the Sirens. Finally, the boat passed the island. The sailors took the
244	wax out of their ears and loosened the knots tying Odysseus.

✔ What danger did Odysseus face near the island of the Sirens?

✔ Why did the crew tie Odysseus to the mast?

Words Read	–	Errors	=	WCPM

☐ Fall (127 WCPM)

☐ Winter (140 WCPM)

☐ Spring (150 WCPM)

WCPM	/	Words Read	=	Accuracy %

PROSODY				
	L1	L2	L3	L4
Reading in Phrases	○	○	○	○
Pace	○	○	○	○
Syntax	○	○	○	○
Self-correction	○	○	○	○
Intonation	○	○	○	○

Making a Home in a New Place

Every year, millions of people move to the United States from other countries. To move from one country to another is called *immigration*. Immigrants come from all over the world, and they have many different reasons for packing up their belongings and seeking a home in a new country. They may be looking for better jobs, or they may be fleeing from a land where their freedom was denied. Natural disasters may have forced them to leave. Maybe they are looking for the chance to have a better education. Whatever their reasons, they leave behind friends, a way of life, and many memories.

After an immigrant family moves to the United States, they may decide not to stay in the same city they first arrived at. Many immigrants first try to establish themselves near other family members who had immigrated earlier. Sooner or later, the new immigrants may discover that they would have better opportunities elsewhere. They might prefer living in another town, or even another state.

At the beginning of the last century, for instance, many immigrants came from Europe on vessels that landed in New York City. Quite a few of them remained there. But millions of them headed elsewhere, traveling by train, boat, or car.

Today, a family may travel conveniently by plane. However, they still face the same old-fashioned challenge of making a home in a strange place.

✔ Why do people immigrate?

✔ What are some of the decisions new immigrants need to make?

Name: _____ **Date:** _____

Making a Home in a New Place

11	Every year, millions of people move to the United States from
22	other countries. To move from one country to another is called
33	*immigration*. Immigrants come from all over the world, and they have
43	many different reasons for packing up their belongings and seeking
58	a home in a new country. They may be looking for better jobs, or they
70	may be fleeing from a land where their freedom was denied. Natural
82	disasters may have forced them to leave. Maybe they are looking for
93	the chance to have a better education. Whatever their reasons, they
103	leave behind friends, a way of life, and many memories.
113	After an immigrant family moves to the United States, they
126	may decide not to stay in the same city they first arrived at.
136	Many immigrants first try to establish themselves near other family
146	members who had immigrated earlier. Sooner or later, the new
155	immigrants may discover that they would have better opportunities
165	elsewhere. They might prefer living in another town, or even
167	another state.
177	At the beginning of the last century, for instance, many
188	immigrants came from Europe on vessels that landed in New York
200	City. Quite a few of them remained there. But millions of them
208	headed elsewhere, traveling by train, boat, or car.
217	Today, a family may travel conveniently by plane. However,
230	they still face the same old-fashioned challenge of making a home in
233	a strange place.

✔ Why do people immigrate?

✔ What are some of the decisions new immigrants need to make?

Words Read	–	Errors	=	WCPM

☐ **Fall (127 WCPM)**

☐ **Winter (140 WCPM)**

☐ **Spring (150 WCPM)**

WCPM	/	Words Read	=	Accuracy %

PROSODY	L1	L2	L3	L4
Reading in Phrases	○	○	○	○
Pace	○	○	○	○
Syntax	○	○	○	○
Self-correction	○	○	○	○
Intonation	○	○	○	○

Costume Party

Rahim's party was less than two days away, and Ken was still undecided about his costume. The problem was that Ken had won the costume award for the last two years, so he was eager to maintain his creative reputation. All he needed was one idea to spark his vision for this year's unique masterpiece.

Ken wandered the house, looking for inspiration. He ended up in the laundry room, where his dad was kneeling by the dryer.

"Can you hand me the new dryer hose?" Mr. Moss asked.

Ken stretched out the shiny, flexible tube before giving it to his dad. It reminded him of the arms and legs of a robot from a science fiction novel.

"If you are going to put the old dryer hose into the garbage, may I have it?" asked Ken.

"Just rinse out the dust if you keep it inside the house," Mr. Moss answered, handing the old hose to Ken.

Ken, examining the foil tube, estimated that it had a six-inch diameter. He knew that the hose could easily slide over his arm, but Ken was doubtful that he could insert his foot through the opening. He decided that he would have to slit the tube and tape the seam together once he wrapped the hose around his leg.

Finally, Ken found his genius idea! He grinned confidently, knowing that he would once again be proclaimed the winner.

✔ Why does Ken have a problem choosing his costume?

✔ What costume does Ken decide to make?

Name: _____ **Date:** _____

Costume Party

11	Rahim's party was less than two days away, and Ken was
22	still undecided about his costume. The problem was that Ken had
36	won the costume award for the last two years, so he was eager to
47	maintain his creative reputation. All he needed was one idea to
55	spark his vision for this year's unique masterpiece.
64	Ken wandered the house, looking for inspiration. He ended
77	up in the laundry room, where his dad was kneeling by the dryer.
88	"Can you hand me the new dryer hose?" Mr. Moss asked.
99	Ken stretched out the shiny, flexible tube before giving it to
114	his dad. It reminded him of the arms and legs of a robot from a
117	science fiction novel.
130	"If you are going to put the old dryer hose into the garbage,
136	may I have it?" asked Ken.
148	"Just rinse out the dust if you keep it inside the house,"
157	Mr. Moss answered, handing the old hose to Ken.
169	Ken, examining the foil tube, estimated that it had a six-inch
181	diameter. He knew that the hose could easily slide over his arm,
192	but Ken was doubtful that he could insert his foot through
205	the opening. He decided that he would have to slit the tube and
217	tape the seam together once he wrapped the hose around his leg.
226	Finally, Ken found his genius idea! He grinned confidently,
236	knowing that he would once again be proclaimed the winner.

✅ Why does Ken have a problem choosing his costume?

✅ What costume does Ken decide to make?

Words Read	–	Errors	=	WCPM

☐ Fall (127 WCPM)
☐ Winter (140 WCPM)
☐ Spring (150 WCPM)

WCPM	/	Words Read	=	Accuracy %

PROSODY				
	L1	L2	L3	L4
Reading in Phrases	○	○	○	○
Pace	○	○	○	○
Syntax	○	○	○	○
Self-correction	○	○	○	○
Intonation	○	○	○	○

Recycled Products

In 2010, people in the United States generated nearly two-hundred-fifty million tons of garbage. Because recycling is an important part of many households, schools, and businesses, almost eighty-five million tons of it was recovered. So what happens to the recovered materials?

Aluminum cans are the most recycled items. They can be made continuously into new cans. Manufacturers also make window frames, electric cables, and even bicycles from them.

Glass is one of the easiest materials to process because it can be melted and remolded into new bottles and jars. The lesser quality glass finds new life in counter tops, flooring, and roads. Some creative manufacturers even crush different colors of bottles and spread the colorful bits in flowerbeds.

Recycled plant material is another important product found in flowerbeds. Vegetable scraps, coffee grounds, leaves, and grass clippings decay and become soil rich in minerals.

Paper is often processed to make new paper, including money and paper towels. However, it is also used to make such interesting products as hospital gowns and lampshades.

Probably the most product variety comes from recycled plastic. Some manufacturers even use plastic to make clothing. Amazingly, the bottle of juice you recycle might be your next ball cap!

✓   What is this the main idea of the passage?

✓   What are two products that might be made from a recycled can?

Name: _____   **Date:** _____

Recycled Products

9	In 2010, people in the United States generated nearly
18	two-hundred-fifty million tons of garbage. Because recycling
28	is an important part of many households, schools, and businesses,
39	almost eighty-five million tons of it was recovered. So what
44	happens to the recovered materials?
54	Aluminum cans are the most recycled items. They can be
62	made continuously into new cans. Manufacturers also make
71	window frames, electric cables, and even bicycles from them.
83	Glass is one of the easiest materials to process because it can
95	be melted and remolded into new bottles and jars. The lesser quality
106	glass finds new life in counter tops, flooring, and roads. Some
115	creative manufacturers even crush different colors of bottles and
121	spread the colorful bits in flowerbeds.
129	Recycled plant material is another important product found
138	in flowerbeds. Vegetable scraps, coffee grounds, leaves, and grass
146	clippings decay and become soil rich in minerals.
155	Paper is often processed to make new paper, including
167	money and paper towels. However, it is also used to make such
174	interesting products as hospital gowns and lampshades.
183	Probably the most product variety comes from recycled plastic.
192	Some manufacturers even use plastic to make clothing. Amazingly,
204	the bottle of juice you recycle might be your next ball cap!

☑ What is the main idea of the passage?

☑ What are two products that might be made from a recycled can?

Words Read	–	Errors	=	WCPM

☐ **Fall (127 WCPM)**
☐ **Winter (140 WCPM)**
☐ **Spring (150 WCPM)**

WCPM	/	Words Read	=	Accuracy %

PROSODY

	L1	L2	L3	L4
Reading in Phrases	○	○	○	○
Pace	○	○	○	○
Syntax	○	○	○	○
Self-correction	○	○	○	○
Intonation	○	○	○	○

Pecos Bill Tames a Cyclone

Of all the cowboys that make up the history of the American West, there is none more famous than Pecos Bill. All the other cowboys might have had animal trouble, but Pecos Bill never got bucked off a horse. In fact, Bill was such a skilled rider that he even saddled and rode a mountain lion one time!

Pecos Bill faced a true test one day when the sky turned black and the winds whirled violently. A cyclone was approaching, which sent the bravest cowboys running—except for Pecos Bill.

"Are you going to let a little puff of wind frighten you?" exclaimed Bill. "I can easily tame that cyclone!"

So when the howling wind came close, Bill grabbed it by the tail and threw it to the ground. After he climbed on top of the cyclone without a saddle, it began to buck, twist, swirl, and jerk, which just made Bill smile.

By the third day, the cyclone decided that it could not get rid of Bill, so it poured out its rain in a mighty flood. The gushing water washed out a big hole in the land, which eventually became known as the Grand Canyon.

Finally, the cyclone stopped swirling and evaporated abruptly, which sent Bill tumbling to the ground with a gigantic thud. And that is how Pecos Bill tamed the cyclone and started the popular sport of rodeo!

- ✔ What happened when other cowboys saw the cyclone?
- ✔ How did Pecos Bill help form the Grand Canyon?

Name: _____   Date: _____

Pecos Bill Tames a Cyclone

12	Of all the cowboys that make up the history of the American
24	West, there is none more famous than Pecos Bill. All the other
35	cowboys might have had animal trouble, but Pecos Bill never got
49	bucked off a horse. In fact, Bill was such a skilled rider that he
58	even saddled and rode a mountain lion one time!
70	Pecos Bill faced a true test one day when the sky turned
80	black and the winds whirled violently. A cyclone was approaching,
90	which sent the bravest cowboys running—except for Pecos Bill.
102	"Are you going to let a little puff of wind frighten you?"
110	exclaimed Bill. "I can easily tame that cyclone!"
121	So when the howling wind came close, Bill grabbed it by
136	the tail and threw it to the ground. After he climbed on top of the
148	cyclone without a saddle, it began to buck, twist, swirl, and jerk,
153	which just made Bill smile.
165	By the third day, the cyclone decided that it could not get
180	rid of Bill, so it poured out its rain in a mighty flood. The gushing
192	water washed out a big hole in the land, which eventually became
197	known as the Grand Canyon.
204	Finally, the cyclone stopped swirling and evaporated
215	abruptly, which sent Bill tumbling to the ground with a gigantic
228	thud. And that is how Pecos Bill tamed the cyclone and started the
232	popular sport of rodeo!

✓ What happened when other cowboys saw the cyclone?
✓ How did Pecos Bill help form the Grand Canyon?

Words Read	–	Errors	=	WCPM

☐ Fall (127 WCPM)
☐ Winter (140 WCPM)
☐ Spring (150 WCPM)

WCPM	/	Words Read	=	Accuracy %

PROSODY				
	L1	L2	L3	L4
Reading in Phrases	○	○	○	○
Pace	○	○	○	○
Syntax	○	○	○	○
Self-correction	○	○	○	○
Intonation	○	○	○	○

Fueled by Grass

Most forms of transportation use gasoline or diesel as their power source. These fuels are made from petroleum, a fossil fuel that is in limited supply. Scientists are currently searching for other natural resources to replace the petroleum-based products in an effort to meet the world's demand for transportation fuels. They are excited that the answer might be growing in your backyard.

Biofuels are energy sources manufactured from living things, including crops, grass, trees, and some garbage. Scientists are interested in biofuels because they are "green" products, materials that can do less harm to Earth's land, water, or air. Corn has been the main source of biofuel, but it is an important food crop. So scientists are concerned that using corn as a fuel could reduce the supply needed to feed both the human and animal populations.

As a result, scientists have begun to experiment with a variety of grasses as biofuel alternatives. They are encouraged by the initial tests and benefits. First, grasses grow in a variety of soils and climates around the world that are often unsuitable for farming food crops. Grasses also have multiple growing seasons, so they could be harvested several times each year. Finally, most grasses need little water, so they are easy and cheap to grow. Presently, producing grass biofuel is expensive and lengthy, but with more testing, scientists are confident this will change.

✔ What is the main idea of the passage?
✔ What are two benefits to using grass as a biofuel?

Oral Reading Fluency Grades 1–6

Name: _____ Date: _____

Fueled by Grass

10	Most forms of transportation use gasoline or diesel as their
21	power source. These fuels are made from petroleum, a fossil fuel
32	that is in limited supply. Scientists are currently searching for other
42	natural resources to replace the petroleum-based products in an
53	effort to meet the world's demand for transportation fuels. They are
63	excited that the answer might be growing in your backyard.
71	Biofuels are energy sources manufactured from living things,
80	including crops, grass, trees, and some garbage. Scientists are
89	interested in biofuels because they are "green" products, materials
103	that can do less harm to Earth's land, water, or air. Corn has been
116	the main source of biofuel, but it is an important food crop. So
128	scientists are concerned that using corn as a fuel could reduce the
138	supply needed to feed both the human and animal populations.
148	As a result, scientists have begun to experiment with a
158	variety of grasses as biofuel alternatives. They are encouraged by
170	the initial tests and benefits. First, grasses grow in a variety of
181	soils and climates around the world that are often unsuitable for
190	farming food crops. Grasses also have multiple growing seasons,
201	so they could be harvested several times each year. Finally, most
213	grasses need little water, so they are easy and cheap to grow.
221	Presently, producing grass biofuel is expensive and lengthy,
231	but with more testing, scientists are confident this will change.

✓ What is the main idea of the passage?

✓ What are two benefits to using grass as a biofuel?

Words Read	–	Errors	=	WCPM

☐ Fall (127 WCPM)

☐ Winter (140 WCPM)

☐ Spring (150 WCPM)

WCPM	/	Words Read	=	Accuracy %

PROSODY				
	L1	L2	L3	L4
Reading in Phrases	○	○	○	○
Pace	○	○	○	○
Syntax	○	○	○	○
Self-correction	○	○	○	○
Intonation	○	○	○	○

2005 National Fluency Norms

Jan Hasbrouck and Gerald Tindal completed an extensive study of oral reading fluency in 2004. The results of their study are published in a technical report entitled, "Oral Reading Fluency: 90 Years of Measurement," which is available on the University of Oregon's Web site, **brt.uoregon.edu/tech_reports.htm.**

This table shows the oral reading fluency rates of students in Grades 1 through 6 as determined by Hasbrouck and Tindal's data.

You can use the information in this table to draw conclusions and make decisions about the oral reading fluency of your students. **Students scoring below the 50th percentile using the average score of two unpracticed readings from grade-level materials need a fluency-building program.** In addition, teachers can use the table to set the long-term fluency goals for their struggling readers.

Average weekly improvement is the average words per week growth you can expect from a student. It was calculated by subtracting the fall score from the spring score and dividing the difference by 32, the typical number of weeks between the fall and spring assessments. For Grade 1, since there is no fall assessment, the average weekly improvement was calculated by subtracting the winter score from the spring score and dividing the difference by 16, the typical number of weeks between the winter and spring assessments.

Grade	Percentile	Fall WCPM*	Winter WCPM*	Spring WCPM*	Avg. Weekly Improvement**
1	90		81	111	1.9
	75		47	82	2.2
	50		23	53	1.9
	25		12	28	1.0
	10		6	15	0.6
2	90	106	125	142	1.1
	75	79	100	117	1.2
	50	51	72	89	1.2
	25	25	42	61	1.1
	10	11	18	31	0.6

*WCPM = Words Correct Per Minute

Oral Reading Fluency Grades 1–6

Grade	Percentile	Fall WCPM*	Winter WCPM*	Spring WCPM*	Avg. Weekly Improvement**
3	90	128	146	162	1.1
	75	99	120	137	1.2
	50	71	92	107	1.1
	25	44	62	78	1.1
	10	21	36	48	0.8
4	90	145	166	180	1.1
	75	119	139	152	1.0
	50	94	112	123	0.9
	25	68	87	98	0.9
	10	45	61	72	0.8
5	90	166	182	194	0.9
	75	139	156	168	0.9
	50	110	127	139	0.9
	25	85	99	109	0.8
	10	61	74	83	0.7
6	90	177	195	204	0.8
	75	153	167	177	0.8
	50	127	140	150	0.7
	25	98	111	122	0.8
	10	68	82	93	0.8
7	90	180	192	202	0.7
	75	156	165	177	0.7
	50	128	136	150	0.7
	25	102	109	123	0.7
	10	79	88	98	0.6
8	90	185	193	199	0.4
	75	161	173	177	0.5
	50	133	146	151	0.6
	25	106	115	124	0.6
	10	77	84	97	0.6

**Average words per week growth

**Placement and
Diagnostic Assessment**

Informal Reading
Inventory

IRI Overview

The **Informal Reading Inventory (IRI)** is an individually-administered diagnostic tool that assesses a student's reading comprehension and reading accuracy. The IRI measures three reading levels: independent, instructional and frustrational. The independent reading level is the level at which a student reads without help from the teacher. To be independent, the student should accurately decode at least 95% of the words and comprehend 90% of the material. The instructional reading level is reached when a student accurately decodes at least 90% of the words and comprehends at least 60% of the material. Below that, a text would be considered to be at a frustrational level: the student decodes 89% or less of the words and can comprehend only 50% of the material.

At each grade level, there are two fiction and two non-fiction reading passages. These passages alternate between oral reading and silent reading as an IRI tests for both oral and silent reading comprehension. To assess the student's comprehension, there are three literal (L) questions, one vocabulary (V) question, and one interpretive (I) question per passage. On the teacher recording sheet, there is a table for each oral reading passage to help identify the student's reading level. This level is based on a combined score of comprehension points and word recognition errors. For each silent reading passage, the total number of comprehension points is used to determine a reading level.

Informal Reading Inventory

The IRI consists of reading passages, teacher recording sheets, and graded word lists for Grades 1–6. The reading passages appear on a reproducible student page. Each passage is ten sentences long and consists of Dolch words in Grades 1–3 and Harris-Jacobson words in Grades 4–6. The reading difficulty of the passages is near the midpoint of each grade level. There is a teacher recording sheet following each student passage that includes the passage, five questions, and a table to determine the appropriate reading level.

How to Use the IRI

Determine reading levels for both oral and silent reading comprehension. Before a student reads a passage, administer the graded word lists to determine the appropriate grade level. These lists span Grades 1–6 and consist of Dolch words, story words, and words that contain appropriate sound-spelling sequences for that level. Teachers should start administering the lists with Grade 1 to obtain a general estimate of the student's independent, instructional, and frustrational reading levels.

Informal Reading Inventory Grades 1–6

The correct instructional level is the level at which the student makes one error. Students who make two errors should go back to the previous list and start reading at that level.

Use this grade level to start administering the oral and silent reading passages, and as a quick assessment of basic sight word knowledge and phonics and structural analysis skills.

Administering the IRI

The IRI is organized by grade level. To administer the IRI efficiently, you should be familiar with Procedures, directions, passages, and questions.

1. Make a copy of all of the graded word lists.

2. Place the Grade 1 word list in front of the student and say, *"Here are some words I would like you to read aloud. Try to read them all, even if you are not sure what some of the words are. Let's begin by reading the words on this list."*

3. If the student is able to easily read these words, this early success may build the student's confidence. If you feel certain that a third-grade student can read above a third-grade level, then begin with a higher list. On the other hand, if a first-grade student misses two words on the first-grade word list, then stop. You should then read the passage aloud and have the student answer the comprehension questions. This activity turns into a listening comprehension inventory. Use the scoring table for the silent reading comprehension passage to determine a reading level for listening comprehension.

4. Record words pronounced correctly with a (✓) mark on the recording sheet that shows each graded word list (p. 171). Write incorrect responses on the line next to the word.

5. Have the student continue reading higher-level lists until one error is made.

6. After the student misses two words, stop the testing, collect the test sheets, and complete the results in the graded word list section on the sheet.

7. Follow these directions to score the graded word list.

   • The highest level at which the student misses zero words is the student's independent reading level.

   • The highest level at which the student misses one word is the student's instructional reading level.

   • The highest level at which the student misses two words is the student's frustrational reading level.

   • If the student scores independent, instructional, or frustrational at more than one level, assign the score to the highest level.

8. Select the first passage for the student to read orally. Make a copy of the teacher recording sheet for that passage. Have the student start reading on the instructional level determined by the graded word lists.

9. Begin by saying, *"I have some passages for you to read. Read the first one aloud. If you find a hard word, try to read it as best you can and continue reading. It is important to remember what you read so you can answer questions at the end."*

10. While the student reads out loud, code the errors or miscues on the scoring sheet. Do not provide any prompting if a student hesitates over a word. If a student hesitates longer than five seconds, simply tell the word to the student.

11. When the student has completed the passage or story, take it away. The student cannot refer to it while answering the questions.

12. Ask the student the comprehension questions as shown on the teacher recording sheet for the passage. Mark correct answers with a point value on the line provided. The point value is in parentheses at the end of each question. A perfect score is 10 points. Interpretive questions are given four points. Vocabulary questions are given three points. Literal questions are given one point. The total number of points that a student earns is the comprehension score. (Instructions for scoring word accuracy and comprehension questions will be provided on page 169.)

At this point, you will have the student shift from oral to silent reading.

13. Give the student the "B" passage next. If the student began with the 1A oral passage, then continue with the 1B silent passage.

14. Say, *"Read this passage to yourself and try to remember what you read so that you can answer questions at the end."*

15. When the student has finished reading the passage, ask the questions on the teacher recording sheet for the passage. Mark the point values that the student earned on the lines provided, and total the number of points earned at the bottom of the questions.

16. After giving the first oral and silent reading passages, use the Scoring Table to determine whether the student has been able to read them at an independent level. If both the oral and silent passages were at the student's independent reading level, continue with the next higher oral reading passage. Then follow with the corresponding silent passage until the frustration level is reached. In many cases, a student will reach frustration level on either oral or silent reading but not both. In these instances, continue with either the oral or silent reading passages until the student reaches frustration level on both.

Informal Reading Inventory Grades 1–6

17. If the student is not reading at the independent level on either or both passages, give an easier oral and silent passage until both oral and silent frustration levels are reached. The goal is that a student should have an independent, instructional and frustrational reading level for both oral and silent reading.

Code for Marking Word Recognition Errors	
Each word recognition error is counted as one error. Never count more than one error on any one word.	
Examples	**Marking Word Recognition Errors**
✔ ✔ ✔ The baby cried	1. Put a check mark over words read correctly.
✔ ✔ My friend (went)	2. Circle omissions.
✔eats ✔ ✔ He ate the pie	3. Draw a line above words that are read with substitutions. Write the substitution above the line.
✔ T ✔ Why are you	4. Place a T above a word that you need to tell student.
✔ ✔ eating R dinner	5. Place an R next to a word the student repeats.
✔ ✔ ✔ See/S a kind person. She	6. Place the student's initial response and an S above a word that is self corrected. Note: Do not score as an error.
✔ ✔ an (red) apple	7. Use parentheses ( ) to enclose a word that is inserted.

Informal Reading Inventory Grades 1–6

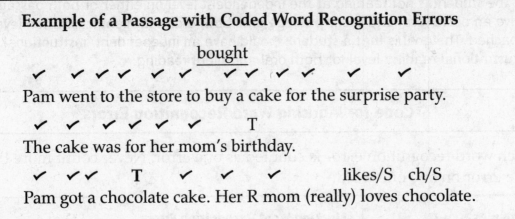

Here is what the teacher heard as the student read the passage. The words in italics are the actual words that the student read.

"Pam went to the store to bought a cake for the surprise party. The cake was for her mom's (after five seconds the teacher produced "birthday"). *Pam got a* (after five seconds the teacher produced "chocolate") *cake. Her . . . Her mom really likes loves ch . . . ch . . . chocolate."*

The student made four mistakes that are to be scored as errors:

     (1) *bought* substituted for *buy*

     (2) *birthday* pronounced by the teacher

     (3) *chocolate* pronounced by the teacher

     (4) *really* inserted

The repetition for *her* is not counted as an error.

The self correction for *likes* is not counted as an error.

The self correction for *ch* is not counted as an error.

This passage is at the frustration level for this student.

Procedure for Scoring Oral Reading Passages

1. Count the total number of scorable errors as outlined in the **Code for Marking Word Recognition Errors**. Write the total number of errors in the space indicated on the teacher recording sheet. Insertions, substitutions, words told to the student by the teacher, and omissions are counted as errors at each occurrence. Words that are self-corrected and repeated are not counted as errors.

2. If a student mispronounces a proper name, count it as one error for the entire passage, even if the student mispronounces the same name again.

Informal Reading Inventory Grades 1-6

3. On the teacher recording sheet, a table follows the set of questions for each oral reading passage. Across the table is a series of numbers to designate the number of word recognition errors. In the column on the left is a series of numbers that show the number of points earned. Locate the number of word recognition errors made by the student in that passage and circle the appropriate number. Then locate the number of points earned on the comprehension questions and draw a circle around that number. Find the point where the two circled numbers intersect. In that space, you will note the following symbols: the (✓) means the student is reading on an independent level; the (*) means the student is reading on an instructional level; and the (—) means the student is reading at a frustrational level.

Scoring Table for Oral Reading

Total Points Earned	# of Word Recognition Errors			Reading Level
	0–4	5–7	8+	
7–10 pts	✓	*	–	Independent ☐
4–6 pts	*	*	–	Instructional ☐
0–3 pts	–	–	–	Frustrational ☑

In the above table, for example, the student has made eight word recognition errors and earned two comprehension points. The student answered two literal questions correctly. These two figures intersect in an area marked with a dash (—). This means the student is reading on a frustrational level; the box to the right of Frustrational is checked.

Procedure for Scoring Silent Reading Passages

1. Add up the number of points earned from the five comprehension questions. If the student answer is not a duplicate of the provided response, points can still be allotted at your discretion (i.e., if answer is a rewording of the provided response or a truncated version of the provided response).

2. There is a table below the questions that follow each silent reading passage on the teacher recording sheet. Look at the table to see which level the student is reading at, based on the number of points earned. In the following example, the student earned three points. This would place the student in the range indicated by 0–3 in the table. This corresponds to the frustrational level; the box to the right of Frustrational is checked.

Scoring Table for Silent Reading

Total Points Earned	Reading Level
7–10 pts	Independent ☐
4–6 pts	Instructional ☐
0–3 pts	Frustrational ☑

Individual Graded Word Lists

Grade 1

mother
could
family
there
said
people
bake
what
three
town

Grade 2

prize
noise
understood
another
piece
trouble
easier
afraid
scare
always

Grade 3

started
lonely
thought
breathe
enough
prepare
actually
waist
earn
delighted

Grade 4

adapted
communicate
bracelet
announced
choice
requires
objects
bulge
gravity
resulting

Grade 5

approaching
crystals
development
territory
astonished
coarse
moisture
luxuries
irregular
resemble

Grade 6

countryside
heroism
consented
mercilessly
appalling
veterinarian
spectacle
emperor
ravenous
exceptional

Informal Reading Inventory Grades 1–6

Recording Sheet for Individual Graded Word Lists

Grade 1

mother _____

could _____

family _____

there _____

said _____

people _____

bake _____

what _____

three _____

town _____

Grade 2

prize _____

noise _____

understood _____

another _____

piece _____

trouble _____

easier _____

afraid _____

scare _____

always _____

Grade 3

started _____

lonely _____

thought _____

breathe _____

enough _____

prepare _____

actually _____

waist _____

earn _____

delighted _____

Grade 4

adapted _____

communicate _____

bracelet _____

announced _____

choice _____

requires _____

objects _____

bulge _____

gravity _____

resulting _____

Grade 5

approaching _____

crystals _____

development _____

territory _____

astonished _____

coarse _____

moisture _____

luxuries _____

irregular _____

resemble _____

Grade 6

countryside _____

heroism _____

consented _____

mercilessly _____

appalling _____

veterinarian _____

spectacle _____

emperor _____

ravenous _____

exceptional _____

Grade 1

mother

could

family

there

said

people

bake

what

three

town

Grade 2

prize

noise

understood

another

piece

trouble

easier

afraid

scare

always

Grade 3

started

lonely

thought

breathe

enough

prepare

actually

waist

earn

delighted

Grade 4

adapted

communicate

bracelet

announced

choice

requires

objects

bulge

gravity

resulting

Grade 5

approaching

crystals

development

territory

astonished

coarse

moisture

luxuries

irregular

resemble

Informal Reading Inventory Grades 1–6

Grade 6

countryside

heroism

consented

mercilessly

appalling

veterinarian

spectacle

emperor

ravenous

exceptional

1A Oral

Sam

Ana was so sad.

She was moving out of town.

They could not take her black cat, Sam.

The new house was just too little for pets.

Ana let a good friend take Sam.

Ana liked her new home, but she missed Sam.

One day, Ana went to open the door.

There was Sam!

He had walked for days and days to find Ana.

Ana's mother now said he could stay.

Passage 1A Oral—Fiction

Sam

Ana *was so* sad. *She was* moving *out of* town. *They could not take her black* cat, Sam. *The new* house *was just too little for* pets. Ana *let a good* friend *take* Sam.

Ana liked *her new* home, *but she* missed Sam. *One* day, Ana *went to open the* door. *There was* Sam! *He had* walked *for* days *and* days *to find* Ana. Ana's mother *now said he could* stay.

(71 words) (44 Dolch Words) Number of Word Recognition Errors _____

Questions

L 1. _____ Where was Ana moving? [Out of town] (1 pt.)

L 2. _____ Who was Sam? [Ana's black cat] (1 pt.)

L 3. _____ Why couldn't Sam go to the new house? [The new house was too little for pets.] (1 pt.)

V 4. _____ What did the story mean when it said that Ana "missed" Sam? [Ana wished he was with her.] (3 pts.)

I 5. _____ What did Sam do that would make you think he loved Ana? [He walked for days and days to find her.] (4 pts.)

Total # of points earned _____

	Scoring Table for Oral Reading			
	# of Word Recognition Errors			
Total Points Earned	**0-4**	**5-7**	**8+**	**Reading Level**
7–10 pts	✓	*	–	Independent ☐
4–6 pts	*	*	–	Instructional ☐
0–3 pts	–	–	–	Frustrational ☐

1B Silent

The Bake Sale

Mrs. Park's class wanted to help people in need.

Mrs. Park said, "We have to make money.

How can we do this?"

"I know what we can do," Ron said.

"We can bake cakes and other foods people like.

Then, we can have a bake sale."

That is just what the class did.

All the children helped make the food.

A lot of hungry people came to eat it.

Soon, the class had money for people in need.

Passage 1B Silent—Fiction

The Bake Sale

Mrs. Park's class wanted to help people in need. Mrs. Park said, "We have to make money. How can we do this?"

"I know what we can do," Ron said. "We can bake cakes and other foods people like. Then, we can have a bake sale."

That is just what the class did. All the children helped make the food. A lot of hungry people came to eat it. Soon, the class had money for people in need.

(78 Words)

Questions

L 1. ____ Who was it that the class wanted to help? [People in need] (1 pt.)

L 2. ____ What did Ron say the class could bake? [Cakes and other foods people like.] (1 pt.)

L 3. ____ What did all the children help to do? [Make the food] (1 pt.)

V 4. ____ The story says, "A lot of hungry people came to eat it." What does *hungry* mean? [Wanting or needing food] (3 pts.)

I 5. ____ Who gave the class the money for the people in need? [The people who paid for food at the bake sale] (4 pts.)

Total # of points earned _____

Scoring Table for Silent Reading	
Total Points Earned	**Reading Level**
7–10 pts	Independent ☐
4–6 pts	Instructional ☐
0–3 pts	Frustrational ☐

School for Clowns

Did you know that there is a clown school?

Clowns go to school to learn to be funny.

They learn how to move in funny ways.

They find out how to run, fall, and jump.

They must make every move look easy.

In school, clowns plan how they will look.

They put on funny pants and tops.

They get into big shoes.

Clowns also put on funny face paint.

They do all this just to make people smile.

Passage 1C Oral—Nonfiction

School for Clowns

Did you know that there is a clown school? Clowns *go to* school *to learn to be funny. They* learn *how to* move *in funny* ways. *They find out how to run, fall, and jump. They must make every* move *look* easy. *In* school, clowns plan *how they will* look. *They* put on *funny* pants *and* tops. *They get into big* shoes. Clowns also *put on funny* face paint. *They do all this just to make* people smile.

(78 words) (57 Dolch words) Number of Word Recognition Errors _____

Questions

L 1. _____ Why do clowns go to school? [To find out how to be funny] (1 pt.)

L 2. _____ To move in funny ways, clowns find out how to run, jump, and what? [How to fall] (1 pt.)

V 3. _____ The passage says, "They must make every move look easy." What does *easy* mean? [Not hard] (3 pts.)

L 4. _____ Other than funny pants and tops, what do clowns get into? [Big shoes] (1 pt.)

I 5. _____ What is the job of a clown? [To make people smile] (4 pts.)

Total # of points earned _____

Scoring Table for Oral Reading				
Total Points Earned	**# of Word Recognition Errors**			**Reading Level**
	0-5	**6-9**	**10+**	
7–10 pts	✔	*	–	Independent ☐
4–6 pts	*	*	–	Instructional ☐
0–3 pts	–	–	–	Frustrational ☐

Houses

Our house is a place we feel safe.

It is the place we like to be with our family.

We can stay in when the weather is bad.

We feel good inside our houses.

You can see that all houses are not the same.

There are wood houses and stone houses.

There are even snow houses!

Some houses are big and some are little.

Some have just one floor.

Others are two and even three floors high.

What is the house that you live in like?

Passage 1D Silent—Nonfiction

Houses

Our house is a place we feel safe. It is the place we like to be with our family. We can stay in when the weather is bad. We feel good inside our houses.

You can see that all houses are not the same. There are wood houses and stone houses. There are even snow houses! Some houses are big and some are little. Some have just one floor. Others are two and even three floors high. What is the house that you live in like?

(86 words)

Questions

L 1. _____ Where do we feel safe? [In our houses] (1 pt.)

L 2. _____ Who do we like to be with in our houses? [Family] (1 pt.)

L 3. _____ How do we feel inside our houses when the weather is bad outside? [Good] (1 pt.)

I 4. _____ Which kind of house would you see in just cold places? [Snow house] (4 pts.)

V 5. _____ The passage says, "Others are two and even three floors high." What does *high* mean? [From top to bottom] (3 pts.)

Total # of points earned _____

Scoring Table for Silent Reading	
Total Points Earned	**Reading Level**
7–10 pts	Independent ☐
4–6 pts	Instructional ☐
0–3 pts	Frustrational ☐

The Race

One day, Tom saw some boys having a race after school.
Tom said, "I would like to be a fast runner like those boys."
Tom began to run every day before and after school.
Each day, he was able to run faster than the day before.
Soon he could run as fast as the other boys. Tom did not win his first few races, but he would not give up.
The next year, there was a race for all the boys at school.
Many of the boys ran fast, but Tom ran faster. The other boys ran hard to catch up with him, but not one could do it.
Tom won the race and took home the first prize.

Passage 2A Oral—Fiction

The Race

One day, Tom *saw some* boys having *a* race *after* school. Tom *said,* "*I would like to be a fast* runner *like those* boys."

Tom began *to run every* day *before and after* school. Each day, *he was* able *to* run faster than *the* day *before. Soon he could run as fast as the* other boys. Tom *did not* win *his first* few races, *but he would not give up.*

The next year, *there was a* race *for all the* boys at school. *Many of the* boys *ran* fast, *but* Tom *ran* faster. *The* other boys *ran* hard *to* catch *up with him, but not one could do it.* Tom won *the* race *and* took home *the first* prize.

(119 words) (76 Dolch words) Number of Word Recognition Errors _____

Questions

L 1. _____ What did Tom see that made him want to be a fast runner? [Some boys having a race] (1 pt.)

L 2. _____ What did Tom do every day before and after school? [He ran.] (1 pt.)

I 3. _____ What did Tom do that would make you think he sticks with something even if things don't go his way? [He did not win the first few races, but he would not give up.] (4 pts.)

V 4. _____ The story says, "The other boys ran hard to catch up with him, but not one could do it." What does "catch up" mean? [Get closer to, or come up to] (3 pts.)

L 5. _____ Why did Tom take home the first prize? [Because he won the race] (1 pt.)

Total # of points earned _____

Scoring Table for Oral Reading

Total Points Earned	# of Word Recognition Errors			Reading Level
	0–6	7–11	12+	
7–10 pts	✓	*	–	Independent ☐
4–6 pts	*	*	–	Instructional ☐
0–3 pts	–	–	–	Frustrational ☐

2B Silent

Kim and Brownie

Kim had a hard time training her new dog, Brownie. He would not do anything that she told him to do. She could not even get him to come when she called him. Then, one day, Kim saw that Brownie did not move when a loud noise went off.

It was then that she understood that Brownie couldn't hear. Kim found out how to train Brownie by using hand signals. To get Brownie to come, she raised her arm up over her head with her hand facing down.

If she wanted him to sit, she would move her arm down with her hand facing up. Brownie learned fast and was soon doing everything Kim asked of him.

Kim felt very lucky that Brownie was her dog.

Passage 2B Silent—Fiction

Kim and Brownie

Kim had a hard time training her new dog, Brownie. He would not do anything that she told him to do. She could not even get him to come when she called him. Then, one day, Kim saw that Brownie did not move when a loud noise went off.

It was then that she understood that Brownie couldn't hear. Kim found out how to train Brownie by using hand signals. To get Brownie to come, she raised her arm up over her head with her hand facing down.

If she wanted him to sit, she would move her arm down with her hand facing up. Brownie learned fast and was soon doing everything Kim asked of him.

Kim felt very lucky that Brownie was her dog.

(126 words)

Questions

L 1. _____ Who was Brownie? [Kim's new dog] (1 pt.)

L 2. _____ What made Kim understand that Brownie couldn't hear? [He did not move when a loud noise went off.] (1 pt.)

V 3. _____ The story says, "Kim found out how to train Brownie by using hand signals." What does the word *signals* mean? [Signs] (3 pts.)

L 4. _____ What signal did Kim use to get Brownie to sit? [Moved her arm down with her hand facing up] (1 pt.)

I 5. _____ What did Brownie do that would make you think he was smart? [He learned fast and was soon doing everything Kim asked of him.] (4 pts.)

Total # of points earned _____

Scoring Table for Silent Reading	
Total Points Earned	**Reading Level**
7–10 pts	Independent ☐
4–6 pts	Instructional ☐
0–3 pts	Frustrational ☐

Bears

Bears are big animals covered with fur. Their legs are short and fat, but they can run very fast. They can also stand up on their back legs and walk like people do.

Bears are mainly colored black, brown, and white. Black bears, which are around five feet, are not as big as brown or white bears. Black and brown bears climb trees to get away from trouble. Both of these bears eat plants, fruit, and animals.

The white bears are called polar bears, and they live on the ice in very cold places. They are great swimmers, and they swim from one piece of ice to another looking for food. These bears eat just meat, and mostly sea animals.

Passage 2C Oral—Nonfiction

Bears

Bears *are big* animals covered *with* fur. *Their* legs *are* short *and fat, but they can run very fast. They can* also stand *up on their* back legs *and walk like* people *do.*

Bears *are* mainly colored *black, brown, and white. Black* bears, *which are around five* feet, *are not as big as brown or white* bears. *Black and brown* bears climb trees *to get away from* trouble. *Both of these* bears *eat* plants, fruit, *and* animals.

The white bears *are* called polar bears, *and they live on the* ice *in very cold* places. *They are* great swimmers, *and they* swim *from one* piece *of* ice *to* another looking *for* food. *These* bears *eat just* meat, and mostly sea animals.

(120 words) (74 Dolch words) Number of Word Recognition Errors _____

Questions

L 1. _____ What are bears covered with? [Fur] (1 pt.)

I 2. _____ What does the passage say that lets you know polar bears are over five feet tall? [Black bears, which are around five feet, are not as big as brown or white bears.] (4 pts.)

V 3. _____ The passage says, "Black and brown bears climb trees to get away from trouble." What does the word *trouble* mean? [A bad situation] (3 pts.)

L 4. _____ Where do polar bears live? [On the ice in very cold places] (1 pt.)

L 5. _____ What do polar bears eat? [Meat, mostly sea animals] (1 pt.)

Total # of points earned _____

Scoring Table for Oral Reading				
Total Points Earned	**# of Word Recognition Errors**			**Reading Level**
	0–6	**7–11**	**12+**	
7–10 pts	✓	*	–	Independent ☐
4–6 pts	*	*	–	Instructional ☐
0–3 pts	–	–	–	Frustrational ☐

2D Silent

About Fire

When people found out how to make fire, their lives became easier. Fire has been around from the days when people lived in caves. Cave people would use fire to stay warm. They also found that they could see more in the dark with the fires going. And many animals like tigers and lions are afraid of fire, so people used fires at night to scare these animals off.

Soon, people found out how to cook over an open fire. Then they made ovens by stacking rocks up over the fires. In these ovens, they baked bread and other good foods. After people found out how to store food, they did not have to go hunting every day. There was always something to eat.

Passage 2D Silent—Nonfiction

About Fire

When people found out how to make fire, their lives became easier. Fire has been around from the days when people lived in caves. Cave people would use fire to stay warm. They also found that they could see more in the dark with the fires going. And many animals like tigers and lions are afraid of fire, so people used fires at night to scare these animals off.

Soon, people found out how to cook over an open fire. Then they made ovens by stacking rocks up over the fires. In these ovens, they baked bread and other good foods. After people found out how to store food, they did not have to go hunting every day. There was always something to eat.

(124 words)

Questions

L 1. _____ What happened to people's lives when they found out how to make fire? [Their lives became easier.] (1 pt.)

L 2. _____ What was one way that cave people used fire? [To stay warm, to see in the dark, or to keep animals away] (1 pt.)

V 3. _____ The passage says, "And many animals like tigers and lions are afraid of fire, so people used fires at night to scare these animals off." What does the word *afraid* mean? [Scared] (3 pts.)

L 4. _____ How did people make ovens? [They stacked rocks up over the fires.] (1 pt.)

I 5. _____ After people found out how to cook and store food, what did they eat when they didn't go hunting? [The stored food] (4 pts.)

Total # of points earned _____

Scoring Table for Silent Reading	
Total Points Earned	**Reading Level**
7–10 pts	Independent ☐
4–6 pts	Instructional ☐
0–3 pts	Frustrational ☐

3A Oral

The Dog Walker

Summer vacation had just started, and Earl was thinking about how to spend his time. Earl liked to read, but he didn't want to spend the whole vacation just reading. He also liked to do things and go places with his friends, but many of them were away for the summer. Then Earl got the idea that it would be wise to try to earn some money.

While playing with his dog, Earl suddenly had a thought. Perhaps people would pay him to walk their dogs. Earl went to the houses of people he knew had dogs, like Mrs. Green. Because she was old and had trouble getting around, she was delighted to hire Earl to walk her big brown dog. In all, Earl was able to find seven people to hire him. By the end of the summer, he was able to buy a new bike.

Passage 3A Oral—Fiction

The Dog Walker

Summer vacation *had just* started, *and* Earl *was* thinking *about how to* spend *his* time. Earl liked *to read, but he* didn't *want to* spend *the* whole vacation *just* reading. *He* also liked *to do* things *and go* places *with his* friends, *but many of them were away for the* summer. *Then* Earl *got the* idea *that it would be* wise *to try to* earn *some* money.

While playing *with his* dog, Earl suddenly *had a* thought. Perhaps people *would* pay *him to walk their* dogs. Earl *went to the* houses *of* people *he* knew *had* dogs, *like* Mrs. Green. *Because she was old and had* trouble getting *around, she was* delighted *to* hire Earl *to walk her big brown* dog. *In all,* Earl *was* able *to find seven* people *to* hire *him. By the* end *of the* summer, *he was* able *to buy a new* bike.

(147 words) (91 Dolch Words) Number of Word Recognition Errors _____

Questions

L 1. _____ Why couldn't Earl spend time with his friends? [Because many were away for the summer] (1 pt.)

L 2. _____ What was Earl doing when he thought about walking dogs for money? [Playing with his dog] (1 pt.)

V 3. _____ The story says, "Because she was old and had trouble getting around, she was delighted to hire Earl to walk her big brown dog." What does the word *delighted* mean? [Very happy] (3 pts.)

L 4. _____ How many people hired Earl? [Seven] (1 pt.)

I 5. _____ Where did Earl get the money to pay for his new bike? [From walking the dogs] (4 pts.)

Total # of points earned _____

	# of Word Recognition Errors			
Total Points Earned	**0–8**	**9–14**	**15+**	**Reading Level**
7–10 pts	✓	*	–	Independent ☐
4–6 pts	*	*	–	Instructional ☐
0–3 pts	–	–	–	Frustrational ☐

Scoring Table for Oral Reading

3B Silent

Lonely Nina

Nina had never felt as lonely as she did at her new school. She had moved to town over a month ago, and she still had not made any friends. As she sat eating her lunch, she listened to Jen and the other girls from her class talk and laugh. Afraid that they wouldn't like her, she thought it best to keep to herself.

All of a sudden, Nina heard Jen start to choke on some food. When she saw that the girl couldn't breathe, Nina rushed over. She put her arms around Jen's waist from the back and pressed in with her fist. The food came out, and Jen began to take in air.

When she could talk, Jen thanked Nina and asked her to join the other girls. "I would have asked you before," Jen said, "but you always seemed to want to be by yourself."

Passage 3B Silent—Fiction

Lonely Nina

Nina had never felt as lonely as she did at her new school. She had moved to town over a month ago, and she still had not made any friends. As she sat eating her lunch, she listened to Jen and the other girls from her class talk and laugh. Afraid that they wouldn't like her, she thought it best to keep to herself.

All of a sudden, Nina heard Jen start to choke on some food. When she saw that the girl couldn't breathe, Nina rushed over. She put her arms around Jen's waist from the back and pressed in with her fist. The food came out, and Jen began to take in air.

When she could talk, Jen thanked Nina and asked her to join the other girls. "I would have asked you before," Jen said, "but you always seemed to want to be by yourself."

(148 words)

Questions

L 1. _____ How did Nina feel at the beginning of the story? [Lonely] (1 pt.)

L 2. _____ Why did Nina keep to herself? [Because she was afraid the other children wouldn't like her] (1 pt.)

V 3. _____ The story says, "When she saw that the girl couldn't breathe, Nina rushed over." What does the word *breathe* mean? [Take in air] (3 pts.)

L 4. _____ What did Jen do as soon as she could talk? [Jen thanked Nina and asked her to join the other girls.] (1 pt.)

I 5. _____ Why didn't Nina make friends? [Because she kept to herself and did not try to talk to the other children] (4 pts.)

Total # of points earned _____

Scoring Table for Silent Reading	
Total Points Earned	**Reading Level**
7–10 pts	Independent ☐
4–6 pts	Instructional ☐
0–3 pts	Frustrational ☐

A Biography

In 1892 a 13-year-old boy beat 25 men to win his first bike race. The boy was Marshall Taylor, and he would become one of the best racers of all time.

Just four years after winning his first race, Taylor became the first black man in the United States to race for money. By the time he was 20 years old, he was setting many records for speed. Sadly, he was not allowed to enter some races because of the color of his skin.

In the years that followed, Taylor raced all over the world. He won almost every race he entered. Millions of people came to see him, and he made friends everywhere he went. Taylor would stop racing in 1924 at the age of 32. But before he did, he broke every speed record there was to earn the title of the fastest bike racer in the world.

Passage 3C Oral—Nonfiction

A Biography

In 1892 *a* 13-year-old boy beat 25 men *to* win *his first* bike race. *The* boy *was* Marshall Taylor, *and he would become* one *of the best* racers *of all* time.

Just four years *after* winning *his first* race, Taylor became *the first black* man *in the* United States *to* race *for* money. *By the* time *he was* 20 years old, *he was* setting *many* records *for* speed. Sadly, *he was not* allowed *to* enter *some* races *because of the* color *of his* skin.

In the years *that* followed, Taylor raced *all over the* world. *He* won almost *every* race *he* entered. Millions *of* people *came to see him, and he made* friends everywhere *he* went. Taylor *would stop* racing *in* 1924 *at the* age *of* 32. *But before he did, he* broke *every* speed record *there was to* earn *the* title *of the* fastest bike racer *in the* world.

(152 words) (86 Dolch words) Number of Word Recognition Errors _____

Questions

L 1. _____ How old was Taylor when he won his first bike race? [13] (1 pt.)

L 2. _____ What was Taylor the first black man to do? [Race for money] (1 pt.)

V 3. _____ What is skin? [Outer covering of the human body] (3 pts.)

I 4. _____ What happened that would make you think Taylor was popular? [Millions of people came to see him, and he made friends everywhere he went.] (4 pts.)

L 5. _____ In what year did Taylor stop racing? [1924] (1 pt.)

Total # of points earned _____

	Scoring Table for Oral Reading			
	# of Word Recognition Errors			
Total Points Earned	**0-8**	**9-15**	**16+**	**Reading Level**
7–10 pts	✓	*	–	Independent ☐
4–6 pts	*	*	–	Instructional ☐
0–3 pts	–	–	–	Frustrational ☐

3D Silent

Sleep

People of all ages need to sleep, but some need more sleep than others do. As people grow older, they need less sleep. Babies sleep about 15 hours a day, while adults need about 8 hours of sleep every night.

Sleep is very important because it will give the body and mind time to rest and prepare for the next day. During the early stages of sleep, the heart does not beat as fast and the brain slows down. If a person dreams while asleep, the heart begins beating faster and the brain goes back into action. At this stage of sleep, your eyes move back and forth very fast under your closed lids.

When people don't get enough sleep, they may be hard to get along with. They also may have trouble thinking and doing things. After five days with no sleep, people will start to see things that are not actually there.

Passage 3D Silent—Nonfiction

Sleep

People of all ages need to sleep, but some need more sleep than others do. As people grow older, they need less sleep. Babies sleep about 15 hours a day, while adults need about 8 hours of sleep every night.

Sleep is very important because it will give the body and mind time to rest and prepare for the next day. During the early stages of sleep, the heart does not beat as fast and the brain slows down. If a person dreams while asleep, the heart begins beating faster and the brain goes back into action. At this stage of sleep, your eyes move back and forth very fast under your closed lids.

When people don't get enough sleep, they may be hard to get along with. They also may have trouble thinking and doing things. After five days with no sleep, people will start to see things that are not actually there.

(154 words)

Questions

I 1. _____ From the passage, you can tell that children sleep somewhere between 8 hours and how many hours? [15] (4 pts.)

L 2. _____ Why is sleep important? [Because it will give the body and mind time to rest and prepare for the next day] (1 pt.)

L 3. _____ What happens to your eyes when you dream? [They move back and forth very fast under your closed lids.] (1 pt.)

L 4. _____ What is one thing that may happen to people when they don't get enough sleep? [They may be hard to get along with, they may have trouble thinking, or they may have trouble doing things.] (1 pt.)

V 5. _____ The reading passage says, "After five days with no sleep, people will start to see things that are not actually there." What does the word *actually* mean? [Really] (3 pts.)

Total # of points earned _____

Scoring Table for Silent Reading	
Total Points Earned	**Reading Level**
7–10 pts	Independent ☐
4–6 pts	Instructional ☐
0–3 pts	Frustrational ☐

4A Oral

A Feel for Music

Having a real feel for music, Cora loved to play the piano for friends and family. The problem was that she made mistakes because she never found enough time to sit down and practice.

One day, Mrs. Ruiz, the music teacher, announced that there was going to be a concert, and she wanted Cora to play a piece of music of her choice. Very excited, Cora decided to play "My Favorite Things."

Mrs. Ruiz called all of the children to her house to play their pieces a few days before the concert. To Cora's horror, Matt had decided to play "My Favorite Things" too. Matt played the piece perfectly, but he did not put any feeling into his music. However, all Cora could think was that he would play without any mistakes, while she would make mistakes and look silly.

The next day, Cora told Mrs. Ruiz that she did not want to be in the concert. The teacher said sadly, "You are a very good player because you feel the music, but this means little unless you believe in your talent and give it the time it requires."

Passage 4A Oral—Fiction

A Feel for Music

Having *a* real feel *for* music, Cora loved *to play the* piano *for* friends *and* family. *The* problem *was that she made* mistakes *because she never* found enough time *to sit down and* practice.

One day, Mrs. Ruiz, *the* music teacher, announced *that there was going to be a* concert, *and she* wanted Cora *to play a* piece *of* music *of her* choice. *Very* excited, Cora decided *to play "My* Favorite Things."

Mrs. Ruiz called *all of the* children *to her* house *to play their* pieces *a few days before the* concert. *To* Cora's horror, Matt *had* decided *to play* "My Favorite Things" *too*. Matt played *the* piece perfectly, *but he did not put any* feeling *into his* music. However, *all* Cora *could* think *was that he would play* without any mistakes, while *she would make* mistakes *and look* silly.

The next day, Cora told Mrs. Ruiz *that she did not want to be in the* concert. *The* teacher *said* sadly, *"You are a very good* player *because you* feel *the* music, *but this* means *little* unless *you* believe *in your* talent *and give it the* time *it* requires."

(189 words) (108 Dolch Words) Number of Word Recognition Errors _____

Questions

L 1. _____ Why did Cora make mistakes when she played? [Because she didn't practice enough] (1 pt.)

L 2. _____ What song did Cora choose to play at the concert? ["My Favorite Things"] (1 pt.)

L 3. _____ Where did the children go a few days before the concert to play their pieces? [To Mrs. Ruiz's house] (1 pt.)

V 4. _____ What does the word *horror* mean in this story? [Shock or disappointment] (3 pts.)

I 5. _____ Why did Cora decide not to be in the concert? [Because she was afraid of looking foolish if Matt played the song better than she did] (4 pts.)

Total # of points earned _____

Scoring Table for Oral Reading			
	# of Word Recognition Errors		
Total Points Earned	**0-11**	**12-18**	**19+**	**Reading Level**
7–10 pts	✓	*	–	Independent ☐
4–6 pts	*	*	–	Instructional ☐
0–3 pts	–	–	–	Frustrational ☐

4B Silent

The Bracelet

Mrs. Dell was delighted when her children gave her a very special present for her birthday. It was a beautiful gold bracelet with five charms, one charm from each of her five children. The clasp on the bracelet was a bit loose, but she planned to have that fixed just as soon as she could get around to it.

Not willing to take the bracelet off, Mrs. Dell wore it always, whether she was at work or doing the household chores. One night before she went to bed, she noticed that the bracelet was not on her wrist. Frantic, she looked for it everywhere, but she just couldn't find it. Feeling miserable, she told the children that she had lost their special gift.

Fifteen years later, all of Mrs. Dell's children were grown and out of the house, so she decided to sell it. The movers had just removed the last piece of furniture, the big sofa, when Mrs. Dell noticed something shiny on the floor. There was her lost bracelet, just like a special gift all over again.

Passage 4B Silent—Fiction

The Bracelet

Mrs. Dell was delighted when her children gave her a very special present for her birthday. It was a beautiful gold bracelet with five charms, one charm from each of her five children. The clasp on the bracelet was a bit loose, but she planned to have that fixed just as soon as she could get around to it.

Not willing to take the bracelet off, Mrs. Dell wore it always, whether she was at work or doing the household chores. One night before she went to bed, she noticed that the bracelet was not on her wrist. Frantic, she looked for it everywhere, but she just couldn't find it. Feeling miserable, she told the children that she had lost their special gift.

Fifteen years later, all of Mrs. Dell's children were grown and out of the house, so she decided to sell it. The movers had just removed the last piece of furniture, the big sofa, when Mrs. Dell noticed something shiny on the floor. There was her lost bracelet, just like a special gift all over again.

(179 words)

Questions

L 1. _____ For what occasion did Mrs. Dell's children give her the bracelet? [Her birthday] (1 pt.)

L 2. _____ When did Mrs. Dell notice that the bracelet was missing? [One night before she went to bed] (1 pt.)

I 3. _____ What probably caused the bracelet to fall off of Mrs. Dell's wrist? [The clasp] (4 pts.)

V 4. _____ What does the word *frantic* mean in this story? [Very excited with worry or fear] (3 pts.)

L 5. _____ Where did Mrs. Dell eventually find her bracelet? [On the floor under where the big sofa had been] (1 pt.)

Total # of points earned _____

Scoring Table for Silent Reading	
Total Points Earned	**Reading Level**
7–10 pts	Independent ☐
4–6 pts	Instructional ☐
0–3 pts	Frustrational ☐

Gravity

The force that draws objects toward one another is called gravity. It is the Earth's gravity that keeps the moon moving around it and holds the ocean waters against it.

Tides are the rise and fall of large bodies of water. They are caused by the gravity of the moon and the sun, which serves to pull on the waters of the Earth. Even though the moon is much smaller than the sun, it has a stronger pull because it is much closer to the Earth than the sun is.

When the moon is directly overhead, its gravity causes the waters of the Earth to move toward it. As the water follows the moon, the oceans puff out in its direction, resulting in a high tide. When this happens, water rises and can come up onto the land for a short distance. A second bulge occurs on the opposite side of our planet because the Earth is also being pulled toward the moon and away from the water on that side. As the moon moves farther away, the water drawn to it will fall back in a low tide.

Passage 4C Oral—Nonfiction

Gravity

The force *that* draws objects toward *one* another *is* called gravity. *It is the* Earth's gravity *that* keeps *the* moon moving *around it and* holds *the* ocean waters against *it.*

Tides *are the* rise *and fall of* large bodies *of* water. *They* are caused *by the* gravity *of the* moon *and the* sun, *which* serves *to pull on the* waters *of the* Earth. Even though *the* moon *is much* smaller than *the* sun, *it has a* stronger *pull because it is much* closer *to the* Earth than *the* sun *is.*

When the moon *is* directly overhead, *its* gravity causes *the* waters *of the* Earth *to* move toward *it. As the* water follows *the* moon, *the* oceans puff out in *its* direction, resulting *in a* high tide. *When this* happens, water rises *and can come* up onto *the* land *for a* short distance. *A* second bulge occurs *on the* opposite side *of our* planet *because the* Earth *is* also being pulled toward *the* moon *and away from the* water *on that* side. *As the* moon moves farther *away, the* water drawn *to it will fall* back *in a* low tide.

(189 words) (102 Dolch words) Number of Word Recognition Errors _____

Questions

L 1. _____ What keeps the moon moving around the Earth and holds the ocean waters against the Earth? [Gravity] (1 pt.)

L 2. _____ Why does the moon have a greater pull on the Earth's water than the sun does? [Because the moon is much closer to Earth] (1 pt.)

L 3. _____ What causes a high tide? [Ocean waters puff out toward the moon when it is directly overhead.] (1 pt.)

V 4. _____ What is a *bulge*? [A part that swells out] (3 pts.)

I 5. _____ Why does the moon affect tides more than the sun does? [Because the moon is closer to Earth and has a stronger pull.] (4 pts.)

Total # of points earned _____

	Scoring Table for Oral Reading			
	# of Word Recognition Errors			
Total Points Earned	**0-11**	**12-18**	**19+**	**Reading Level**
7–10 pts	✓	*	–	Independent ☐
4–6 pts	*	*	–	Instructional ☐
0–3 pts	–	–	–	Frustrational ☐

4D Silent

A Biography of Sequoya

Born around 1765, Sequoya was a member of the Cherokee tribe. He was always fascinated by the white people's ability to communicate with one another by making marks on paper, which he would call "talking leaves." In 1809, he decided that the Cherokee should have a written language of their own. In spite of constant teasing by friends and family, Sequoya gave 12 years of his life to creating an alphabet for his people.

Sequoya found out that the Cherokee language was made up of a particular group of sounds. His alphabet gave a symbol for each of these sounds, resulting in 85 letters in all.

In 1821, Sequoya showed the leading men of the Cherokee Nation how his new alphabet worked. These wise men at once recognized the great worth of the alphabet and quickly adopted it for their people. In just a matter of months, thousands of Cherokee were able to read and write their own language for the first time. Because of Sequoya's vision, the Cherokee could now keep a written record of their great history to be handed down to generations to come.

Passage 4D Silent—Nonfiction

A Biography of Sequoya

Born around 1765, Sequoya was a member of the Cherokee tribe. He was always fascinated by the white people's ability to communicate with one another by making marks on paper, which he would call "talking leaves." In 1809, he decided that the Cherokee should have a written language of their own. In spite of constant teasing by friends and family, Sequoya gave 12 years of his life to creating an alphabet for his people.

Sequoya found out that the Cherokee language was made up of a particular group of sounds. His alphabet gave a symbol for each of these sounds, resulting in 85 letters in all.

In 1821, Sequoya showed the leading men of the Cherokee Nation how his new alphabet worked. These wise men at once recognized the great worth of the alphabet and quickly adopted it for their people. In just a matter of months, thousands of Cherokee were able to read and write their own language for the first time. Because of Sequoya's vision, the Cherokee could now keep a written record of their great history to be handed down to generations to come.

(187 words)

Questions

L 1. _____ What were "talking leaves"? [What Sequoya called the marks on paper used by white people to communicate with one another] (1 pt.)

L 2. _____ What did Sequoya spend 12 years of his life doing? [Creating an alphabet for his people] (1 pt.)

V 3. _____ What does the word *adopted* mean in this passage? [Accepted] (3pts.)

I 4. _____ How do you know that Sequoya's alphabet was easy to use? [In just a matter of months, thousands of Cherokee were able to read and write their own language for the first time.] (4 pts.)

L 5. _____ What did Sequoya's alphabet allow the Cherokee to do? [Keep a written record of their history to be handed down to generations to come] (1 pt.)

Total # of points earned _____

Scoring Table for Silent Reading	
Total Points Earned	**Reading Level**
7–10 pts	Independent ☐
4–6 pts	Instructional ☐
0–3 pts	Frustrational ☐

The Wolf and the Dog

A scrawny wolf was almost dead with hunger when he happened to meet a house dog who was passing by. "Cousin," said the dog, "your irregular life will soon be the ruin of you. Why don't you work steadily as I do, and get your food regularly given to you?"

"I would have no objection," said the wolf, "if I could only get a place."

"I will arrange that for you if you come with me to my master and share my work," said the dog.

So the wolf and dog went towards the town together. On the way there, the wolf noticed that the hair on a certain part of the dog's neck was very much worn away, so he asked him how that had come about.

"Oh," said the dog, "that is only the place where the collar is put on at night to keep me chained up. It does irritate the neck a bit, but you'll soon get used to it."

"Goodbye to you," said the wolf, "for it is better to be free and starve than be a fat slave."

Passage 5A Oral—Fiction

The Wolf and the Dog

A scrawny wolf was almost dead with hunger when he happened to meet a house dog who was passing by. "Cousin," said the dog, "your irregular life will soon be the ruin of you. Why don't you work steadily as I do, and get your food regularly given to you?"

"I would have no objection," said the wolf, "if I could only get a place."

"I will arrange that for you if you come with me to my master and share my work," said the dog.

So the wolf and dog went towards the town together. On the way there, the wolf noticed that the hair on a certain part of the dog's neck was very much worn away, so he asked him how that had come about.

"Oh," said the dog, "that is only the place where the collar is put on at night to keep me chained up. It does irritate the neck a bit, but you'll soon get used to it."

"Goodbye to you," said the wolf, "for it is better to be free and starve than be a fat slave."

(184 Words) Number of Word Recognition Errors _____

Questions

L 1. _____ Why was the wolf almost dead? [Lack of food] (1 pt.)

I 2. _____ What did the dog do that would make you think he liked the wolf? [He offered to arrange for the wolf to work for his master.] (4 pts.)

L 3. _____ Why was the hair on the dog's neck worn away? [He had to wear a collar at night.] (1 pt.)

V 4. _____ What does the word *irritate* mean in this story? [Make sore] (3 pts.)

L 5. _____ Why does the wolf say goodbye to the dog? [Because he'd rather starve than be chained up] (1 pt.)

Total # of points earned _____

	# of Word Recognition Errors			
Scoring Table for Oral Reading				
Total Points Earned	**0–10**	**11–18**	**19+**	**Reading Level**
7–10 pts	✓	*	–	Independent ☐
4–6 pts	*	*	–	Instructional ☐
0–3 pts	–	–	–	Frustrational ☐

5B Silent

Tracy's Find

Life in Tracy's household became very challenging after her father lost his job. Now the entire family had to watch what they spent, and simple pleasures like buying new clothes or eating out were luxuries that Tracy rarely enjoyed.

With winter fast approaching and Tracy in desperate need of boots, she and her mother visited the used clothing store. Embarrassed and miserable, Tracy searched through the boots until she spied a pair in her size that weren't too worn. When she picked one up to try it on, she noticed something stuffed inside. She was stunned when she stuck in her hand and pulled out a little over $1,000 in cash.

Thrilled, she raced over to her mother and said excitedly, "Mom, I found all this money in these boots! The person who gave the boots away won't miss it, so we can keep it, can't we?"

Tracy's mother didn't respond, but the sad and disappointed expression on her face spoke volumes. Ashamed of herself, Tracy knew what her mother expected of her, and she did not hesitate to do it.

Passage 5B Silent—Fiction

Tracy's Find

Life in Tracy's household became very challenging after her father lost his job. Now the entire family had to watch what they spent, and simple pleasures like buying new clothes or eating out were luxuries that Tracy rarely enjoyed.

With winter fast approaching and Tracy in desperate need of boots, she and her mother visited the used clothing store. Embarrassed and miserable, Tracy searched through the boots until she spied a pair in her size that weren't too worn. When she picked one up to try it on, she noticed something stuffed inside. She was stunned when she stuck in her hand and pulled out a little over $1,000 in cash.

Thrilled, she raced over to her mother and said excitedly, "Mom, I found all this money in these boots! The person who gave the boots away won't miss it, so we can keep it, can't we?"

Tracy's mother didn't respond, but the sad and disappointed expression on her face spoke volumes. Ashamed of herself, Tracy knew what her mother expected of her, and she did not hesitate to do it.

(181 words)

Questions

L 1. _____ Why did life in Tracy's household become challenging? [Because her father lost his job] (1 pt.)

L 2. _____ Why was Tracy in the used clothing store? [She needed boots for winter.] (1 pt.)

V 3. _____ What does the word *stunned* mean in this story? [Amazed] (3 pts.)

L 4. _____ What did Tracy want to do with the money she found? [Keep it] (1 pt.)

I 5. _____ What did Tracy's mother expect her to do? [Return the money] (5 pts.)

Total # of points earned _____

Scoring Table for Silent Reading	
Total Points Earned	**Reading Level**
7–10 pts	Independent ☐
4–6 pts	Instructional ☐
0–3 pts	Frustrational ☐

5C Oral

Clouds

Throughout history, people have found clouds to be both interesting and beautiful. Clouds begin to form when warm, damp air is pushed up by cool, dry air. As the warm air rises, it begins to expand and cool. The cooling air is no longer able to hold all of the moisture in gas form that it was able to hold when it was warm. Eventually, tiny drops of water or ice crystals begin to form on bits of dust, taking the shape of a cloud. After the drops or ice crystals form, they can collide with each other and grow by joining together to such a large size that they fall to the ground as rain or snow.

There are four basic families of clouds, with each forming at a different distance above the earth. High clouds form above 20,000 feet, middle clouds appear between 6,500 feet and 20,000 feet, and low clouds appear below 6,500 feet. Finally, there are clouds that are moving upward while their bases are near the ground. These clouds with vertical development range from 1,600 feet to over 20,000 feet.

Passage 5C Oral—Nonfiction

Clouds

Throughout history, people have found clouds to be both interesting and beautiful. Clouds begin to form when warm, damp air is pushed up by cool, dry air. As the warm air rises, it begins to expand and cool. The cooling air is no longer able to hold all of the moisture in gas form that it was able to hold when it was warm. Eventually, tiny drops of water or ice crystals begin to form on bits of dust, taking the shape of a cloud. After the drops or ice crystals form, they can collide with each other and grow by joining together to such a large size that they fall to the ground as rain or snow.

There are four basic families of clouds, with each forming at a different distance above the earth. High clouds form above 20,000 feet, middle clouds appear between 6,500 feet and 20,000 feet, and low clouds appear below 6,500 feet. Finally, there are clouds that are moving upward while their bases are near the ground. These clouds with vertical development range from 1,600 feet to over 20,000 feet.

(185 words) Number of Word Recognition Errors _____

Questions

L 1. _____ What happens to the warm air as it rises? [It begins to expand and cool.] (1 pt.)

V 2. _____ What does the word *moisture* mean in this reading passage? [Wetness] (3 pts.)

L 3. _____ What makes the shape of a cloud? [Tiny drops of water or ice crystals forming on bits of dust] (1 pt.)

L 4. _____ At what distance above earth do middle clouds appear? [Between 6,500 feet and 20,000 feet] (1 pt.)

I 5. _____ Which family of clouds would produce the tallest clouds? [Clouds with vertical development] (4 pts.)

Total # of points earned _____

	Scoring Table for Oral Reading			
	# of Word Recognition Errors			
Total Points Earned	**0–10**	**11–18**	**19+**	**Reading Level**
7–10 pts	✓	*	–	Independent ☐
4–6 pts	*	*	–	Instructional ☐
0–3 pts	–	–	–	Frustrational ☐

5D Silent

Deserts

Most people think of a desert as a wide, empty stretch of coarse sand and low dunes. Although some parts of large deserts do resemble this description, there are other regions that do not fit this picture.

To be a desert, a territory must have less than ten inches of rain a year. These dry areas are widely scattered over the Earth, covering one-fifth of its land surface. The Sahara is the world's largest desert, stretching 3,200 miles across northern Africa and covering an area almost as large as the United States. The Sahara is the driest and hottest of all the world's deserts, creating one of the harshest environments on Earth.

You might be astonished to learn that only one-fifth of the entire area of the Sahara is covered with sand. If you travel through the Sahara, you'll see snow-capped mountains, such as the Tibesti, which are higher than 10,000 feet. There are also lakes such as Lake Chad, which is the size of the state of New Jersey. Also native to the Sahara are canyons, stony plains, and fifty oases, which are desert areas containing water.

Passage 5D Silent—Nonfiction

Deserts

Most people think of a desert as a wide, empty stretch of coarse sand and low dunes. Although some parts of large deserts do resemble this description, there are other regions that do not fit this picture.

To be a desert, a territory must have less than ten inches of rain a year. These dry areas are widely scattered over the Earth, covering one-fifth of its land surface. The Sahara is the world's largest desert, stretching 3,200 miles across northern Africa and covering an area almost as large as the United States. The Sahara is the driest and hottest of all the world's deserts, creating one of the harshest environments on Earth.

You might be astonished to learn that only one-fifth of the entire area of the Sahara is covered with sand. If you travel through the Sahara, you'll see snow-capped mountains, such as the Tibesti, which are higher than 10,000 feet. There are also lakes such as Lake Chad, which is the size of the state of New Jersey. Also native to the Sahara are canyons, stony plains, and fifty oases, which are desert areas containing water.

(191 words)

Questions

V 1. _____ What does the word *resemble* mean in this reading passage? [Look like] (3 pts.)

L 2. _____ To be a desert, what must a territory have? [Less than ten inches of rain a year] (1 pt.)

L 3. _____ Where is the Sahara located? [Northern Africa] (1 pt.)

I 4. _____ What in the passage would make you think that relatively few people live in the Sahara? [It is the driest and hottest of all the world's deserts, creating one of the harshest environments on Earth.] (4 pts.)

L 5. _____ How much of the entire area of the Sahara is covered with sand? [One-fifth] (1 pt.)

Total # of points earned _____

Scoring Table for Silent Reading	
Total Points Earned	**Reading Level**
7–10 pts	Independent ☐
4–6 pts	Instructional ☐
0–3 pts	Frustrational ☐

6A Oral

Androcles and the Lion

A slave named Androcles once escaped from his master and fled to the forest. As he wandered about there, he came upon a lion moaning and groaning in acute pain. At first he turned to flee, but then he saw that the lion's paw was all swollen and bleeding due to the presence of a huge thorn. Androcles pulled out the thorn and bound up the paw, after which the lion licked the man's hand in appreciation and the two became fast friends.

Shortly afterwards both Androcles and the lion were captured, and the slave was sentenced to be thrown to the lion after the latter had not been fed for several days. The emperor and all his court came to see the spectacle, and Androcles was led out into the middle of the arena. Soon the ravenous lion was let loose and rushed roaring toward his victim. But as soon as he approached Androcles, he recognized his friend and licked his hand. The emperor, astounded at this, summoned Androcles to him. After hearing the slave's exceptional story, the emperor freed him and released the lion to his native forest.

Passage 6A Oral—Fiction

Androcles and the Lion

A slave named Androcles once escaped from his master and fled to the forest. As he wandered about there, he came upon a lion moaning and groaning in acute pain. At first he turned to flee, but then he saw that the lion's paw was all swollen and bleeding due to the presence of a huge thorn. Androcles pulled out the thorn and bound up the paw, after which the lion licked the man's hand in appreciation and the two became fast friends.

Shortly afterwards both Androcles and the lion were captured, and the slave was sentenced to be thrown to the lion after the latter had not been fed for several days. The emperor and all his court came to see the spectacle, and Androcles was led out into the middle of the arena. Soon the ravenous lion was let loose and rushed roaring toward his victim. But as soon as he approached Androcles, he recognized his friend and licked his hand. The emperor, astounded at this, summoned Androcles to him. After hearing the slave's exceptional story, the emperor freed him and released the lion to his native forest.

(190 words) Number of Word Recognition Errors _____

Questions

L 1. _____ Why was Androcles in the forest? [He fled there after escaping from his master.] (1 pt.)

I 2. _____ What in the story supports the idea that Androcles is both brave and considerate? [He tends to the wounded lion despite the danger.] (4 pts.)

L 3. _____ What was Androcles's sentence after he was captured? [He was to be thrown to the lion after it had not been fed for several days.] (1 pt.)

L 4. _____ Why didn't the lion attack Androcles? [Because he recognized the friend who had helped him in the forest] (1 pt.)

V 5. _____ What does the word *exceptional* mean in this story? [Extraordinary] (3 pts.)

Total # of points earned _____

Scoring Table for Oral Reading			
	# of Word Recognition Errors		
Total Points Earned	**0-11**	**12-19**	**20+**	**Reading Level**
7–10 pts	✓	*	–	Independent ☐
4–6 pts	*	*	–	Instructional ☐
0–3 pts	–	–	–	Frustrational ☐

6B Silent

Morgan's Escape

After making her escape, Morgan glanced nervously around as she slowly moved into the deserted street. Hearing someone approaching from behind, she crouched behind some trash cans and peeked out to see the figure of a man. As he called her name, she recognized the familiar voice of Ben, someone she had once foolishly trusted. He had lost her trust by taking her to that appalling place where a woman in a white coat had placed her on a cold table. Luckily, she had managed to escape and make a run for her life.

As Ben stepped closer to the spot where Morgan was hiding, she crouched down lower, hoping that he would not detect her. Frozen with fear, she reacted too late when Ben grabbed her.

Indignant and humiliated, Morgan struggled to be free, but Ben held her resolutely and said, "You shouldn't have run out of the veterinarian's office, you silly cat. Now let's go home so we can both get something to eat." At the mention of food, Morgan decided to forgive Ben and go quietly home with him.

Passage 6B Silent—Fiction

Morgan's Escape

After making her escape, Morgan glanced nervously around as she slowly moved into the deserted street. Hearing someone approaching from behind, she crouched behind some trash cans and peeked out to see the figure of a man. As he called her name, she recognized the familiar voice of Ben, someone she had once foolishly trusted. He had lost her trust by taking her to that appalling place where a woman in a white coat had placed her on a cold table. Luckily, she had managed to escape and make a run for her life.

As Ben stepped closer to the spot where Morgan was hiding, she crouched down lower, hoping that he would not detect her. Frozen with fear, she reacted too late when Ben grabbed her.

Indignant and humiliated, Morgan struggled to be free, but Ben held her resolutely and said, "You shouldn't have run out of the veterinarian's office, you silly cat. Now let's go home so we can both get something to eat." At the mention of food, Morgan decided to forgive Ben and go quietly home with him.

(182 words)

Questions

L 1. _____ Where did Morgan hide when she heard someone approaching? [Behind some trash cans] (1 pt.)

L 2. _____ Who was looking for Morgan? [Ben] (1 pt.)

V 3. _____ What does the word *appalling* mean in this story? [Awful] (3 pts.)

I 4. _____ Who was the woman in the white coat? [The veterinarian] (4 pts.)

L 5. _____ Why did Morgan decide to go quietly home with Ben? [He mentioned food.] (1 pt.)

Total # of points earned _____

Scoring Table for Silent Reading	
Total Points Earned	**Reading Level**
7–10 pts	Independent ☐
4–6 pts	Instructional ☐
0–3 pts	Frustrational ☐

6C Oral

Comets

People have long been both awed and alarmed by comets flashing across the sky. To people of the past who didn't understand the movement of heavenly bodies, the ominous sight of a comet was often linked to terrible events such as wars or plagues. The earliest known record of a comet sighting was made in China around 1059 B.C. Since then, these regular visitors have been observed by astronomers like Edmond Halley, who first proved that comets return as they orbit the sun.

Comets, sometimes called "dirty snowballs," are lumps of dust and rock held together by ice. They orbit the sun in an oval path that brings them very close to it and swings them deep into space. As a dark, cold comet approaches the sun, it goes through a spectacular change. Usually, heated ice turns to water first and then evaporates to form a gas. However, when a comet gets close to the sun, the intense heat changes the surface ice directly into gases, which begin to glow. Fountains of dust and gas squirt out for millions of miles, forming a long tail that glows from reflected sunlight.

Passage 6C Oral—Nonfiction

Comets

People have long been both awed and alarmed by comets flashing across the sky. To people of the past who didn't understand the movement of heavenly bodies, the ominous sight of a comet was often linked to terrible events such as wars or plagues. The earliest known record of a comet sighting was made in China around 1059 B.C. Since then, these regular visitors have been observed by astronomers like Edmond Halley, who first proved that comets return as they orbit the sun.

Comets, sometimes called "dirty snowballs," are lumps of dust and rock held together by ice. They orbit the sun in an oval path that brings them very close to it and swings them deep into space. As a dark, cold comet approaches the sun, it goes through a spectacular change. Usually, heated ice turns to water first and then evaporates to form a gas. However, when a comet gets close to the sun, the intense heat changes the surface ice directly into gases, which begin to glow. Fountains of dust and gas squirt out for millions of miles, forming a long tail that glows from reflected sunlight.

(190 words) Number of Word Recognition Errors _____

Questions

V 1. _____ What does the word *ominous* mean in this reading passage? [Threatening or alarming] (3 pts.)

L 2. _____ Who first proved that comets return as they orbit the sun? [Edmond Halley] (1 pt.)

L 3. _____ What are comets made of? [Lumps of dust and rock held together by ice] (1 pt.)

L 4. _____ What does the intense heat of the sun do to the comet? [Changes the surface ice directly into gases, which begin to glow] (1 pt.)

I 5. _____ How does the comet change as it moves away from the sun in its orbit? [It grows cold once more and the ice refreezes.] (4 pts.)

Total # of points earned _____

Scoring Table for Oral Reading				
	# of Word Recognition Errors			
Total Points Earned	**0-11**	**12-19**	**20+**	**Reading Level**
7–10 pts	✓	*	–	Independent ☐
4–6 pts	*	*	–	Instructional ☐
0–3 pts	–	–	–	Frustrational ☐

6D Silent

Sybil's Ride

Everyone has heard of Paul Revere's ride to warn a sleeping countryside that the British were coming. About two years later, there was another essential ride—this time made by a girl named Sybil Ludington.

The eldest child of Colonel Henry Ludington, Sybil was with her family in New York on the night of April 26, 1777, when a messenger knocked on the door. He related that the British were burning the town of Danbury, Connecticut, only 25 miles away. With his men scattered over a wide area, Colonel Ludington had to alert them and organize his troops to fend off the British raid. Not being able to do both, he consented to let Sybil ride to summon the men.

It was raining hard that night, but Sybil rode her horse over 40 miles on dark, unmarked roads to notify the men to gather at her home. When, soaked and exhausted, she returned home, most of the soldiers were ready to march. The men whom she gathered arrived in time to drive the British back to their ships in Long Island Sound. After the battle, General George Washington congratulated Sybil for her heroism.

Passage 6D Silent—Nonfiction

Sybil's Ride

Everyone has heard of Paul Revere's ride to warn a sleeping countryside that the British were coming. About two years later, there was another essential ride—this time made by a girl named Sybil Ludington.

The eldest child of Colonel Henry Ludington, Sybil was with her family in New York on the night of April 26, 1777, when a messenger knocked on the door. He related that the British were burning the town of Danbury, Connecticut, only 25 miles away. With his men scattered over a wide area, Colonel Ludington had to alert them and organize his troops to fend off the British raid. Not being able to do both, he consented to let Sybil ride to summon the men.

It was raining hard that night, but Sybil rode her horse over 40 miles on dark, unmarked roads to notify the men to gather at her home. When, soaked and exhausted, she returned home, most of the soldiers were ready to march. The men whom she gathered arrived in time to drive the British back to their ships in Long Island Sound. After the battle, General George Washington congratulated Sybil for her heroism.

(193 words)

Questions

V 1. ___ What does the word *essential* mean in this reading passage? [Very important] (3 pts.)

L 2. ___ What did the messenger tell Sybil and her family? [The British were burning the town of Danbury, Connecticut.] (1 pt.)

L 3. ___ What did Colonel Ludington consent to let Sybil do? [Ride to summon the men] (1 pt.)

I 4. ___ How do you know that Sybil was a skillful horsewoman? [Because she successfully rode over 40 miles in the rain and dark over unmarked roads] (4 pts.)

L 5. ___ What did the men whom Sybil gathered succeed in doing? [Driving the British back to their ships in Long Island Sound] (1 pt.)

Total # of points earned _____

Scoring Table for Silent Reading	
Total Points Earned	**Reading Level**
7–10 pts	Independent ☐
4–6 pts	Instructional ☐
0–3 pts	Frustrational ☐

Informal Reading Inventory Record

Graded Word Lists

	Grade Level	Date Administered
Independent		
Instructional		
Frustrational		

Oral Reading Passage

	Grade Level	Date Administered
Independent		
Instructional		
Frustrational		

Silent Reading Passage

	Grade Level	Date Administered
Independent		
Instructional		
Frustrational		

Comments:

Placement and Diagnostic Assessment

Spelling

- ## Inventories of Developmental Spelling

Spelling Grades K–6

Inventories of Developmental Spelling

Skills Assessed

- Spelling
- Orthographic Knowledge
- Phonics and Morphology

Grade Levels

- Primary K–3
- Elementary 1–6
- Upper Level, 6–8

Whole Class, Group/Individual

Approximate Testing Time

10–15 Minutes

Materials

Pencil or pen

Lined paper

McGraw-Hill IDSs

▶ **WHAT** There are three Inventories of Developmental Spelling: one for primary students in grades K–3, one for elementary students in grades 1–6, and one for upper-level students in grades 6–8 and above. Each inventory is administered in the same way as a standard spelling test. The focus of these inventories is to examine what students are learning about words and what they are ready to study in their spelling and word study.

▶ **WHY** The words and word patterns spelled correctly, as well as the qualities of students' spelling errors, open a window to understanding what they are ready to study in phonics, spelling, and morphology. Through this examination, students' skills can be classified as falling into particular developmental stages of spelling.

Donald Bear and his colleagues have identified five developmental spelling stages listed below, along with examples of spelling errors typical for each stage.

Spelling Stages and Types of Errors	
Stage 1. Emergent	Squiggles, random letters, *F* for *fed*
Stage 2. Letter Name—Alphabetic	*FD* and *FAD* for *fed*, *DS* and *DES* for *dish*
Stage 3. Within-Word Pattern	*DRANE* for *drain*, *FOYL* for *foil*
Stage 4. Syllables and Affixes	*BERRYS* for *berries*, *MODLE* for *model*
Stage 5. Derivational Constancy	*publicity* for *publicity* (spelled correctly)

Copyright © McGraw-Hill Education

Spelling Grades K–6

▶ HOW General Directions for Administering the Inventories

Tell students that the spelling inventory is not a part of their grade and that knowing more about their spelling will help you to teach them more about words, reading, and spelling. They should not study these words before taking the test.

You could say something like the following:

> *Please spell the words I call out. Some of the words are easy and some will be harder for you to spell. Spell the words the best you can; write down all the sounds you hear and feel when I say the word. Spelling the best you can will help me to be a better teacher.*

Provide paper and have students write the numbers down the side of the page, or prepare a form with the numbering and a line for their names. Say each word in a natural voice. Read the sample sentence and say the word a second time. You may break the list into parts and stop the assessment when students have missed several words in a row.

Setting for the Inventories

These assessments can be administered to the whole class (at least by second grade), in small groups, and individually. How many words you ask students to spell depends on your purpose, and you may wish to divide the administration into different sessions. Make sure to collect enough errors to be able to determine a stage of spelling. As you call out the words, see if you can read what students have written. For individual assessment, there may be times when you can ask a student to spell to you as you write the letters down. If you do not administer the entire list, draw a line on the feature guide under the last word called. Adjust the possible total points at the bottom of each feature column.

TWO WAYS TO SCORE, INTERPRET, AND PLAN

After you collect the papers, you can score them in one of two ways, using either (1) the Feature Guide and the Planning and Organization Chart or (2) the Words Spelled Correctly Planning Chart.

The forms provided with the Inventories of Developmental Spelling are used to plan and organize instruction in word study and spelling: phonics, vowel patterns, and the junctures and meaning parts of words. What you learn about your students' word knowledge also can guide your thinking about the composition of different reading groups.

IDS Feature Guides and Planning and Organizational Chart

Feature Guides A deeper understanding of students' progress is found in the IDS Feature Guide that follows each inventory (*see* **IDS-P pages 234-235, IDS-E pages 236-238, and IDS-U pages 240-242**) and in students' first-draft writing.

Make a copy of the Feature Guide for each student. Check the correct instructional features, and note errors. Check the features and words correct in the last two columns. The total from the last two rows should match the total of the final row.

How do you interpret these scores? A general rule of thumb is to begin instruction at the first place where students miss two or more features in the total column at the bottom of the Feature Guide. Look for a gradual drop in the scores across columns. There can be overlap in the study of digraphs and blends and long and short vowels during the letter name and within word pattern stages of development.

Find the instructional features at the top of the page to determine a spelling stage and gradation within the stage. Circle this stage and complete the score summaries in the third row.

Planning Guide On the class Planning Guide (*see* **page 231**), write each student's name under the stage and gradation, and form groups by drawing circles around reasonable instructional groups; use a pencil at first. In these groups, students focus on specific features in their word study.

For most classroom settings, three groups are ideal unless other teachers are available to provide small group instruction. One group will be with the teacher, another at stations, and another completing independent activities.

Words Spelled Correctly Planning Chart

The Words Spelled Correctly Planning Chart (*see* **pages 232-233**) is a quick guide to instruction. To use the chart, count the number of words spelled correctly in the first three columns. Refer to the fourth column for the spelling stage and the instructional features to study. Track progress and write students' names in the boxes on the right of the chart. Once completed, you will be able to see what instructional groups to consider for word study in phonics, spelling, and upper-level morphological and generative word study for the study of syllables and word meanings. Research has shown a significant correlation between word and feature totals.

Spelling Grades K–6

Planning Guide for Inventories of Developmental Spelling

Directions: This Planning Guide can be used to organize the students by stages, based on analysis of how they spell the words on the Inventories of Developmental Spelling. Write the names of students underneath the stages and gradations for spelling. Consider groups for instruction, and draw a line around the students to place in a group. The groups may span stages; students within a column can be divided to have more even numbers across groups.

Instructional Features →	Consonants: Beginning & Ending	Beginning Digraphs & Blends	Short Vowels	Final Digraphs and Blends	Common Long Vowel Patterns	Other Vowels	Plurals & Inflected Endings	Syllable Junctures & Final Unaccented Syllables	Harder Affixes: Less Frequent Prefixes, & Suffixes, & Consonant & Vowel Alterations and Changes	Bases or Roots & Absorbed Prefix
Spelling Stages & Gradations →	EMERGENT	LETTER NAME - ALPHABETIC		WITHIN-WORD PATTERN			SYLLABLES & AFFIXES		DERIVATIONAL RELATIONS	
	LATE	EARLY MIDDLE LATE		EARLY LATE	MIDDLE LATE		EARLY MIDDLE LATE		EARLY MIDDLE LATE	
Students										

Words Spelled Correctly Planning Chart – page 1

Teacher _____

Words Spelled Correctly			Spelling Stages & Gradations	Instructional Features for Word Study	Dates & Students		
IDSP 25	IDSE 26	IDSU 25					
0	-	-	Emergent Early Scribbles, different directions, two-fisted, to mock linear, no concept of word in text				
0	-	-	Emergent Middle Includes prominent, usually beginning, sounds, inconsistent concept of word in text				
0	-	-	Emergent Late Beginning and final consonant letter-sound correspondences, rudimentary concept of word in text				
0-2	1	-	Letter Name Early Beginning and final consonants, consonant, beginning digraphs and blends				
3-5	2-3	-	Letter Name Middle Short vowel families, short vowel sounds, the CVC pattern				
6-7	3-4	1-2	Letter Name Late Continue CVC pattern, final consonant digraphs and blends				
8-10	5-6	3-4	Within Word Pattern Early Common long vowel patterns beginning with CVCe				
11-14	7-9	5-6	Within Word Pattern Middle Long vowel patterns, final blends & digraphs				

(continued)

Words Spelled Correctly Planning Chart – page 2

Teacher _____

Words Spelled Correctly			Spelling Stages & Gradations	Instructional Features for Word Study	Dates & Students	
IDSP 25	IDSE 26	IDSU 25				
15-18	10-12	7-8	Within Word Pattern Late	Other vowel patterns		
19-21	13-14	9-11	Syllables & Affixes Early	Inflected endings, consonant doubling, easy affixes (prefixes & suffixes)		
22-25	15-17	12-15	Syllables & Affixes Middle	Syllable junctures, unaccented syllables		
-	18-20	16-19	Syllables & Affixes Late	Syllable structures, open and closed syllables, accent & stress, less frequent prefixes & suffixes, consonant & vowel alterations and changes		
-	21-22	20-22	Derivational Relations Early	Harder affixes, reduced and altered vowels, bases, roots and derivations, spelling-meaning connections		
-	23-24	23-26	Derivational Relations Middle	Bases, roots & derivational morphology		
-	25-26	27-30	Derivational Relations Late	Bases, roots & derivational morphology, absorbed prefixes		

Inventory of Developmental Spelling–Primary (IDS-P) Grades K–3

This assessment can be administered whole class (at least by second grade), in small group, and individually. How many words students spell depends on your purpose and procedures in your school. You may administer this inventory over two days. Make sure to collect enough errors to be able to determine a stage of spelling. For example, Emergent spellers need not spell more than four or five words before it is obvious what stage they are in. If you do not administer the whole list, draw a line on the feature guide under the last word called. Adjust the possible total points at the bottom of each feature column.

1. *top*   Hair grows on top of your head.   *top*

2. *can*   I can do anything!   *can*

3. *wig*   I wore a wig on Halloween.   *wig*

4. *bell*   The bell rings when school starts.   *bell*

5. *lost*   I lost my mittens.   *lost*

6. *brick*   The third little pig built a brick house.   *brick*

7. *lump*   There is a lump on his head where the ball hit him.   *lump*

8. *dress*   She is wearing a red dress.   *dress*

9. *strong*   The strong woman picked up the heavy box.   *strong*

10. *scratch*   Don't scratch your mosquito bite.   *scratch*

11. *shape*   The shape with three sides is a triangle.   *shape*

12. *chain*   The chain fell off my bike.   *chain*

13. *clear*   There were no clouds in the clear, blue sky.   *clear*

14. *fright*   The actor had stage fright.   *fright*

15. *stool*   The little boy sat on a high stool.   *stool*

16. *flutes*   Flutes are wind instruments.   *flutes*

17. *blinded*   I was blinded by the bright light.   *blinded*

18. *crown*   The king wore a crown of gold.   *crown*

19. *taught*   My friend taught me how to jump rope.   *taught*

20. *gliding*   The flying squirrel is gliding through the air.   *gliding*

21. *worries*   My mother always worries that I won't finish my homework.   *worries*

22. *sparkles*   The star sparkles like a diamond in the sky.   *sparkles*

23. *fountain*   I stopped to get a drink at the water fountain.   *fountain*

24. *chopped*   My aunt chopped tomatoes and put them in the sauce.   *chopped*

25. *follower*   I became a loyal follower of the show.   *follower*

Spelling Grades K–6

Name _____ **Grade** _____ **Date** _____ **Teacher** _____

Stage and Gradation of Spelling _____ *Total Feature Score* _____ /55 *Words Spelled Correctly* _____ /25 *Total Features & Words* _____ /80

Spelling Stages & Gradations →	EMERGENT (LATE · EARLY)	LETTER NAME–ALPHABETIC (MIDDLE)	(MIDDLE)	(LATE · EARLY)	WITHIN-WORD PATTERN (EARLY · MIDDLE)	(LATE)	SYLLABLES & AFFIXES (EARLY)	(MIDDLE)		
Instructional Features → / Words	Consonants: Beginning & Ending	Beginning Digraphs & Blends	Short Vowels	Final Digraphs & Blends	Common Long Vowel Patterns	Other Vowels	Plurals & Inflected Endings	Syllable Junctures & Final Unaccented Syllables	Feature Points	Words Spelled Correctly
1. top	t p		o							
2. can	c n		a							
3. wig	w g		i							
4. bell	b		e	ll						
5. lost			o	st						
6. brick		br	i	ck						
7. lump			u	mp						
8. dress		dr	e	ss						
9. strong		str	o	ng						
10. scratch		scr	a	tch						
11. shape		sh			ape					
12. chain		ch			ain					
13. clear		cl			ear					
14. fright		fr			ight					
15. stool						ool				
16. flutes					ute		s			
17. blinded				nd			ed			
18. crown						own				
19. taught						aught				
20. gliding							ing			
21. worries							ies	rr		
22. sparkles							s	le		
23. fountain						oun	tain			
24. chopped							ed	pp		
25. follower						ow	er	ll		
Totals	7	8	10	8	5	5	8	4	55	25

Inventory of Developmental Spelling – Elementary (IDS-E) Grades 1 - 6

This assessment can be administered whole class, in small group, and individually. You may administer this inventory over two days. Unless there is an established process, consider discontinuing when students have misspelled eight words in a row. If you do not administer the whole list, draw a line on the feature guide under the last word called. Adjust the possible total points at the bottom of each feature column.

1. *fed*   I fed my dog an apple.   *fed*

2. *dish*   The dish broke when my brother dropped it on the floor.   *dish*

3. *job*   I did a great job on my homework.   *job*

4. *trap*   The mouse was caught in a trap.   *trap*

5. *bump*   Please don't bump my desk while I'm writing.   *bump*

6. *gate*   My mom left the gate open and my dog got out.   *gate*

7. *shore*   The boat came to shore after sailing all morning.   *shore*

8. *drain*   The bubbly water went down the drain.   *drain*

9. *slight*   It was a slight exaggeration to say that he was the tallest boy in town.   *slight*

10. *reach*   I have to reach up high to get the glasses off the shelf.   *reach*

11. *foil*   My father wrapped his sandwich in foil and put it in his lunch.   *foil*

12. *ridge*   The hiker stood on the mountain ridge.   *ridge*

Inventory of Developmental Spelling - Elementary (IDS-E) Grades 1 - 6

13. *chopped*   My aunt chopped tomatoes and put them in the sauce. *chopped*

14. *model*   The students made a model of the solar system. *model*

15. *soothing*   My mother's soothing voice put me to sleep. *soothing*

16. *berries*   The berries on my ice cream were delicious. *berries*

17. *stumbled*   He stumbled over a crack in the sidewalk. *stumbled*

18. *treasures*   The pirates were searching for treasures. *treasures*

19. *divinity*   The all-seeing eye is an ancient symbol of divinity. *divinity*

20. *renounce*   She would not renounce her personal beliefs for any reason. *renounce*

21. *aquarium*   If you want to keep sharks in an aquarium you will need a large tank. *aquarium*

22. *publicity*   It is important for politicians to use the publicity they get from the media wisely. *publicity*

23. *alliance*   The players formed an alliance in order to beat the other team. *alliance*

24. *perspiration* Spicy food increases perspiration, which cools the body when it evaporates. *perspiration*

25. *susceptible* A wound is less susceptible to infection when it is clean and bandaged. *susceptible*

26. *occasionally* Lower the heat and simmer for 5 minutes, stirring occasionally. *occasionally*

Name _____ **Grade** _____ **Date** _____ **Teacher** _____

Stage and Gradation of Spelling _____ *Total Feature Score* _____ /59 *Words Spelled Correctly* _____ /26 *Total Features & Words* _____ /85

Spelling Stages & Gradations →

Stage →	EMERGENT (LATE · EARLY)	LETTER NAME–ALPHABETIC (MIDDLE · LATE · EARLY)			WITHIN-WORD PATTERN (MIDDLE · LATE · EARLY)		SYLLABLES & AFFIXES (EARLY · MIDDLE)		DERIVATIONAL RELATIONS (LATE · EARLY · MIDDLE · LATE)			
Instructional Features → / **Words ↓**	Consonants; Beginning & Ending	Beginning Digraphs & Blends	Short Vowels	Final Digraphs & Blends	Common Long Vowel Patterns	Other Vowels	Plurals & Inflected Endings	Syllable Junctures & Final Unaccented Syllables	Harder Affixes: Less Frequent Prefixes & Suffixes, & Consonant & Vowel Alterations & Changes	Bases or Roots & Absorbed Prefix	Feature Points	Words Spelled Correctly
1. fed	f		e									
2. dish	d		i	sh								
3. job	j		o									
4. trap	p	tr	a									
5. bump	b		u	mp								
6. gate	g				ate							
7. shore		sh			ore							
8. drain		dr			ain							
9. slight		sl			ight							
10. reach				ch	ea							
11. foil	l					oi						
12. ridge						idge						
13. chopped		ch					ed	pp				
14. model			o					el				
15. soothing				th		oo	ing					
16. berries							ies	rr				
17. stumbled							ed	le				
18. treasures						ea	s		ure			
19. divinity							ity			divin		
20. renounce						ounce			re-			
21. aquarium									rium	aqua		
22. publicity									ity	public		
23. alliance									ance	alli		
24. perspiration									ation	spir		
25. susceptible									ible			
26. occasionally									ionally	oc		
Totals	6	5	6	4	5	5	6	4	8	6	59	26

Inventory of Developmental Spelling – Upper (IDS-U) Grades 6 - 8

This assessment can be administered whole class, in small group, and individually. You may administer this inventory over two days. Unless there is an established process, consider discontinuing when students have misspelled eight words in a row. If you do not administer the whole list, draw a line on the feature guide under the last word called. Adjust the possible total points at the bottom of each feature column.

1. *fresh*   The fresh fruit was juicy and delicious.   *fresh*

2. *sauce*   I would like more sauce on my pasta.   *sauce*

3. *toadstool*   A toadstool grows on the forest floor.   *toadstool*

4. *filthy*   My mom said my hands were filthy.   *filthy*

5. *torch*   She carried a torch into the dark cave.   *torch*

6. *chewed*   He chewed gum and blew a bubble.   *chewed*

7. *sunken*   The diver searched for sunken treasure.   *sunken*

8. *cleaver*   The butched chopped the meat with a cleaver.   *cleaver*

9. *quarreling* The girls were quarreling about who was first.   *quarreling*

10. *stubbornly* Stubbornly, the dog held on to the bone.   *stubbornly*

11. *bundle*   Before the performance, I was a bundle of nerves.   *bundle*

12. *funnel*   We poured the liquid through a funnel.   *funnel*

13. *moisture*   Moisture in the air is called humidity.   *moisture*

14. *notification* A notification came in the mail today.   *notification*

15. *divinity*   The all-seeing eye is an ancient symbol of divinity.   *divinity*

Inventory of Developmental Spelling – Upper (IDS-U) Grades 6 – 8

16.	*invitation*	I sent you an invitation to my birthday party. *invitation*
17.	*technician*	A technician came to install our cable. *technician*
18.	*hemisphere*	The United States is in the northern hemisphere. *hemisphere*
19.	*dissection*	We watched a frog dissection in class. *dissection*
20.	*correspondent*	The foreign correspondent reported on the war. *correspondent*
21.	*inquisitive*	An inquisitive child asks many questions. *inquisitive*
22.	*aggression*	Filled with agression, he clenched his fists. *aggression*
23.	*terrarium*	He looked at the tiny plants in the terrarium. *terrarium*
24.	*deprivation*	Sleep deprivation is common among teenagers. *deprivation*
25.	*sufficient*	His excuse was not sufficient to get him out of trouble. *sufficient*
26.	*exhalation*	Exhalation is the movement of air out of the lungs. *exhalation*
27.	*corroborate*	He was able to corroborate the findings. *corroborate*
28.	*irresistible*	The warm chocolate chip cookies were irresistible. *irresistible*
29.	*condescend*	The queen does not condescend to eat with her servants. *condescend*
30.	*architecture*	The unique architecture of the house made it easy to find. *architecture*

Spelling Grades K–6

Name _____   Grade _____   Date _____   Teacher _____

Stage and Gradation of Spelling _____ *Total Feature Score* _____ /64 *Words Spelled Correctly* _____ /30 *Total Features & Words* _____ /94

Spelling Stages & Gradations →	LETTER NAME-ALPHABETIC LATE	WITHIN-WORD PATTERN EARLY MIDDLE	WITHIN-WORD PATTERN LATE	SYLLABLES & AFFIXES EARLY	SYLLABLES & AFFIXES MIDDLE	SYLLABLES & AFFIXES LATE	DERIVATIONAL RELATIONS EARLY	DERIVATIONAL RELATIONS MIDDLE LATE	Feature Points	Words Spelled Correctly
Instructional Features → / Words	Final Digraphs & Blends	Common Short & Long Vowel Patterns	Other Vowels	Plurals & Inflected Endings	Syllable Junctures & Final Unaccented Syllables	Consonant & Vowel Alterations & Changes	Harder Affixes: Less Frequent Prefixes & Suffixes	Bases or Roots & Absorbed Prefix		
1. fresh	sh									
2. sauce		e	auce							
3. toadstool		oa	ool							
4. filthy	lth	i		y						
5. torch	ch		or							
6. chewed		ew		ed						
7. sunken		unk		en						
8. cleaver		ea			er					
9. quarreling			uar		el					
10. stubbornly	st		orn	ly	bb					
11. bundle		un			dle					
12. funnel					nnel					
13. moisture	st		oi			tif	ure			
14. notification						vin	cation			
15. divinity						vit	ity			
16. invitation							ation			
17. technician							ian	technic		
18. hemisphere							hemi	sphere		
19. dissection							dis	ssect		
20. correspondent							ent	corr		
21. inquisitive						ui	ive	quisi		
22. aggression							ssion	aggres		
23. terrarium							ium	terra		
24. deprivation						i	ation			
25. sufficient							suff	fici		
26. exhalation							ex	hal		
27. corroborate							ate	corrobor		
28. irresistible						e	ible	irr		
29. condescend						e		descend		
30. architecture						i		arch		
Totals	5	6	7	4	5	8	16	13	64	30

**Placement and
Diagnostic Assessment**

Vocabulary

• Critchlow Verbal Language Scales

Critchlow Verbal Language Scales

SKILL ASSESSED
Vocabulary

Grade Level
K–6

Language
• English

Grouping
Individual

Approximate Testing Time
15 Minutes

Materials
• English Record Form (p. 246)

Source
From *Dos Amigos Verbal Language Scales* by Donald E. Critchlow.

WHAT The *Critchlow Verbal Language Scales* assess a student's vocabulary in English. Vocabulary is assessed by asking a student to say the "opposite" of a series of words spoken by the examiner. The words on this assessment are arranged in increasing order of difficulty. The scale contains 75 English stimulus words.

WHY As students progress through the grades, they build larger and larger vocabularies. A more advanced vocabulary enables students to better comprehend what they read and hear as well as to better express their thoughts. Measuring vocabulary provides an index of what a student has learned and how well equipped the student is for future learning.

HOW Before beginning the test, determine that the student understands what an opposite is and can demonstrate this knowledge. For example say: "If it is not daytime, it is _____" or "If a child is not a boy, it is a _____" to help establish the concept of opposite.

Explain to the student that you are going to say a word and he or she is to respond with the opposite of that word. Begin with item 1 for all students, and discontinue testing after the child misses five consecutive words or completes the scale. Do not give credit for a response that is not listed.

Note that alternatives are sometimes provided for an acceptable response. For example, the response to *absent* is listed as *present-here,* indicating that either response is correct.

Vocabulary Grades K–6

WHAT IT MEANS Count the number correct and refer to the scoring criteria below to identify the approximate vocabulary grade level. For students who score below their current grade level, provide direct instruction in specific vocabulary needed for school success.

Number Correct English	Vocabulary Grade Level
1–8	Grade K and below
9–12	Grade 1
13–17	Grade 2
18–21	Grade 3
22–26	Grade 4
27–30	Grade 5
31–34 and above	Grade 6 and above

WHAT'S NEXT? For students with limited vocabulary, more intense support in developing other underlying reading skills may be warranted. Further testing of fluency, phonics, or phoneme segmentation ability may be indicated.

Permission granted by ATP Assessments and Arena Press, publishers of Assessing Reading: Multiple Measures (www.academictherapy.com)

Critchlow Verbal Language Scale

Name: _____ Grade: _____ Date: _____

Directions: Ask the student to say the opposite of each word. Discontinue testing after five consecutive errors.

	STIMULUS	RESPONSE		STIMULUS	RESPONSE
____	1. boy	girl	____	39. multiply	divide
____	2. up	down	____	40. friend	enemy
____	3. front	back	____	41. difficult	easy
____	4. hot	cold	____	42. narrow	wide
____	5. brother	sister	____	43. wild	tame
____	6. dirty	clean	____	44. dangerous	safe
____	7. wet	dry	____	45. entrance	exit
____	8. crooked	straight	____	46. sharp	dull
____	9. young	old	____	47. imprisoned	free
____	10. off	on	____	48. falsehood	truth
____	11. shut	open	____	49. public	private
____	12. noisy	quiet	____	50. costly	cheap
____	13. dead	alive	____	51. lengthen	shorten
____	14. early	late	____	52. succeed	fail
____	15. empty	full	____	53. victory	defeat
____	16. near	far	____	54. stale	fresh
____	17. come	go	____	55. timid	bold-brave
____	18. north	south	____	56. maximum	minimum
____	19. lost	found	____	57. unite	separate
____	20. pretty	ugly-homely	____	58. profit	loss
____	21. sick	well	____	59. complex	simple
____	22. sour	sweet	____	60. create	destroy
____	23. add	subtract	____	61. vertical	horizontal
____	24. daughter	son	____	62. former	latter
____	25. remember	forget	____	63. bless	curse
____	26. false	true	____	64. loiter	hurry
____	27. love	hate	____	65. discord	harmony
____	28. heavy	light	____	66. gradual	sudden
____	29. tight	loose	____	67. diminish	increase
____	30. after	before	____	68. naive	sophisticated
____	31. laugh	cry	____	69. superfluous	necessary
____	32. smooth	rough	____	70. asset	liability
____	33. absent	present-here	____	71. tentative	permanent
____	34. strong	weak	____	72. clergy	laity
____	35. evening	morning	____	73. corpulent	slender
____	36. raw	cooked	____	74. epilogue	prologue
____	37. begin	end-stop	____	75. autocracy	democracy
____	38. same	different		Score:	/75

Permission granted by ATP Assessments and Arena Press, publishers of Assessing Reading: Multiple Measures (www.academictherapy.com)

**Placement and
Diagnostic Assessment**

Reading
Comprehension

- **Comprehension Tests Grades K–6**
- **Metacomprehension Strategy Index**
- **McLeod Assessment of Reading Comprehension**

Comprehension Tests K-6

▶ **WHAT** The *Comprehension Tests* assess overall reading comprehension and grade-level reading proficiency. Students read a series of passages that get progressively harder and answer accompanying comprehension questions. There is one set of passages and questions for each grade level. It is useful to test frequently in the elementary and middle school grades.

▶ **WHY** Comprehension is the ultimate goal of reading. This assessment requires students to accurately decode words, to apply their knowledge of vocabulary, and to use critical reading strategies that aid in the literal and inferential comprehension of what is read. When administered to everyone in a class, the assessment serves as a valuable screening for identifying students who may have reading difficulties and who may benefit from additional assessment that focuses on specific skills underlying reading. It can also be used to place students in appropriate-leveled materials to work on critical prerequisite skills and to build overall reading fluency. Since the goal of all instruction is access to core, grade-level content and reading materials, students should only use lower-level materials as needed to work on targeted skills. They should also have exposure to grade-level text and receive ample preteaching and reteaching during small group instructional periods to access this material.

▶ **HOW** Make booklets for students by copying the passages and questions in grade-level order. Begin with passages two grade levels below the students' current grade and end two grade levels above the current grade (if applicable). For example, a grade 4 student would receive a booklet containing grades 2–6 passages and questions. Distribute the booklets to the students.

Explain to students that this test will help you find their instructional reading levels so that they can enjoy reading and build their reading skills. Make sure students are sitting in a comfortable setting with minimal distractions, and encourage them to do their best on the test.

Reading Comprehension Grades K–6

In order to administer the test efficiently and make the directions understandable, you should be familiar with the directions and the test items before the test is given. During the administration, monitor students closely to make sure that each student is following the directions, is on the correct item, and is marking the test form correctly.

▶ **WHAT IT MEANS** The assessment can be scored using the Answer Key at the end of this section (page 295). It lists the correct response for each question. Mark each incorrect item on the student's test, and record the number of correct items. To find the percentage for each score, use the Scoring Chart at the end of this section (page 296).

If students achieve a score of 80%–90%, then they should receive instruction on that grade level. If students receive a score below 80%, then administer additional assessments to determine specific skill needs. These students may need targeted skills-based instruction during small group time to build mastery of prerequisite skills. These students may struggle with grade-level text and will need ample preteaching and reteaching of core content. If students score higher than 90%, monitor their progress in the weeks following the assessment. You might consider providing advanced, or beyond-level, instruction and practice to accelerate their reading growth and enrich the grade-level activities provided.

Reading Comprehension Grades K–6

Directions

Give the child a copy of the Comprehension Test. Read the story and the questions aloud. The child will answer the questions by circling pictures.

Now I am going to read a story. Listen to the story. Then I will ask you some questions. Here is the story.

The Amazing Fish

One day, a fisherman caught an amazing fish with his fishing pole. The fish asked to be let go. "I will grant you three wishes if you let me go," the fish said.

"Very well," said the fisherman. "I wish to be a king."

The fish granted the fisherman's first wish, but the fisherman was not happy.

"I wish for a castle," said the fisherman. So the fish granted the fisherman's second wish, but the fisherman was not happy.

"I wish for a bigger castle," said the fisherman. "I want one that reaches up to the sun!"

"That is not possible," said the fish. "Wish again."

The fisherman became very angry and stomped his foot. "Oh, how I wish I had never met you!" he screamed.

So the fish granted the fisherman's last wish. In an instant, the fisherman was no longer a king with a castle. He was a fisherman fishing in the sea.

Now I will read some questions.

Have the child look at page 252.

1. *Point to the star. Look at the pictures. Which picture shows what the fisherman wished for first? Circle the picture.*

2. *Point to the sun. Look at the pictures. Which picture shows what happened to the fisherman at the end of the story? Circle the picture.*

Have the child look at page 253.

3. *Point to the circle. Look at the pictures. Which picture shows what the fisherman wanted his castle to reach up to? Circle the picture.*

4. *Point to the triangle. Look at the pictures. Which picture shows something the fisherman used to catch fish? Circle the picture.*

Have the child look at page 254.

5. *Point to the moon. Look at the pictures. Which picture shows something that could __not__ really happen? Circle the picture.*

6. *Point to the square. Look at the pictures. Which picture shows what will happen to the fisherman next? Circle the picture.*

Comprehension

1.

  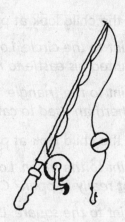

2.

Comprehension

3.

4.

Comprehension

5.

6.

Reading Comprehension Grades K–6

Directions

Make a copy of the Comprehension Test. There are two reading passages in this section. You will read the passages and the questions aloud. Children will answer the questions by filling in circles under the pictures.

Now I am going to read some stories. Listen to the first story. Then I will ask you some questions. Here is the story.

> Have you ever seen a real bear? Most bears live in the mountains or the forest. Bears like to eat many different foods. They eat lots of nuts and berries. Some bears catch and eat fish from the rivers. One of the bear's favorite foods is honey, which is made by bees. The bear finds a beehive and takes the honey.
>
> All through the summer, bears eat a lot and get very big. When fall comes, the weather gets colder. When the leaves fall off the trees, the bear knows that winter will come soon. The bear finds a good place to go for winter, such as a cave or a hole in the ground. The bear climbs in and goes to sleep for the winter. In the spring, the bear will wake up and start eating again.

Have the child look at page 257.

Now I will read some questions.

1. *Point to the star at the top of the page. Look at the pictures. What is the story mostly about? Fill in the circle under the picture that shows what the story is mostly about.*

2. *Point to the moon. Which picture shows where a bear gets honey?*
   Fill in the circle under the picture that shows where the bear gets honey.

3. *Point to the sun. Which picture shows how the bear knows when winter is coming? Fill in the circle under the picture that shows how the bear knows that winter is coming.*

4. *Point to the heart. Which picture shows where a bear likes to sleep for the winter? Fill in the circle under the picture that shows where a bear likes to sleep.*

Go to page 256.

Now I am going to read another story. Listen carefully. Here is the story.

Working with Mom

Maya and Sam were excited about spending the day at the flower shop with their moms. Maya and Sam were best friends. Their families lived in the same apartment building, and their moms worked together in the same flower shop.

On Saturday morning, the four of them rode the bus together to the shop. When they got there, Maya's mom opened the door with a key. When the door opened, a little bell jingled.

"That bell will let us know when someone comes to buy something," said Sam's mom.

A minute later, the bell jingled. The first customer walked in.

"Hello, may I help you?" asked Maya's mom.

The man told them he would like a bouquet of fresh flowers.

"We'll make that for you, and it will be beautiful," said Maya's mom. "We have lots of help today."

Sam and Maya helped their moms choose the flowers. Sam's mom snipped the stems and put everything into a vase. "It's so pretty," said Maya.

The man was happy, too. "I think you should let these two come to work with you more often!" he said, smiling at Maya and Sam.

Maya and Sam were happy with the work they had done.

Have the child look at page 258.

Now I will read some questions.

5. *Point to the star at the top of the page. Look at the pictures. Which picture shows what this story is mostly about? Fill in the circle under the picture.*

6. *Point to the moon. Which picture shows how Maya and Sam and their moms got to work? Fill in the circle under the picture that shows how they got to work.*

7. *Point to the sun. Which picture shows something that happens at the **beginning** of the story? Fill in the circle under the picture that shows something that happens at the **beginning** of the story.*

8. *Point to the heart. Which picture **best** shows how the two families feel about each other? Fill in the circle under the picture that **best** shows how the two families feel about each other.*

Reading Comprehension Grades K–6

Comprehension

1. ⭐   Ⓐ   Ⓑ   Ⓒ

2. 🌙   Ⓐ   Ⓑ   Ⓒ

3. ☀️   Ⓐ   Ⓑ   Ⓒ

4. ❤️   Ⓐ   Ⓑ   Ⓒ

Comprehension

5.

6.

7.

8.

Directions:

Have children turn to the Comprehension section of the test. Then give them these directions.

This part of the test has two reading passages and 8 questions. Read each passage and answer the questions that follow. Mark your answers.

Have children read the passages and answer questions 1–8 independently.

Comprehension

Read this story about a boy named Sam. Then answer questions 1–4. Mark your answers.

Forever Minutes

Sam looked out the apartment window. He saw many people walking along the sidewalk. He was looking for one special person, though. He was looking for Aunt Jazzy. Aunt Jazzy was an artist, and her paintings were in an art show. Aunt Jazzy had asked Sam to go see the paintings with her. So Sam was very happy.

Soon Sam saw a tall woman at the end of the block. She was wearing a shirt that had big splashes of color. It was Aunt Jazzy!

"She's here!" Sam called to his mother. He ran to open the door. Aunt Jazzy stepped into the room and gave Sam a big bear hug.

"Are you ready?" asked Aunt Jazzy.

"Let's go!" yelled Sam.

Before long Sam and Aunt Jazzy were walking along the sidewalk. After several blocks, Aunt Jazzy stopped in front of a tall building. She led Sam up the stairs. A man walked up to meet them.

"We are happy to have you visit today, Ms. Wilson," the man said. "Your paintings are hanging in that room."

Sam looked to where the man pointed. There was a big sign above the door that said *Forever Minutes by Jazzy Wilson.*

"That's you!" Sam laughed. He took his aunt by the hand and pulled her quickly toward the room. Sam looked around the room. There were many colorful paintings hanging on the walls. They made Sam think of the shirt Aunt Jazzy was wearing.

"Did you paint all of these?" Sam asked. Aunt Jazzy smiled and nodded.

"Each painting shows something special in my life," Aunt Jazzy explained. "Some paintings show people, while others show places. I wanted to remember all of these special minutes forever, so I painted pictures of them."

Aunt Jazzy took Sam to look at each painting and told him why each one was special. Finally, they looked at the last picture.

"This is my favorite," Aunt Jazzy said with a smile.

Sam's mouth dropped open. "That's me and you!" he said. "I remember that day. We took a picnic to the park and fed the ducks. It was a very special day!"

"Just like today!" added Aunt Jazzy. "Now I have one more forever minute that I want to paint when I get home!"

Reading Comprehension Grades K–6

1 What is the central idea of this story?

Ⓐ Families remember special times they spend together.

Ⓑ Art helps us see beauty in the world around us.

Ⓒ Members of a family take care of each other.

Ⓓ Artists look at the world in a special way.

2 What evidence from the text shows that Sam and Aunt Jazzy care about each other?

Ⓐ They finally looked at the last picture.

Ⓑ "She's here!" Sam called to his mother.

Ⓒ Aunt Jazzy had asked Sam to go see the paintings with her.

Ⓓ Aunt Jazzy stepped into the room and gave Sam a big bear hug.

3 What happens AFTER Sam sees the sign?

Ⓐ Sam looks out the window to find Aunt Jazzy.

Ⓑ Sam and Aunt Jazzy walk along the sidewalk.

Ⓒ A man meets Sam and Aunt Jazzy in the building.

Ⓓ Sam pulls Aunt Jazzy toward the room with the paintings.

4 How does Sam feel when he sees himself in a painting?

Ⓐ angry

Ⓑ puzzled

Ⓒ surprised

Ⓓ unhappy

Comprehension

Read this passage about beavers. Then answer questions 5–8. Mark your answers.

Beavers

Beavers belong to the same animal family as mice. Beavers and mice have big front teeth. The teeth on both animals never stop growing. However, beavers and mice are very different. First, beavers are much bigger. They can grow up to four feet long. They can weigh over 40 pounds. Also, beavers can swim. Unlike mice, beavers spend most of their life in the water.

All beavers live near rivers or small lakes. Some beavers dig holes in the bank of a river. This hole is their home. However, most beavers build their homes in the middle of the water. They cut down trees with their sharp teeth. They chew off the branches. Beavers pile the branches in the water. They use mud to hold them together. The door is under the water. So beavers swim under the water to get inside. They climb up to a big room that is above water. Then the beavers can breathe air.

Beavers live in places that can get cold. A beaver's body is built to keep the animal warm. First, it has very thick fur. It also makes a special oil that it uses on its fur. The oil keeps the fur dry. Finally, a beaver has lots of fat under its skin. The fat is like a blanket. It keeps the inside body parts extra warm.

Beavers are great swimmers. They can stay under the water for 15 minutes before they need air. Beavers can close their ears and noses. Then water cannot get inside. A clear skin slides over their eyes. Now beavers can see as they swim. Moving around in the water is easy, too. Their back feet look like swimming fins. There is skin between the toes. These webbed feet help beavers glide as they swim.

Beavers have a round, flat tail. There is no hair on it. The tail helps beavers turn and stop as they swim. It helps in other ways, too. Sometimes beavers will strike their tail on the water. The big, loud splash scares away animals that are not friendly. The sound also tells other beavers that there is trouble close by. Beavers know they must find a place to hide. For most beavers, that is their home in the middle of the water.

5 Which is the BEST summary of this article?

Ⓐ Beavers are good swimmers.

Ⓑ A beaver's body helps it live in the water.

Ⓒ Beavers and mice are in the same animal family.

Ⓓ Beavers can live in a river bank hole or a pile of sticks in the water.

6 Beavers are the SAME as mice because

Ⓐ they live in the water.

Ⓑ their back feet are webbed.

Ⓒ they have fat under their skin.

Ⓓ they have teeth that do not stop growing.

7 Why would a beaver hide in its home if other animals come near?

Ⓐ Their home is in the middle of the water.

Ⓑ Other beavers help keep everyone safe.

Ⓒ Most animals are scared of sticks and mud.

Ⓓ A beaver can block the door with its webbed feet.

8 How long can beavers swim under water before coming up for air?

Ⓐ 4 minutes

Ⓑ 15 minutes

Ⓒ 40 minutes

Ⓓ as long as they want

Comprehension

Read each passage and answer the questions that follow.

The Fox and the Tiger

A long time ago, a tiger hunted in a dark forest. He walked quietly through the trees, swinging his shaggy head from side to side. He was searching for something to eat. The striped beast paused every few steps and sniffed the air before moving on.

As the tiger got close to a river, he saw a fox drinking the cool water. The tiger rushed at the fox with a fierce roar and jumped on the smaller animal. Instantly, the tiger's huge paws caught the fox. The fox was pinned to the ground and not able to wiggle free. The tiger opened his huge mouth, showing off his sharp teeth. The future of the fox's life seemed very clear. No animal had ever escaped from a hungry tiger. Yet the fox was a very smart animal. Even though he was in immediate danger, the fox was determined to escape. He needed a plan.

"How dare you attack me!" the fox announced loudly. "Turn me loose at once! Don't you know who I am?"

Surprised, the tiger stopped roaring and closed his mouth. Then he relaxed his grip just a bit.

"You are just a little fox," the tiger growled. "I can eat you as a snack in one bite. Why are you demanding that I let you go?"

"Of all the animals in this forest, you should know that the emperor has made me king of the beasts," exclaimed the fox proudly. "If you kill me, you will show that you do not respect the emperor's wishes. Then he will be very unhappy with you."

The tiger laughed out loud, but eyed the fox with care. He wanted to discover if the fox was telling the truth.

Seeing that the tiger did not totally believe him, the fox spoke again. "Let's have a test. I can prove to you that I am king of the forest animals. Follow me as I walk through the forest. Then you will see that the animals are frightened of me. They will run away and hide."

The tiger agreed and let the fox go. The fox calmly brushed off his fur. Then he started to walk proudly along the forest path. The tiger followed just a few steps behind. Just like the fox had said, the animals raced away in fear. The squirrels scrambled high up into the trees. The deer ran deeper into the forest. However, the tiger did not notice that the eyes of the animals were locked on him, not the fox.

The fox smiled and turned to the tiger. "As you can see, I speak the truth," the fox boldly stated. "I am the king of the forest animals!"

The tiger bowed down in front of the fox. Then he turned and walked back along the forest path.

1 What is the MAIN problem in the story?

(A) The fox wants to be king of the forest animals.

(B) The fox does not want to be eaten by the tiger.

(C) The tiger is hungry and searching for something to eat.

(D) The tiger does not want the fox to be king of the forest animals.

2 The tiger agrees to let the fox go when

(A) the fox demands it.

(B) the tiger learns about the emperor's wishes.

(C) the tiger sees the fox drinking from the cool water.

(D) the fox tells the tiger about a test to prove that he is king.

3 What lesson do you learn from the story?

(A) People of power make the rules.

(B) Listen to what powerful people say.

(C) A brave person can get out of trouble.

(D) Using someone else's power often hurts others.

4 The reader knows that the tiger believes the fox because

(A) the tiger bows and walks away.

(B) the emperor makes the fox the king.

(C) the squirrels scamper higher into the trees.

(D) the fox says he is king of the forest animals.

Lighting the Way

A long time ago, ships were the only way for people to journey across the sea. These ships used sails and were pushed by the wind. Trips could take weeks and even months to complete. So ships traveled both day and night. They sailed in all kinds of weather, too. It was easy to see when the sun lit the way. However, being on the sea at night or during a storm was dangerous. If the sailors were not careful, the ship sailed too close to shore. Some places had sharp cliffs. Others had shallow water filled with jagged rocks. The boat could easily crash. So sailors depended on lighthouses. These shining lights told them that danger was near. The lighthouses warned them to stay away.

The first lighthouse was built in ancient Egypt. It was not until the 1700s that lighthouses became an important part of sea life. They were especially necessary in the early history of the United States. Many people had come from other countries. They missed the food, clothes, and goods from their home lands. Merchants often sailed to these other countries. They returned with full ships. Lighthouses helped ships get safely into many harbors.

Lighthouses were found along the coast. They were built in places that could cause problems for a ship. They stood high above ground so their lights could be seen a long way out at sea. The tallest lighthouse was almost 200 feet tall.

Lighthouses were made of materials that could stand up to terrible storms. The earliest lighthouses were built from rock and brick. The top room was called the "lantern room." It had glass windows that allowed the light to shine out to sea. Lighthouses were often painted different colors. Some had interesting patterns, such as diamonds or stripes. Sailors knew where they were by the way the lighthouse looked.

Lighthouse keepers lived in the bottom of the buildings. Every night and during storms, the keepers climbed up hundreds of stairs to the lantern room. They put whale oil into a large tub. They lit a rope-like cloth that stood up in the middle. The light burned just like a flame on a candle. Later, keepers burned different kinds of oils to make the light. Around the 1800s, inventors used mirrors and glass to send beams of light greater distances.

Today, lighthouses still use mirrors and glass to help send out light beams. However, electricity and light bulbs replaced the burning oil to make the actual light. Now it is possible to see a lighthouse light from over twenty-five miles away. Some lights flash, while others move in a circle. Also, lighthouses no longer have keepers. Instead, rays from the sun charge batteries which power the lighthouse. However, lighthouses still perform the same, very important job. They keep all ships and sailors safe!

5 The evidence in the text gives you reason to believe that

Ⓐ lighthouse keepers were not serious about their jobs.

Ⓑ sailors often avoided sailing at night or during storms.

Ⓒ every dangerous place along the coast had a lighthouse.

Ⓓ lighthouse keepers lost their jobs when people stopped sailing.

6 When did keepers burn the lights?

Ⓐ night and day

Ⓑ just during storms

Ⓒ on the darkest nights

Ⓓ at night and during storms

7 According to text evidence, the light early keepers made was SIMILAR to a candle because

Ⓐ it was in a tub.

Ⓑ it made a flame.

Ⓒ it used whale oil.

Ⓓ it was made of wax.

8 What makes the light in lighthouses today?

Ⓐ mirrors and glass

Ⓑ flashes and circles

Ⓒ electricity and light bulbs

Ⓓ whale oil and rope-like cloth

Comprehension

Directions:

Read each passage and answer the questions that follow.

What to Do?

Tamika sat on the front step of her house and sighed deeply. It was only the second day of summer vacation, and she was bored.

Mrs. Addison, Tamika's mother, looked out the door. "Mrs. Bryan is on the phone," she said. "She is working from home today and needs to make several business calls. She wants to know if you would watch Sally while she is on the phone."

The Bryans were Tamika's neighbors, and Sally was their six-year-old daughter. While Tamika was not old enough to baby-sit, she sometimes went to help take care of Sally if the parents were home and needed to focus on something else.

"Yes, I will watch Sally," said Tamika. "It will give me something to do."

Mrs. Bryan met Tamika at the door. "Thank you for coming over," she said. "I should be on the phone for about an hour. If Sally gets hungry, would you please make a sandwich and cut up an apple for her?"

Tamika nodded and said, "I can stay as long as you need me." Then she turned to Sally. "What do you want to do first?" Tamika asked.

"I want to have a tea party with my bear, clown, and my doll Anna," Sally announced.

"To have a proper tea party, you have to send invitations," said Tamika. "Then you have to get all dressed up, set the table, and make the food."

Sally clapped her hands and twirled in a circle. "This is going to be so much fun!" she squealed.

Tamika got out the paper and crayons and helped Sally make invitations. When the cards were done, Sally ran to her bedroom to deliver them to her guests.

"Everyone will be coming to the tea party!" Sally announced with a giggle when she returned. "Now we all need to get ready in our best party clothes!"

Sally excitedly grabbed Tamika's hand and pulled her to the bedroom. Sally got out a box of dress-up clothes and slipped a tutu over her jeans. She added several long necklaces and a crown. Then Sally helped Tamika put clothes on the toys.

"Now it is time to set the table and make the food," Tamika said. Sally put dishes and silverware on the table, while Tamika made two sandwiches and sliced an apple. Then Tamika poured milk into a tiny teapot. Once the table was ready, all the guests arrived. The tea party was ready to begin.

Mrs. Bryan entered the room and exclaimed, "What a nice tea party! Tamika, this gives me an idea. I plan to work at home three days a week while Sally is home this summer. Would you be interested in coming over on those days to watch Sally? I would happily pay you to be my helper."

"And I would be happy to help at any time," answered Tamika.

Reading Comprehension Grades K–6

1 What is the theme of this story?

(A) Families work together.

(B) Helping others can help you.

(C) Imagination is the best toy there is.

(D) Children around the world are the same.

2 What is the MAIN problem in the story?

(A) Tamika misses school.

(B) There is no tea at the tea party.

(C) Tamika is bored during summer vacation.

(D) Mrs. Bryan needs someone to watch Sally.

3 How is the setting important to the story?

(A) It is summer, so it is too hot to play outside.

(B) It is summer, so the children are out of school.

(C) It is in the Bryan's house, so Sally had to stay inside.

(D) It is during the week, so Mrs. Bryan had to make phone calls.

4 What happens AFTER Sally delivers the invitations but BEFORE the girls dress the toys?

(A) Sally sets the table.

(B) Sally puts on a crown.

(C) Mrs. Bryan enters the bedroom.

(D) Tamika pours milk into the teapot.

Copyright © McGraw-Hill Education

5 One conclusion that can be made about the tea party is that

(A) Tamika is serving lunch.

(B) the guests arrived too late.

(C) the guests are very hungry.

(D) Tamika could not find the tea.

6 Based on text evidence, what will MOST LIKELY happen to the characters next?

(A) Tamika will go home.

(B) Mrs. Bryan will fix lunch.

(C) Tamika and Sally will eat.

(D) Mrs. Addison will join the tea party.

7 Which word BEST describes Tamika at the end of the story?

(A) bored

(B) interested

(C) tired

(D) upset

White House Pets

The White House is home to the president of the United States and the president's family. Just like many families, they often have pets. In all, there have been over 200 different pets that called the White House home. Many of the animals have lived in the private quarters where the family eats, sleeps, and plays. Others have lived on the lawn, in the garden, or even in the garage. Of course, most of the pets were dogs and cats. However, several of the first families have favored more unusual critters.

John Quincy Adams was the country's sixth president. In 1826, a French general gave President Adams an alligator. The reptile stayed in the East Room of the White House. It lived in the bathtub. Sometimes Adams let the alligator out on purpose to shock his guests.

President Woodrow Wilson was in office during World War I. At that time, many men wanted to become soldiers to support their country. The White House gardeners wanted to join the war effort, too. So Wilson got a flock of sheep to replace the gardeners. The sheep nibbled the grass, keeping the lawn neatly mowed. The sheep helped in another way, too. Their heavy coats were clipped, and the wool was sold. Wilson gave the money to a group of people who helped soldiers.

The six children of President Theodore Roosevelt had many pets, including a pony. A pony was not an unusual pet; however, it did visit inside the White House one time. Roosevelt's son Archie got the measles. Quentin, another son, wanted to cheer up his brother. So Quentin led the pony inside the house. Then he took it for a ride on the elevator to get to Archie's bedroom!

Calvin Coolidge was known for his love of animals. During his presidency, President Coolidge was given geese, a wallaby, lion cubs, a bear, and a raccoon. Many were eventually moved to a zoo. However, the raccoon seemed to be tame, so Coolidge kept it. He named the raccoon Rebecca. At night, Rebecca stayed outside in a special house in a tree. Some people say that Coolidge walked her on a leash like a dog. Rebecca was also allowed to run freely inside the White House. Her favorite activity was to sit in a bathtub filled with a little water. Rebecca played with a bar of soap.

President Warren Harding had a dog named Laddie Boy. While a dog is a common pet, Laddie Boy got special treatment. This favored pet attended government meetings with Harding. Laddie Boy even had his own hand-carved chair. Harding and his wife threw a birthday party for Laddie Boy. They invited the neighborhood dogs. All the guests enjoyed eating a dog biscuit cake covered in frosting!

Reading Comprehension Grades K–6

8 Which is the BEST summary statement of this article?

(A) Some United States presidents have had unusual pets.

(B) The presidents' most unusual pets were moved to a zoo.

(C) The president of the United States lives in the White House.

(D) Pets often live in the White House with the presidents' families.

9 What pet did John Quincy Adams have?

(A) a bear

(B) a goose

(C) an otter

(D) an alligator

10 Adams let his pet loose because he

(A) wanted to give it exercise.

(B) hoped it would swim in the bathtub.

(C) hoped to keep it out of the East Room.

(D) wanted to shock people visiting the White House.

11 Which event was caused by White House gardeners leaving to fight in World War I?

(A) White House pets stayed inside.

(B) Archie Roosevelt got the measles.

(C) President Wilson got a flock of sheep.

(D) President Coolidge moved some of his pets to a zoo.

12 From evidence in the text, the reader can conclude that

(A) Quentin cared about his brother.

(B) Archie got better after seeing the pony.

(C) the pony started to live in the White House.

(D) Quentin got in trouble for taking the pony inside.

Comprehension

Read each passage and answer the questions that follow.

City Girl, Country Girl

Jenna opened her eyes and stretched. She noticed that the other bed in the room was neatly made, so she knew that her cousin Beth had already gotten up and dressed. Looking at the clock, Jenna saw it was nearly eight o'clock. Jenna was a little surprised that she had slept so late because she was usually an early morning riser. However, she had not slept well. She missed the honking horns and the rumble of the buses that sounded day and night. To Jenna, they were the lullaby that helped her sleep.

Jenna rolled out of bed and scrambled into a white T-shirt and navy blue shorts. After brushing her hair, she pinned up the sides. Jenna slipped on her sandals and tossed a silver chain around her neck before leaving the room. A quick glance in the mirror showed Jenna that she was ready for the day.

"Good morning, Jenna," Beth called out. "I have to go to the barn to feed the animals, but I thought you might like to go. There is a new foal that we can play with after the barn chores are done."

"I haven't been around animals since my visit last year," replied Jenna excitedly. "Thanks for waiting for me!"

After Jenna ate breakfast, the girls walked to the door. Beth finally noticed Jenna's shoes. "We had lots of rain yesterday, so it is really muddy in the yard," Beth said. "You will ruin your sandals if you wear them outside. I have an extra pair of rain boots that you might prefer to wear." Beth ran to get the boots.

Soon Beth and Jenna were chatting merrily as they walked out the door. Even with the boots on, the girls were careful to step around the biggest mud puddles that dotted the yard. Before long, Beth's St. Bernard, Silas, spotted the pair. He had been out most of the morning, so his fur was slick with mud. Howling excitedly, Silas raced to greet Beth and Jenna. His giant paws dug into the rain-soaked ground, churning up chunks of mud as he dashed forward. Splatters of mud flew wildly from his coat with each stride.

"Sit down, Silas," Beth called out firmly, as she tried to halt the filthy dog's approach. But it was too late. Silas gave a final joyous bark and leapt towards Beth and Jenna. Both girls frantically darted away to avoid the heavily-caked brown paws and slinging mud.

SPLASH! When Beth looked around, she found Jenna sprawled in a puddle with Silas on top of her.

"I am so sorry, Jenna!" Beth gasped, pushing Silas away. She was surprised when she heard Jenna giggle. Beth extended her hand to help her very wet and muddy cousin get up.

"I haven't visited you in so long," Jenna laughed cheerfully. "I totally forgot what it was like to be on the farm, especially after it has rained. I should be wearing jeans and an old shirt, instead of looking like I am going to the mall!"

"Did you bring different clothes?" Beth asked. Jenna shook her head. "Luckily, we are about the same size, so I will happily let you wear some of my clothes."

"Thank you, Beth," answered Jenna. "I think it would be a good idea. I'm going to need them if I am going to be a country girl this week, but first I need to find the garden hose."

Reading Comprehension Grades K–6

1 From the way Jenna describes the sounds of the city, the reader can tell that she

   (A) is ready to move.

   (B) likes living there.

   (C) prefers the country.

   (D) wants to go outside.

2 Why does Beth get a pair of rain boots for Jenna?

   (A) Jenna forgot to bring her rain boots.

   (B) Jenna wants to trade shoes with Beth.

   (C) Beth knows that Silas will knock Jenna over.

   (D) Beth does not want Jenna's sandals to get ruined.

3 From evidence in the text, the reader can conclude that Jenna and Beth

   (A) enjoy being together.

   (B) like to shop at the mall.

   (C) do not agree on anything.

   (D) both take care of animals.

4 What happens when Silas leaps towards the girls?

   (A) He howls excitedly.

   (B) The girls move away.

   (C) Beth puts on the rain boots.

   (D) Jenna looks for a garden hose.

5 How does Jenna feel about Silas knocking her into the mud puddle?

Ⓐ She is angry at Silas.

Ⓑ She is scared of Silas.

Ⓒ She thinks it is funny.

Ⓓ She is worried about her clothes.

6 What is the message of the selection?

Ⓐ The country is better than the city.

Ⓑ Family is the same wherever you go.

Ⓒ Expensive things are not always better.

Ⓓ Think ahead to best prepare for a situation.

7 Which paragraph BEST supports the theme?

Ⓐ paragraph 2, p. 279

Ⓑ paragraph 5, p. 279

Ⓒ paragraph 2, p. 280

Ⓓ paragraph 5, p. 280

8 Based on what you read, what will the characters most likely do next?

Ⓐ rinse off

Ⓑ go swimming

Ⓒ feed the animals

Ⓓ give Silas a bath

Elephant Artists

The artist studies the canvas before applying the next stroke of paint. Soon, a green vine with red flowers appears on the white background. When the painting is done, the artist hands the small brush to a helper. The crowd claps loudly and cheers with pleasure. The artist, an Asian grey elephant, raises its trunk. It enjoys the attention.

Elephant artists have been a hot topic in both the animal and art worlds. Elephants are one of the smartest animals on Earth; they are able to show emotion and can communicate with others. Elephants also have great strength. They have worked for decades lifting and carrying heavy loads. However, these strong, giant creatures also have very good fine motor control in their trunks. They are able to grasp a single blade of grass with their flexible trunks.

People wondered if elephants could paint because of their intelligence and trunk control. Some early experiments convinced the owners of the Maesa Elephant Camp in Thailand that elephants could be excellent painters. So they began an elephant art program. Handlers started working with young elephants. They helped the animals grasp the brush. Next, the handler dipped the brush in the paint and showed the elephant how to apply the paint. After much practice, elephants were able to make simple designs and shapes. The experienced elephants painted flowers, trees, and elephant heads. After five years, the program proved to be a success. Art lovers often bought the elephant paintings.

The owners of the Maesa Elephant Camp wanted to show off their talented elephants. So they contacted Guinness World Records, the authority that records amazing and historical feats. The camp owners submitted a request to make a world record for the largest painting done by a group of elephants. Guinness approved the event. They set the date for February 19, 2005.

Since the world would be watching, the camp owners decided to have a practice session. Many people gathered to watch eight elephants in action on December 13, 2004. Record keepers from Thailand's Ripley's Believe It or Not, another organization that keeps unusual records, also joined the crowd. Eight panels were placed next to each other. Together, they measured about 23 feet long and 7 feet tall. The elephants worked for six hours. The handlers made sure that the artists took a 20-minute break every hour to eat and cool down with water.

Each elephant added its own unique style to the painting. The younger elephants painted with strokes, lines, and dots. The older animals that had more experience painted with precise movements. When finished, the canvas displayed flowers and trees against a blue sky. It was called "Cold Wind, Swirling Mist, Charming Lanna." That day the elephants received their first record of "The Largest Painting by a Group of Elephants." It came from Thailand's Ripley's Believe It or Not.

On February 19, 2005, an even bigger crowd visited the Maesa Elephant Camp. The elephants once again painted the same landscape. This second painting was called "Cold Wind, Swirling Mist, Charming Lanna I." This time it earned the record of "The Largest Painting by a Group of Elephants" from Guinness World Records.

The day of record making was not over yet, though. A businesswoman bought the elephants' painting for $39,000. This time Guinness awarded a record for "The Most Expensive Painting by a Group of Elephants." The painting was divided into two sections. One part was displayed at the Maesa Elephant Camp. The other was donated to the Thailand government.

9 Which is the main idea of the article?

Ⓐ Elephants are good artists.

Ⓑ Elephants are intelligent animals.

Ⓒ Eight elephant artists won two world records.

Ⓓ Elephant owners know that elephants are good painters.

10 The details in the second paragraph on page 283 help the reader to understand

Ⓐ how an elephant learns to paint.

Ⓑ how the trunk is able to hold a brush.

Ⓒ what jobs elephants have done in the past.

Ⓓ the qualities that make elephants good painters.

11 Based on evidence in the text, why can elephants paint?

Ⓐ They are intelligent, so they like to paint.

Ⓑ They are intelligent and have strong trunks.

Ⓒ They are intelligent and have good trunk control.

Ⓓ Their trunks are strong, so they have good trunk control.

12 From evidence in the text, the reader can conclude that

Ⓐ all elephants can paint.

Ⓑ the elephants choose the colors to paint.

Ⓒ the handlers teach the elephants to paint.

Ⓓ elephant paintings hang in many museums.

13 The article gives you reason to believe that

Ⓐ elephants know how to paint.

Ⓑ elephants learn how to paint quickly.

Ⓒ elephants can learn how to paint at any age.

Ⓓ elephants must learn to paint when they are young.

14 According to the article, the painting of the younger elephants is different from the older elephants because

Ⓐ the older elephants mostly paint designs.

Ⓑ the older elephants use mostly bright colors.

Ⓒ the younger elephants use mostly bright colors.

Ⓓ the younger elephants are not as experienced.

15 The Maesa Elephant Camp owners contacted Guinness World Records because

Ⓐ they wanted to make money on the art.

Ⓑ the owners were proud of their elephants.

Ⓒ the elephants had just finished the painting.

Ⓓ their elephants were the best elephant artists.

16 After winning the Guinness World Record for "The Largest Painting by a Group of Elephants,"

Ⓐ the elephants won a Ripley's Believe It or Not record.

Ⓑ the elephants made another painting that looked like the first.

Ⓒ the elephants got a 20-minute break to eat and cool down with water.

Ⓓ the elephants won "The Most Expensive Painting by a Group of Elephants."

Comprehension

Read each passage and answer the questions that follow.

Phaeton and the Chariot of the Sun

In ancient times, there lived a young man named Phaeton. His father was Apollo, the sun god who drove his gleaming chariot daily across the sky. Phaeton often bragged about his powerful father to his friends as they tested their skills and strength in friendly competitions. Eventually, Phaeton's friends got tired of hearing his boasts and challenged him to prove his words.

One night Phaeton traveled to the tallest mountain in the land and climbed the steep and jagged slope. Upon reaching the peak, Phaeton found a glittering palace decorated with sparkling gems and bathed in a brilliant light. He boldly entered the palace and saw a regal being that radiated a fiery light. It was Apollo! Apollo beckoned to his son to approach the golden throne.

"Welcome, Phaeton!" greeted Apollo. "Why have you journeyed here to see me?"

"I have been told that I am your son," answered Phaeton. "I have come to find out if it is true."

"Indeed, you are my son," responded Apollo. "As proof, I will grant you one wish."

Phaeton wanted more than anything to prove to his friends that Apollo was his father, so the young man made a bold request. "I wish to drive your chariot, Father."

Immediately, Apollo regretted his decision and pleaded with young Phaeton to choose another wish. "The horses are mighty beasts that breathe fire, and the chariot is blazing hot. The powerful steeds need a firm hand to control their climb to the dizzying heights of the sky and then to restrain the race back down."

Phaeton held firm in his request, and a saddened Apollo led his son to the fiery chariot. The horses pawed the ground and snorted fire, anxious for their daily exercise. Apollo made a final plea for his son to choose another wish, but Phaeton stood fast in his choice. He knew that his friends would now believe his words.

Then Apollo anointed his son with an oil to keep the heat of the chariot from burning his human skin. Sighing, Apollo transferred the flaming crown to Phaeton's head. Phaeton gripped the reins as the team bolted forward. The steeds sensed the weaker hand and thundered upward at a frightening speed. The carriage swayed, but young Phaeton managed to steady the horses. At the top of the sky, Phaeton looked out at the extreme height. Feeling dizzy, he dropped the reins and the fierce horses veered off course.

The horses galloped closer to Earth, pulling the fiery chariot. The sun's extreme heat dried up the rivers and lakes. It scorched the cities and towns. As the chariot crossed the continent of Africa, it torched the great Sahara Forest. The land was reduced to glowing ashes and blistering hot sand. In anguish, the people and animals on Earth pleaded for relief from the extreme heat and burning destruction.

Mighty Zeus heard the cries. He reached for a thunderbolt and released the jagged light with a roar. It sped straight toward the chariot, striking with deadly accuracy. The oil Apollo used to protect Phaeton from the sun could not keep him safe from the thunderbolt. The chariot shattered into pieces. Phaeton fell into the sea and drowned.

The sun's horses raced home. Apollo, seeing them without the chariot or Phaeton, realized what had happened. In sorrow, he declared that the sun would never rise again. Zeus visited Apollo and pleaded that the Earth and all its creatures needed the sun to live. Apollo, still grieving, knew his duty, so he called for a new chariot to be built. The next morning, Apollo climbed into the sun's fiery chariot and once again raced across the sky.

Reading Comprehension Grades K–6

1 Phaeton went to see Apollo because he wanted

Ⓐ to see the chariot.

Ⓑ to listen to his friends.

Ⓒ to prove Apollo was his father.

Ⓓ to brag about the trip to his friends.

2 Why does Phaeton want his friends to see him driving the sun's chariot?

Ⓐ It will prove that Phaeton is Apollo's son.

Ⓑ It will show that Apollo likes Phaeton the best.

Ⓒ It will give Phaeton something else to brag about.

Ⓓ It will prove that Phaeton is the strongest of his friends.

3 Which word BEST describes Phaeton?

Ⓐ brave

Ⓑ careful

Ⓒ proud

Ⓓ thoughtful

4 Based on evidence in the text, what protects Phaeton from the sun's heat?

Ⓐ oil

Ⓑ jewels

Ⓒ a crown

Ⓓ the horses

Copyright © McGraw-Hill Education

Placement and Diagnostic Assessment · Comprehension Test Grade 6   **289**

5 Why does Apollo grant Phaeton's wish?

Ⓐ Apollo wants to keep his word to Phaeton.

Ⓑ Apollo wants to punish the people on Earth.

Ⓒ Apollo wants to punish Phaeton for being too proud.

Ⓓ Apollo thinks Phaeton will be able to drive the chariot.

6 From evidence in the text, the reader can conclude that the myth explained

Ⓐ how to drive a chariot.

Ⓑ why there are deserts on Earth.

Ⓒ why lightning flashes in the sky.

Ⓓ why the sun does not always shine.

7 Why does Zeus throw a thunderbolt?

Ⓐ to destroy the chariot and save Earth

Ⓑ to keep the chariot from falling into the sea

Ⓒ to scare the horses so they return to the route

Ⓓ to make light for Earth once the chariot shatters

8 What message about human nature does this myth tell?

Ⓐ Promises are easily broken.

Ⓑ Strength overcomes carelessness.

Ⓒ Pride can cause people to make poor choices.

Ⓓ Bragging can hurt your friends and friendships.

The Mother Goose Mystery

Children around the world have been raised on Mother Goose nursery rhymes, games, and fairy tales. The rhymes are fun to repeat. The rhythm and words of the alphabet and the counting games help children learn and remember important skills. Moreover, the famous fairy tales inspire the imagination with amazing places, characters, and events. Even adults enjoy the Mother Goose verses and stories as they recite them to children. So who was Mother Goose? Who was the person with the wonderful imagination and writing skills?

The first mention of the name *Mother Goose* appears in a book published in France in 1650. One translated phrase reads "Like a Mother Goose story." These words show that the name *Mother Goose* was already familiar to people in that country. Some historians believe that the author was talking about Queen Bertha Greatfoot. Queen Bertha was also called *Goosefoot*. She lived in the 700s and was known to support the interests of children.

It was not until 1697 that the name *Mother Goose* was actually printed on the cover of a book. Frenchman Charles Perrault published *Histories and Tales of Long Ago, with Morals*. The picture on the front of the book showed an old woman who was telling stories. There was a subtitle that said "Tales from My Mother Goose." The book was made up of a group of fairy tales, including "Cinderella" and "Little Red Riding Hood." These stories were familiar to most people because they had been orally passed down through the generations. Perrault simply recorded the tales and published them. Historians agree that the book was intended to be read by wealthy adults, though. At that time, few people could read or write. Moreover, books took a long time to make and were very expensive.

Thirty years later Perrault's book was translated into English in Great Britain. The book's title was *Mother Goose's Fairy Tales*. The title was an important event in literature for two reasons. First, the name *Mother Goose* officially appeared in a title. Second, it gave proof that the name *Mother Goose* had finally spread from France. Wealthy adults were still the target audience, so the book did not attract much attention.

In 1760, John Newbery, of Newbery Award fame, published a book specifically for children. He titled it *Mother Goose's Melody*. The book included fairy tales, but Newbery also added popular children's rhymes. The book was a huge success and established the format of nursery rhymes being paired with fairy tales in Mother Goose books.

The first Mother Goose book in the United States was published in the late 1700s. It was titled *Mother Goose's Melody: or Sonnets for the Cradle*. The book contained about fifty of the most popular rhymes children recite today, such as "Jack and Jill" and "Little Tommy Tucker." The Mother Goose name was now recognized around the world.

When historians began searching for the origin of Mother Goose, they followed many leads. One story identified Elizabeth Goose of Boston, Massachusetts, as the famed storyteller. Information suggested that she entertained her grandchildren by reciting nursery rhymes. Her son-in-law, a publisher, recorded them and printed the verses in a book called *The Only True Mother Goose*. Because Elizabeth's last name was *Goose,* people believed that she was the real Mother Goose. Later, people began visiting the grave of a woman named Mary Goose, saying that she was Mother Goose. However, research showed that neither of these women was the original Mother Goose.

As the research about the true Mother Goose continued, historians traced the origin to France. Sadly, they could never prove if there was a Mother Goose who lived long ago. They all believed that Mother Goose was a collection of imaginative stories, games, and rhymes gathered by book publishers from around the world over several centuries. While the words were originally meant to entertain adults, they soon became a central part of childhood around the world.

9 Which sentence best expresses the main idea of the article?

Ⓐ Historians have tried to discover who Mother Goose was.

Ⓑ Mother Goose is a collection of rhymes, games, and fairy tales.

Ⓒ Children all around the world know and love Mother Goose books.

Ⓓ Mother Goose verses and stories were passed down through the generations.

10 The evidence in the text gives you reason to believe that Queen Bertha might have been the first Mother Goose because

Ⓐ she lived in France.

Ⓑ she lived around the 700s.

Ⓒ she was called *Goosefoot*.

Ⓓ she was mentioned in a book.

11 Based on evidence in the text, which of the following might be found in Perrault's book?

Ⓐ Sleeping Beauty, a fairy tale

Ⓑ Little Boy Blue, a nursery rhyme

Ⓒ The Alphabet Song, a children's song

Ⓓ I Caught a Fish Alive, a nursery rhyme and children's song

12 Based on what you read, what most likely happened to Mother Goose books soon after 1730?

Ⓐ Readers became less and less interested in Mother Goose.

Ⓑ Printers in France were forbidden to publish Mother Goose.

Ⓒ Schools began teaching lessons based on Mother Goose.

Ⓓ Mother Goose was read in English-speaking countries.

13 Which of the following appears in both the Perrault and Newbery books?

Ⓐ rhymes

Ⓑ fairy tales

Ⓒ alphabet songs

Ⓓ counting songs

14 According to text evidence, what happened to the popularity of Mother Goose after John Newbery's Mother Goose publication?

Ⓐ Mother Goose became popular with children.

Ⓑ People in the United States could read the book.

Ⓒ People finally found out who Mother Goose was.

Ⓓ The book became part of early childhood education.

15 Who is believed to have first used a mix of rhymes and stories in Mother Goose?

Ⓐ Queen Bertha

Ⓑ Elizabeth Goose

Ⓒ Charles Perrault

Ⓓ John Newbery

16 What conclusion can you draw from "The Mother Goose Mystery"?

Ⓐ Mother Goose was a French queen.

Ⓑ People still do not know if there was a Mother Goose.

Ⓒ The Mother Goose books were popular with adults in 1697.

Ⓓ An American grandmother wrote some of the Mother Goose rhymes.

Answer Key

GRADE 2
1. A
2. D
3. D
4. C
5. B
6. D
7. A
8. B

GRADE 3
1. B
2. D
3. C
4. A
5. C
6. D
7. B
8. C

GRADE 4
1. B
2. C
3. B
4. B
5. A
6. C
7. B
8. A
9. D
10. D
11. C
12. A

GRADE 5
1. B
2. D
3. A
4. B
5. C
6. D
7. D
8. C
9. C
10. D
11. C
12. C
13. D
14. D
15. B
16. D

GRADE 6
1. C
2. A
3. C
4. A
5. A
6. B
7. A
8. C
9. A
10. C
11. A
12. D
13. B
14. A
15. D
16. B

Scoring Chart

The Scoring Chart is provided for your convenience in grading your students' work.

- Find the column that shows the total number of items on the test.
- Find the row that matches the number of items answered correctly.
- The intersection of the column and the row provides the percentage score.

NUMBER CORRECT	TOTAL NUMBER OF ITEMS										
	6	7	8	9	10	11	12	13	14	15	16
1	17	14	13	11	10	9	8	8	7	7	6
2	33	29	25	22	20	18	17	15	14	13	13
3	50	43	38	33	30	27	25	23	21	20	19
4	67	57	50	44	40	36	33	31	29	27	25
5	83	71	63	56	50	45	42	38	36	33	31
6	100	86	75	67	60	55	50	46	46	40	38
7		100	88	78	70	64	58	54	50	47	44
8			100	89	80	73	67	62	57	53	50
9				100	90	82	75	69	64	60	56
10					100	91	83	77	71	67	63
11						100	92	85	79	73	69
12							100	95	86	80	75
13								100	93	87	81
14									100	93	88
15										100	94
16											100

Metacomprehension Strategy Index Grades 4 - 6

▶ **WHAT** The *Metacomprehension Strategy Index* (developed by Schmitt, 1988, 1990) assesses students' independent use of strategies before, during, and after reading. Students read a series of questions about their reading behaviors. Questions cover broad areas such as predicting and verifying, previewing, purpose setting, self-questioning, drawing from background knowledge, summarizing, and using appropriate fix-up strategies.

Predicting and Verifying: Items numbered 1, 4, 13, 15, 16, 18, 23

Predicting the content of a story promotes active comprehension by giving readers a purpose for reading. Evaluating predictions and generating new ones as necessary enhances the constructive nature of the reading process.

Previewing: Items numbered 2, 3

Previewing the text facilitates comprehension by activating background knowledge and providing information for making predictions.

Purpose Setting: Items numbered 5, 7, 21

Reading with a purpose promotes active, strategic reading.

Self-Questioning: Items numbered 6, 14, 17

Generating questions to be answered promotes active comprehension by giving readers a purpose for reading.

Drawing from Background Knowledge: Items numbered 8, 9, 10, 19, 24, 25

Activating and incorporating information from background knowledge contributes to comprehension by helping readers make inferences and generate predictions.

Summarizing and Applying Fix-Up Strategies: Items numbered 11, 12, 20, 22

Summarizing the content at various points in the story serves as a form of comprehension monitoring. Rereading when comprehension breaks down represents strategic reading.

(from *Metacognition in Literacy Learning;* S. Israel, C. C. Block, K. Bauserman, K. Kinnucan-Welsch, 2005, page 105)

▶ **WHY** Comprehension is the ultimate goal of reading. Developing skilled, independent, strategic readers is the goal of comprehension instruction. This assessment helps you determine if students are using strategies before, during, and after reading and which ones they might be using. The assessment can provide insights into each student's strategic processing of text and affect the amount and types of strategy instruction you provide to students.

▶ **HOW** Make booklets for students by copying the series of questions. Distribute the booklets to the students.

Explain to students that this test will help you determine the strategies they use while reading so you can help them become more skilled and strategic readers. Make sure students are sitting in a comfortable setting with minimal distractions, and encourage them to do their best on the test.

In order to administer the test efficiently and make the directions understandable, you should be familiar with the directions and the test items before the test is given. During the administration, monitor students closely to make sure that each student is following the directions, is on the correct item, and is marking the test form correctly.

▶ **WHAT IT MEANS** This assessment can be scored using the Answer Key at the end of this section (page 305). It lists the correct response for each question. Mark each incorrect item on the student's test and record the number of correct items by category: Before Reading, During Reading, After Reading. In addition, use the item analysis information on pages 297–298 to determine which types of strategies students are not using (e.g., summarizing and fix-up strategies as indicated by items 11, 12, 20, and 22).

Use the results of the assessment to form small groups based on strategy needs. Provide additional instruction on these strategies during small-group time, and help students apply the strategies using the Skills-Based Practice Readers. In addition, reinforce those strategies not mastered during whole- group reading sessions in which students are asked to explain their self-selected strategy use.

METACOMPREHENSION STRATEGY INDEX

Directions: Think about what kinds of things you can do to understand a story better before, during, and after you read it. Read each of the lists of four statements and decide which one of them would help *you* the most. *There are no right answers.* It is just what *you* think would help the most. Circle the letter of the statement you choose.

I. In each set of four, choose the one statement which tells a good thing to do to help you understand a story better *before* you read it.

1 Before I begin reading, it's a good idea to

Ⓐ see how many pages are in the story.

Ⓑ look up all of the big words in the dictionary.

Ⓒ make some guesses about what I think will happen in the story.

Ⓓ think about what has happened so far in the story.

2 Before I begin reading, it's a good idea to

Ⓐ look at the pictures to see what the story is about.

Ⓑ decide how long it will take me to read the story.

Ⓒ sound out the words I don't know.

Ⓓ check to see if the story is making sense.

3 Before I begin reading, it's a good idea to

Ⓐ ask someone to read the story to me.

Ⓑ read the title to see what the story is about.

Ⓒ check to see if most of the words have long or short vowels in them.

Ⓓ check to see if the pictures are in order and make sense.

4 Before I begin reading, it's a good idea to

Ⓐ check to see that no pages are missing.

Ⓑ make a list of words I'm not sure about.

Ⓒ use the title and pictures to help me make guesses about what will happen in the story.

Ⓓ read the last sentence so I will know how the story ends.

METACOMPREHENSION STRATEGY INDEX (continued)

5 Before I begin reading, it's a good idea to

Ⓐ decide on why I am going to read the story.

Ⓑ use the difficult words to help me make guesses about what will happen in the story.

Ⓒ reread some parts to see if I can figure out what is happening if things aren't making sense.

Ⓓ ask for help with the difficult words.

6 Before I begin reading, it's a good idea to

Ⓐ retell all of the main points that have happened so far.

Ⓑ ask myself questions that I would like to have answered in the story.

Ⓒ think about the meanings of the words which have more than one meaning.

Ⓓ look through the story to find all of the words with three or more syllables.

7 Before I begin reading, it's a good idea to

Ⓐ check to see if I have read this story before.

Ⓑ use my questions and guesses as a reason for reading the story.

Ⓒ make sure I can pronounce all of the words before I start.

Ⓓ think of a better title for the story.

8 Before I begin reading, it's a good idea to

Ⓐ think of what I already know about the things I see in the pictures.

Ⓑ see how many pages are in the story.

Ⓒ choose the best part of the story to read again.

Ⓓ read the story aloud to someone.

9 Before I begin reading, it's a good idea to

Ⓐ practice reading the story aloud.

Ⓑ retell all of the main points to make sure I can remember the story.

Ⓒ think of what the people in the story might be like.

Ⓓ decide if I have enough time to read the story.

METACOMPREHENSION STRATEGY INDEX (continued)

10 Before I begin reading, it's a good idea to

(A) check to see if I am understanding the story so far.

(B) check to see if the words have more than one meaning.

(C) think about where the story might be taking place.

(D) list all of the important details.

II. **In each set of four, choose the one statement which tells a good thing to do to help you understand a story better *while* you are reading it.**

11 While I'm reading, it's a good idea to

(A) read the story very slowly so that I will not miss any important parts.

(B) read the title to see what the story is about.

(C) check to see if the pictures have anything missing.

(D) check to see if the story is making sense by seeing if I can tell what's happened so far.

12 While I'm reading, it's a good idea to

(A) stop to retell the main points to see if I am understanding what has happened so far.

(B) read the story quickly so that I can find out what happened.

(C) read only the beginning and the end of the story to find out what it is about.

(D) skip the parts that are too difficult for me.

13 While I'm reading, it's a good idea to

(A) look all of the big words up in the dictionary.

(B) put the book away and find another one if things aren't making sense.

(C) keep thinking about the title and the pictures to help me decide what is going to happen next.

(D) keep track of how many pages I have left to read.

METACOMPREHENSION STRATEGY INDEX (continued)

14 While I'm reading, it's a good idea to

Ⓐ keep track of how long it is taking me to read the story.

Ⓑ check to see if I can answer any of the questions I asked before I started reading.

Ⓒ read the title to see what the story is going to be about.

Ⓓ add the missing details to the pictures.

15 While I'm reading, it's a good idea to

Ⓐ have someone read the story aloud to me.

Ⓑ keep track of how many pages I have read.

Ⓒ list the story's main character.

Ⓓ check to see if my guesses are right or wrong.

16 While I'm reading, it's a good idea to

Ⓐ check to see that the characters are real.

Ⓑ make a lot of guesses about what is going to happen next.

Ⓒ not look at the pictures because they might confuse me.

Ⓓ read the story aloud to someone.

17 While I'm reading, it's a good idea to

Ⓐ try to answer the questions I asked myself.

Ⓑ try not to confuse what I already know with what I'm reading about.

Ⓒ read the story silently.

Ⓓ check to see if I am saying the new vocabulary words correctly.

18 While I'm reading, it's a good idea to

Ⓐ try to see if my guesses are going to be right or wrong.

Ⓑ reread to be sure I haven't missed any of the words.

Ⓒ decide on why I am reading the story.

Ⓓ list what happened first, second, third, and so on.

METACOMPREHENSION STRATEGY INDEX (continued)

19 While I'm reading, it's a good idea to

(A) see if I can recognize the new vocabulary words.

(B) be careful not to skip any parts of the story.

(C) check to see how many of the words I already know.

(D) keep thinking of what I already know about the things and ideas in the story to help me decide what is going to happen.

20 While I'm reading, it's a good idea to

(A) reread some parts or read ahead to see if I can figure out what is happening if things aren't making sense.

(B) take my time reading so that I can be sure I understand what is happening.

(C) change the ending so that it makes sense.

(D) check to see if there are enough pictures to help make the story ideas clear.

III. In each set of four, choose the one statement which tells a good thing to do to help you understand a story better *after* you have read it.

21 After I've read a story, it's a good idea to

(A) count how many pages I read with no mistakes.

(B) check to see if there were enough pictures to go with the story to make it interesting.

(C) check to see if I met my purpose for reading the story.

(D) underline the causes and effects.

22 After I've read a story, it's a good idea to

(A) underline the main idea.

(B) retell the main points of the whole story so that I can check to see if I understood it.

(C) read the story again to be sure I said all of the words right.

(D) practice reading the story aloud.

METACOMPREHENSION STRATEGY INDEX (continued)

23 After I've read a story, it's a good idea to

Ⓐ read the title and look over the story to see what it is about.

Ⓑ check to see if I skipped any of the vocabulary words.

Ⓒ think about what made me make good or bad predictions.

Ⓓ make a guess about what will happen next in the story.

24 After I've read a story, it's a good idea to

Ⓐ look up all of the big words in the dictionary.

Ⓑ read the best parts aloud.

Ⓒ have someone read the story aloud to me.

Ⓓ think about how the story was like things I already knew about before I started reading.

25 After I've read a story, it's a good idea to

Ⓐ think about how I would have acted if I were the main character in the story.

Ⓑ practice reading the story silently for practice of good reading.

Ⓒ look over the story title and pictures to see what will happen.

Ⓓ make a list of the things I understood the most.

METACOMPREHENSION STRATEGY INDEX (continued)

DIRECTIONS FOR SCORING

Responses that indicate metacomprehension strategy awareness.

I. Before Reading:	II. During Reading:	III. After Reading:
1. C	11. D	21. C
2. A	12. A	22. B
3. B	13. C	23. C
4. C	14. B	24. D
5. A	15. D	25. A
6. B	16. B	
7. B	17. A	
8. A	18. A	
9. C	19. D	
10. C	20. A	

McLeod Assessment of Reading Comprehension

▶ **WHAT** The *McLeod Assessment of Reading Comprehension* assesses reading comprehension by means of the "cloze" technique, in which students read a series of passages and supply words that have been deleted from sentences within each passage. Supplying the correct word requires comprehension of the sentences within the passage. While the passages are ordered in respect to difficulty, individual passages do not represent a specific grade level like those that appear in the *Fry Oral Reading Test.* Interpretation is based on the total number of correct words supplied for all passages administered. Two levels of the test assess reading comprehension in grades 2–5 and in grades 6 and above.

▶ **WHY** Comprehension is the ultimate goal of reading. This assessment requires students to accurately decode words, to apply their knowledge of grammar, syntax, and vocabulary, and to use critical reading strategies that aid in the literal and inferential comprehension of what is read. When administered to everyone in a class, the *McLeod Assessment of Reading Comprehension* serves as a valuable screening tool for identifying students who may have reading difficulties and who may benefit from additional assessment that focuses on specific skills underlying reading. It is useful to test frequently in the elementary and middle school grades.

▶ **HOW** Make booklets for students by copying either the elementary or upper level test pages that follow. For the youngest students, you may want to use only the first two to four passages of the elementary level. Distribute the booklets to the students.

Permission granted by ATP Assessments and Arena Press, publishers of Assessing Reading: Multiple Measures (www.academictherapy.com)

Reading Comprehension Grades K–6

SAY: *Do not open your booklets. There are some silent reading puzzles in these booklets. Some words are missing from sentences, and you have to write in the word that you think should go in each blank space. Let's do the first sample together.*

Work through the example paragraph aloud with the students. Read the first sentence, pausing for the blank, and have the students suggest an answer. Have them write the answer in the proper space. Repeat this process with the second sentence. Then have the students read the third sentence to themselves and fill in the answer. Check their work.

SAY: *In the paragraphs inside the booklet, write the one word in each blank that you think should go there. Just write one word in each blank space. If you can't think of a word, go on to the next one. When you come to the end of the first page, go straight to the second without waiting to be told, and continue until you come to the end.*

You have 15 minutes to complete the test. If you do finish before the time is up, look over your work. Don't worry about the correct spelling—this is not a spelling test. Try to spell each word as best you can.

After answering any questions, have students begin. After the time has expired or when students appear to have finished, ask students to stop.

This is not a strictly timed test. Students should be given a reasonable amount of time to complete the test. You may want to adjust the time limit if you are giving students fewer passages to complete.

▶ **WHAT IT MEANS** Use the scoring key that follows each form to correct the students' work. Place the total number of words correctly scored in the box after each passage. Then determine the total score and enter it on page 1 of the test booklet. Refer to the scoring criteria on the following page to determine approximate reading grade level. For those students whose reading comprehension is below their current grade level, additional assessments should be administered that evaluate specific reading comprehension skills.

Permission granted by ATP Assessments and Arena Press, publishers of Assessing Reading: Multiple Measures (www.academictherapy.com)

Reading Comprehension Grades K–6

Scoring Criteria   Elementary Level

Score	Reading Grade Level
1–4	Grade 1 and below
5–8	Grade 2, Early
9–14	Grade 2, Late
15–20	Grade 3, Early
21–25	Grade 3, Late
26–30	Grade 4, Early
31–34	Grade 4, Late
35–38	Grade 5, Early
39–42	Grade 5, Late
43–46	Grade 6, Early
47–49	Grade 6, Late
50–56	Grade 7 and above

Scoring Criteria   Upper Level

Score	Reading Grade Level
1–40	Administer Elementary Level
41–55	Grade 7 and above

▶ **WHAT'S NEXT?** Students who score below grade level will benefit from an assessment provided by the *Fry Oral Reading Test,* the *San Diego Quick Assessment of Reading Ability,* and the *Critchlow Verbal Language Scales* (pp. 243–246) to determine if fluency, word recognition, or vocabulary deficits are the underlying causes of poor comprehension.

McLeod Assessment of Reading Comprehension, Elementary Level

Name: _____ **Grade:** _____ **Date:** _____

DO NOT TURN OVER THE PAGE UNTIL YOU ARE TOLD.

Pat Has a Cold

Pat did _____ feel very well.

Dad gave her _____ hot milk. She

drank the milk and went to rest _____ her bed.

TOTAL SCORE

A Hungry Cat

Kitty jumped up and sat on the table. She watched the fish swim round _____ round in the glass bowl. She tried _____ push the bowl with _____ paw, but could not tip _____ over.

A Trip to the Hospital

Mike woke up in the middle of the night _____ called out for his mother and father. He _____ them that he was _____ feeling well and that _____ was a sharp pain _____ his side. Wrapping him _____ a blanket, Mike's parents rushed _____ to the hospital. A _____ examined him and informed his _____ that an operation was necessary.

GO TO THE NEXT PAGE.

Permission granted by ATP Assessments and Arena Press, publishers of Assessing Reading: Multiple Measures (www.academictherapy.com)

Scottie Raises the Alarm

Something seemed to be wrong with Scottie, the family dog, when she woke up suddenly late one winter evening. _____ air was filled with smoke, and flames _____ coming from the stove in the corner _____ the kitchen. She ran upstairs to where the family was sleeping and began _____ bark loudly. Suddenly, the lights were switched _____ in each bedroom and Scottie watched _____ waited until the family _____ gone downstairs. Then she followed them _____ of the house and into _____ cool night air.

A Modern Pirate

Carol had just finished reading a book about the pirates who used _____ sail the seven seas. She closed _____ eyes and soon she was asleep and dreaming _____ she was a pirate. She was not like the pirate in the book but one who flew _____ spaceship and attacked other spaceships. Instead _____ gold, silver, and diamonds, her booty included precious fuels _____ expensive computers.

GO TO THE NEXT PAGE.

Permission granted by ATP Assessments and Arena Press, publishers of Assessing Reading: Multiple Measures (www.academictherapy.com)

Joshua

Each day Joshua woke at six in the morning. For most boys of
his age, _____ to school was only a dream. Joshua
himself had to _____ to provide money for the
members _____ his family. Each day he had an hour's
walk _____ the capital city where _____
would pick up a box containing plastic jewelry. For _____
next ten hours he _____ walk the streets, stopping
tourists and begging them to buy some of the jewelry. The only
_____ he rested was during the hottest part of the
_____, when he was able to drink _____
tepid water and to _____ the orange that he had
picked up at the market. At the _____ of the day he
would receive the few coins that made up his pay, walk _____,
eat a small supper, and then _____ asleep. He was
always _____ tired to enjoy the normal life of a young boy.

GO TO THE NEXT PAGE.

Permission granted by ATP Assessments and Arena Press, publishers of Assessing Reading: Multiple Measures (www.academictherapy.com)

In the Valley of the Unknown Planet

Listen. Can you hear that whistling noise? It seems to be

_____ from that mountain. Kris and Michael

volunteered to _____ out and investigate. They put on

their _____ suits and grabbed their laser pistols. They

_____ the safety of their underground headquarters and

began _____ cross the empty terrain that lay before

_____. Without encountering any problems they

reached _____ mountain. Their bulky space

suits _____ climbing difficult but after a few hours

_____ reached the summit of the _____.

Before them stood a huge monument that _____ been

constructed by previous settlers. The whistling started _____

and now the two spacemen _____ the cause.

STOP. LOOK OVER YOUR WORK UNTIL TIME IS UP.

Permission granted by ATP Assessments and Arena Press, publishers of Assessing Reading: Multiple Measures (www.academictherapy.com)

Scoring Key – Elementary Level

Correct responses for each passage are listed below. Mark errors in the test booklet. Do not count misspellings as an error. Count the number of correct responses and record this number in the space provided on the first page of the test booklet.

Pat Has a Cold

n't; not
some
in; on

A Hungry Cat

and
to
her
it

A Trip to the Hospital

and
told
not; n't
there
in
in
him
doctor
parents

Scottie Raises the Alarm

The; the
were
of
to
on
and
had
out
the

A Modern Pirate

to
her
that
a
of
and

Joshua

going
work
of
to
he
the
would
time
day
some
eat
end
home
fall
too

In the Valley of the Unknown Planet

coming
go
space
left
to
them
the
made
they
mountain
had
again
knew

Permission granted by ATP Assessments and Arena Press, publishers of Assessing Reading: Multiple Measures (www.academictherapy.com)

McLeod Assessment of Reading Comprehension, Upper Level

Name: _____ Grade: _____ Date: _____

DO NOT TURN OVER THE PAGE UNTIL YOU ARE TOLD.

Pat Has a Cold

Pat did _____ feel very well. Dad gave her _____ hot milk. She drank the milk and went to rest _____ her bed.

TOTAL SCORE

Copyright © McGraw-Hill Education

Mrs. Hill and Her Garden

Everyone on West Street knows Mrs. Hill.

_____ is the little old lady who lives _____ the little white house.

All summer long _____ is out working in her garden. This _____ is what she likes to do best _____ all.

"Hello, Mrs. Hill," her friends say _____ they go by. "May we help you?"

Mrs. _____ always says with a smile, "No, _____ you." And she goes on working with _____ many plants and flowers.

One day last month, Mrs. Hill looked around _____ her garden. She looked _____ at the sky. "It is _____ to take my house plants in," she _____. "It will start to get cold soon."

_____ by one, Mrs. Hill took her plants _____ the house.

GO TO THE NEXT PAGE.

Permission granted by ATP Assessments and Arena Press, publishers of Assessing Reading: Multiple Measures (www.academictherapy.com)

The Enemy

In a corner of Mrs. Smith's living _____ hangs a golden cage. The cage is _____ home of Goldie, the parrot. Mrs. Smith also _____ a very haughty cat who, come what may, _____ be the master of the _____.

For several days now the cat has noticed _____ Mrs. Smith has been paying more _____ to Goldie. She never stops saying: "What _____ darling he is! How sweet he is! _____ well he talks!"

The cat is fed _____. He notices that it is easy for _____ mistress to open the cage to feed _____ bird. So he takes advantage of her absence and, by _____ the cage door with _____ paw, lets the bird escape.

GO TO THE NEXT PAGE.

The Clever Crow

A thirsty crow found a water jug. Since there _____ only a little water in _____, she could not reach it with her _____. She hopped back a few steps and _____ flew against the jug. The jug did _____ move from its place. The crow saw _____ it was too heavy. But now she brought little stones _____ the field and threw _____ into the jug, so that the _____ soon rose higher. At last she could dip _____ beak into the water and quench her _____.

GO TO THE NEXT PAGE.

Permission granted by ATP Assessments and Arena Press, publishers of Assessing Reading: Multiple Measures (www.academictherapy.com)

Once Upon a Time

Once upon a time there was a prisoner whom nobody ever

_____ to see, and to whom no friend ever came to say

_____ kind word in his dark _____. He led a

dreary, wretched life, but one _____ a little mouse came out

of a _____ in the corner. As it was _____ timid, it

disappeared as soon as the _____ moved, but soon it came

back. _____ threw it a crumb from his scanty meal. From

then on the little mouse _____ back to see him every day.

It _____ to come and snuggle up against his

neck or play on _____ hands. To cut a long story

_____, they became real friends, and his dark

_____ never seemed as lonesome _____ the

prisoner when the little mouse _____ there.

STOP. LOOK OVER YOUR WORK UNTIL TIME IS UP.

Reading Comprehension Grades K–6

Scoring Key – Upper Level

Correct responses for each passage are listed below. Mark errors in the test booklet. Do not count misspellings as an error. Count the number of correct responses and record this number in the space provided on the first page of the test booklet.

Pat Has a Cold

n't; not
some
in; on

Mrs. Hill and Her Garden

She; she
in
she
work
of
as
Hill
thank
her
at
up
time
said
One
into

The Enemy

room
the
has
will
house
that
attention
a
How
up
his/the
the
opening
his

The Clever Crow

was
it
beak
then
not
that
from
them
water
her
thirst

Once Upon a Time

came
a
cell
day
hole
very
prisoner
He
came
used
his
short
cell
to
was

Permission granted by ATP Assessments and Arena Press, publishers of Assessing Reading: Multiple Measures (www.academictherapy.com)

**Placement and
Diagnostic Assessment**

Writing

Writing Assessment

▶ **WHAT** The Writing Assessment is designed to provide students practice with crafting written responses related to source texts.

▶ **WHY** In Grades 2–6, the Writing Assessment should be administered at the start of the year to determine students' understanding of genre writing and to help identify instructional needs. In Grade 1, the assessment should be administered closer to the mid-point of the year.

▶ **HOW** Provide students with a section of a grade-appropriate narrative and ask them to write the conclusion **OR** provide students with a narrative situation and ask them to continue the story. (For example, *Mom and I knew the sound in the garage was unusual. We went to grab some flashlights . . .* or *I had finished packing my bag when Dad came inside the house. "We're not going to the campground, Stella," he said. "I have a better idea."*)

Have students create a multi-paragraph response that connects to the source material and advances the narrative. Remind students to maintain a consistent point of view and to employ narrative techniques, such as dialogue, description, and foreshadowing.

Review key writing traits with students as they prepare to craft their narratives:

- **Focus and Coherence**
  Writing "on-topic" and avoiding extraneous information that impairs the readers' understanding of and interest in the written performance.

- **Organization**
  Writing that evidences a clear organizational strategy and that features a logical ordering of ideas and use of effective transitions.

- **Ideas and Support**
  Writing that explains and develops ideas with supportive details.

- **Word Choice**
  Writing that shows varied and precise word choice.

- **Voice/Sentence Fluency**
  Writing features a tone appropriate to the genre and sounds authentic and original. Sentence structure is varied, and sentences flow smoothly.

- **Conventions**
  Writing that evidences understanding of grammar and punctuation rules and features words that are spelled correctly.

Provide students with grade-level Checklists from the core program. You can structure the experience as a timed-writing event or something students craft over a number of days.

Writing Grades 1–6

▶ **WHAT IT MEANS** The assessment can be viewed as a baseline of writing performance. As students progress through the program, this early achievement can be compared to later narratives and other genre work to see if consistent achievement or improved achievement is apparent.

The narratives can be scored using the grade-level rubrics provided in the core program. If students receive a score below "3," use the written response to identify specific weaknesses in writing traits that may require targeted instruction during small group time to build mastery. If students score higher than "3," monitor their work in unit writing projects to see if achievement is consistent or improving.